INSIDE
OUTSOURCING

How Remote Work, Offshoring & Global
Employment is Changing the World

DEREK GALLIMORE

INSIDE OUTSOURCING:
How Remote Work, Offshoring, and Global Employment
is Changing the World

Copyright (c) 2022 by Derek Gallimore
Paperback ISBN: 978-1-7396230-0-5
First edition: May 2022

Published by: Outsource Accelerator
801 Tung Hip Commercial,
244-248 Des Voeux Road,
Hong Kong

Book Production by: MRD Publishing
Book Design by: Ideas We Form Studio
Printed in the Philippines

Address requests for information to:
info@outsourceaccelerator.com

Contents

Introduction

A Wild Ride

I arrived late into the night, jostled throngs of passengers, and edged my way through the shabby customs counters. Emerging from a long 10-hour flight, I found myself in an unmistakably developing-world airport. After collecting my suitcase from the mucky luggage belt, I pushed through the arrival hall crowds, strode through the sliding doors into thick humid air, and jumped into a rickety old cab.

It was 2011 and the first time I had ever set foot in the Philippines. Just two years before, I hadn't even heard of the country.

As my hastily matched cab driver drove us off into the heavy darkness, I contemplated our destination.

I was in Manila, a city of almost 20 million people, where every inch of space was competed for by bustling crowds, indignant traffic, street-side stalls, pollution, smoke, and noise. We were driving towards a place called Eastwood, which I only knew by name, and nothing else.

My cab driver was wire-framed and ruddy with a grimy red taxi-issue T-shirt. It was so worn and blackened that he looked more mechanic than driver. He was completely disinterested in me, but spoke good English, which was at least a little reassuring. We had little to talk about though, as he negotiated his way through the dimly lit metropolis. As we zoomed away from the airport's familiarity towards the unknown, I soon realized that my driver and I had only one thing in common—neither of us knew where we were going.

My knowledge of the Philippines, its people, and culture was almost zero.

I'd had an employee working for me for the last year, from something called a 'BPO,' based in the country I now find myself in. She wasn't strictly my employee, and I really didn't know anything about her, but she did work for me. I had no idea what a BPO was. I was just about to get an education.

The impromptu taxi adventure had us exploring the city's blackened streets, back alleys, and frenetic highways. Most were tightly lined with ad hoc convenience stores, karaoke bars, and tire repair shops perching on the curbside like tracks on a pinball machine. I knew that I was an early adopter of outsourcing, but at that moment, I felt more like a dodgy drug dealer about to make a drop.

The whole experience caused a wary unease. There was nothing explicitly menacing, but it was very different—this was no Kansas City, Toto. I was instinctively on edge and ready for fight or flight.

After appeals for help from pedestrians, store owners, and tricycle drivers, the driver gradually made his way to our destination.

Manila is a huge city with numerous distributed centers across the metro. Eastwood is one of those recently built business districts quickly thrown up in a knee-jerk response to the early explosive years of BPO growth.

Driving into Eastwood off the chaotic highway was like

entering a kooky Hollywood movie set. It felt like a cross between an outdoor shopping mall, The Truman Show, and Universal Studios, with a touch of Bollywood panache. High-density, intense, and upbeat. The area, no bigger than a few football fields in size, had dozens of looming modern towers packed tightly together, shooting 50 stories up into the sky. It was late at night, but there were thousands of people busily doing their thing. Hundreds of offices, restaurants, bars, and shops were crammed into a handful of indoor and outdoor malls and up into the high-rises above.

As we approached the hotel's lobby, I straightened up and prepared for the new dimension I was about to enter. What was I doing here? I might be a frontier businessman, but this seemed a little ridiculous…

If you had told me then that just three years later, the Philippines would become my adopted country—that I would settle, fall in love with a Brazilian fintech CFO, and eventually adopt a dog and get married here—I would have fallen off my chair, or even out of the rickety cab.

But for now, I was here to learn about the world of outsourcing.

Humble Beginnings

In 1975, the Homebrew Computer Club was an obscure meetup for outcast geeks dabbling in a niche hobby. It was written off by most as thoroughly uncool or, at best, completely unremarkable. However, its members were passionate about a technological movement that would dominate the world for the next half-century and beyond. Unbeknownst to the members, their nerdy 'personal computing' pastime would spawn the technology, software, and internet revolution that would go on—to borrow a phrase from Marc Adressen—'eat the world.'

Based in an otherwise small sleepy town, Hombrew Club's

influence transformed an unassuming Menlo Park into the epicenter of the Silicon Valley zeitgeist, and ground zero for the world's technological metamorphosis.

Steve Jobs, Steve Wozniak, and Bill Gates were members, as were numerous other Silicon Valley luminaries such as Harry Garland and Roger Melen of Cromemco; Paul Terrell, Repco partner; Todd Fischer of Fischer-Freitas Company; George Morrow of Morrow Designs; and Adam Osborne of Osborne Computer.

No one could ever envisage the power and potential that computers and computing power would have had on the world. But that's not necessarily surprising. It turns out that humanity is bad at foreseeing trends. History is littered with now hilarious ill-fated predictions, cast by the leading experts of the time.

In 1943, Thomas Watson, president of IBM, pronounced: "I think there is a world market for maybe five computers."

In 1949, Popular Mechanics Magazine predicted that "computers in the future may weigh no more than 1.5 tons."

In 1977: "There is no reason anyone would want a computer in their home," said Ken Olsen, founder of Digital Equipment Corporation, a predecessor of Compaq.

In 1989, Bill Gates of Microsoft proclaimed: "We will never make a 32-bit operating system."

In 1992: "The idea of a personal communicator in every pocket is a "pipe dream driven by greed," said Andy Grove, CEO of Intel.

1995: "I predict the Internet will soon go spectacularly supernova and in 1996 catastrophically collapse," said Robert Metcalfe, inventor of Ethernet.

2007: "There's no chance that the iPhone is going to get any significant market share," said Steve Ballmer, Microsoft CEO.

And it has never really been any different:

1876: "The Americans have need of the telephone, but we do not. We have plenty of messenger boys," said Sir William Preece, chief engineer, British Post Office.

1903: "The horse is here to stay but the automobile is only a novelty—a fad," said the president of the Michigan Savings Bank advising Henry Ford's lawyer.

1946: "Television won't be able to hold on to any market it captures after the first six months. People will soon get tired of staring at a plywood box every night," said Darryl Zanuck, co-founder of 20th Century Fox.

It seems that people tend to dramatically underestimate the capabilities and likely impact of things that have not yet emerged. Which is completely understandable—no one knows what they don't yet know. Prior to the motor car, cities relied on horse-drawn carriages to get around. As populations grew, experts predicted that cities would become buried under towering piles of steaming horse manure in just a few short years. No one had seen the motor car coming. But it did come, and quickly nullified the mounting manure dilemma. As Steve Jobs says, "you can only connect the dots looking backward."

From the early days of the Homebrew Computer Club, computer technology and its far-reaching applications have created seismic shifts in the way that society functions. We now treat miraculous technology like e-mail, video calls, Google Earth, Uber, smartphones, e-commerce, social media, and websites as normal. Only 20 years ago, these things would have been firmly in the realm of magic.

◇◇◇◇◇◇◇◇◇◇◇◇◇

Things are slow to change. Habits die hard. But unquestionably, change is underway.

As the world transitions from a physical economy to bits and bytes, it is functionally shrinking every day. Trade borders are vanishing, cultures are homogenizing, and it no longer matters where you're sitting when working, shopping, or socializing.

Humanity is quickly moving from an infinite number of small isolated silos, defined by geographical locations such as homes, offices, suburbs, towns, cities, and countries, toward a singular global community, interfaced by a laptop and internet connection. This new global forum is where we all increasingly shop for clothes, buy food, build friendships, find dates, book taxis, reminisce with old friends, and binge-watch our favorite shows. And it will soon be the place we all go to hire our employees.

The remote work culture, distributed workforces, online economy, digital nomads, and offshore staffing are all a bit fringe right now. Some people understand and embrace the concept, but the majority still see it as a kooky alternative to the mainstream— just like a computer club in the 70s.

With the COVID pandemic, the world has faced unprecedented change over the last couple of years. It has forced people to adopt a physically segregated life, and pushed them towards an immersive digital reality online.

Only a few short years ago, remote work, work-from-home, and distributed workforces were a fanciful pipe dream. Now, with pandemic-induced 'new normals'—and with technology doing its part in enabling such realities—the old way of physical confinement to a single geographical market has gone forever.

The strongly visible trend lines of technology, globalization, and online work, suggest that the next 10 to 20 years will see a complete switch from localized jobs to a globalized workforce. The new wave of globalized employment is resetting the labor-cost equilibrium and redistributing access and opportunity. With easy access to a world-wide pool of labor, it is becoming normal to contemplate hiring an accountant in New York for $6,000 per month, or an equally qualified one in Manila for $600.

No one would have thought that the Home Brew Computer Club would have ignited a world movement. At the time, it was just an obscure passion project for a few nerds. And the same is true for globalized employment.

The offshore staffing industry started 30 years ago and is the early progenitor of this new way of working. Like many things, it took a long time to get initial traction and recognition, but like a snowball, it has been building size, sophistication, and momentum ever since. With the advent of better technology to support global working, it is gradually reaching an inevitable tipping point where the world's workforce amalgamate into a single talent pool.

This is outsourcing. And it is the brave new world of a single global economy.

Despite global employment being here and now, most company's are as yet unaware of it, or circumspect of its efficacy. Despite powering 99% of the Fortune 500, outsourcing faces strong headwinds of controversy and quality complaints which dissuade most small and medium-sized businesses from starting. For the most part, there is a huge knowledge, comfort, and culture gap on the topic. While for many business owners, the concept of hiring someone far, far away is still just a little too weird.

I want to help you close these 'gaps' over the following chapters. It is not essential for a business to outsource—yet. But outsourcing is now so powerful that it cannot be ignored. It is important to make an informed decision on its applicability to your business. The single global economy is fast approaching. It's fine to opt-out, but it's likely that your competitors will not.

This book is split into four parts, where we work from broad concepts to higher-level theory and eventually down into actionable tactics and takeaways. First, Part 1 charts the progress of human cooperation and globalization. Part 2 introduces outsourcing in concept. Part 3 dives into the specifics of the 30-year old offshore industry. And Part 4 takes a deeper look at outsourcing in practice, offering some clear, actionable guidelines for getting started, and optimizing your own offshore team.

Global employment can give you access to deep talent pools of highly capable staff for a 70% discount. It is, without doubt, the single most powerful tool available to businesses today.

I hope this book will help people become a little more educated and aware of the opportunities and possible downsides that outsourcing brings.

Part 1

Business: Past, Present, and Future

Evolution of Business

Canals to Hyperloops

Venice, in Italy, is world-famous for its web of romantic winding canals. The 'floating city,' as it's called, is synonymous with romantic getaways, wedding proposals, and picturesque gondolas that effortlessly glide through its endless winding waterways.

Birmingham, a slightly depressing midsized city in England, on the other hand, is much lesser known for its canal system. However, this old industrial conclave was once the beating heart of an elaborate national network of canals connecting all corners of the country. In fact, Birmingham's canals stretched 270 kilometers around the city, compared to just 40 kilometers in Venice.

Canals are man-made waterways. Almost absurdly, it was discovered that they were an efficient means for carrying heavy and bulk goods across long distances. They were first engineered in the 17th century but really hit their stride in the early 1800s—coinciding with the boom of the industrial revolution.

The concept of a nationwide canal system almost beggars belief. The thing about water is that it needs to be completely horizontal, otherwise it will quickly empty as it heads 'downstream.' Despite this significant complication, in its peak, the UK had built a national network of canals covering 6,500 kilometers. This is an incredible engineering feat when you consider that the entire system needed to be completely flat, had to accommodate intersections and junctions with other canals without leakage, and were required to cross all manner of terrain.

As you know, with any stream, water travels downwards. Quickly. It is impossible, on any scale, to make water standstill on an incline, never mind travel upwards. So, for a national system of waterways to work, they would have to traverse all manner of hills, valleys, troughs, and gorges. Think of building 6,500 kilometers of highways that were made of water, had to stay flat, and could not leak. At first blush, it might seem an impossible task. However, the industrious engineers found solutions for these problems.

To cross gorges and valleys, they built enormous stone aqueducts to support the watery highways high in the air. The Pontcysyllte Aqueduct in Wales is a prime example, which is both the longest and highest aqueduct in the world. The stone and cast iron UNESCO World Heritage site still stands proudly today, spanning 307 meters across a valley, and rising nine stories in the air.

To enable the horse-drawn canal boats to travel up and down hillsides, they designed a system of watertight 'locks' that would open and close, one boat at a time. These locks acted like mammoth-sized steps, working their way up the side of a hill and breaking any incline, or decline, into stages. Each lock accommodates one boat at a time. When inside, the water level adjusts to the new height, letting the boat out the other side and into another giant stepping-stone lock. This monumental engineering feat allows boats to work their way up the side of hills or down through gorges, while staying horizontal and afloat.

In today's world, it's hard to even consider that this would ever seem to be an efficient means of transport. But in the 1770s, the only other option was a horse and cart. While these were satisfactory for shorter distances and lighter loads, they could not carry the growing volumes of tonnage that the emerging industrial revolution was beginning to produce.

Back in the early 19th century, Birmingham was known as the 'workshop of the world.' It was the epicenter of western manufacturing in the 1800s, creating some of the world's cutting-edge merchandise. Things like weapons, machines, toys, jewelry, clocks, clothing, homeware, and eventually, steam engines, trains, and automobiles. These things all represented the latest technology of its time, and Birmingham was very much the Silicon Valley of its era.

The canal system was an essential part of the infrastructure puzzle to move its merchandise. Birmingham's complex web of canals supported the movement of materials into its factories and the finished products out to the neighboring towns and across Britain.

The building and maintenance of the canal system involved tens of thousands of people, and hundreds of private companies. They spawned hundreds of other auxiliary businesses—like boat builders and civil engineers—to service the sector.

It was an incredibly vibrant ecosystem that was cutting edge for its time—and essential for the economy's success. The canal system reached a glorious crescendo sometime in the late 1820s. By this time, it had evolved into a complex network of 1,569 locks, 53 tunnels, 3112 bridges, 370 aqueducts, and 74 reservoirs.

Then, all of a sudden, something changed. And the canal system, in one fell swoop, was doomed. Something new came along, almost overnight, that made the canal system quickly irrelevant and a quaint vestige of the past.

Birmingham also invented the steam-powered engine. It was the steam engine that powered the factories back then, and the machines that enabled the mass production of the Industrial Age.

One of the evolutionary descendants of the steam engine was the steam locomotive, or train. And it proved to be a game changer. The steam-powered trains were enormously powerful, traveling five times faster than a horse-drawn boat, along efficient railway lines, and capable of carrying enormous loads.

Virtually overnight, a railway network was built, and the canal system quickly slipped into decline and complete demise.

Thousands of people lost their jobs, and hundreds of businesses folded due to this severe pivot. An entire industry was basically destroyed on the spot.

Allow me to dwell on this for a moment.

The canal system was built over a period of 75 years. An incredible web of 6,500 kilometers of watertight highways, crossing and connecting an entire country. It employed tens of thousands of people, facilitated the country's manufacturing, represented the latest cutting-edge technology, and was a dominant economic force.

Then—all of a sudden—it was rendered obsolete, and within a few short years, it all but disappeared from social conscience. Incredible.

Change happens. And sometimes the change is monumental, and can happen with little or no notice.

Time

Something else pretty remarkable happened due to Britain's faster train system. *Time.* Time happened.

Can you believe that it wasn't until the late 19th century that the world had a standardized system of time?

It's almost beyond comprehension that no one had deemed

it necessary to have a standardized system of timekeeping before this period. In simple terms, this meant that different towns had different times.

The world has always been subject to different times in different places, because it is big and round, and so the sun reaches different parts of the globe at disparate times. However, before 1880, it's pretty amazing to think that there just wasn't a need for a centralized, coordinated time. This is basically because no one traveled far enough, quickly enough, or often enough, to warrant or even understand the need for a standardized time. If you are young, 140 years might sound like a long time. However, modern humans in some form have been roaming around for the last 300,000 years, so in the grand scheme of things, it's really only like yesterday.

It wasn't until the 1880s that the United Kingdom invented and launched a national network of steam engines and train travel. For the first time, large numbers of people could quickly and reliably move between UK towns. However, when they tried to create the first train timetable, they realized that the different stations along the line were all working to varying times. So it was impossible to have a unifying agenda linking them all together. Finally, humanity had seen a need to standardize time. As a result, on 1 November 1884, the Greenwich Mean Time was universally adopted at the International Meridian Conference in Washington, D.C. Twenty-four time zones covering the globe's surface were created, and time was unified within each time zone.

Previously, standardized time was simply irrelevant as neighboring towns had never been before in close, frequent, and fast communication. There was no need for everyone to be reading the same time. This demonstrates that distance and its impact are contextual. It used not to matter if two towns, only 100 miles apart, were working to different times if it took you three days to connect with or communicate with that town. In the 1800s, most people would never have left their hometown—so it just didn't matter.

Today, the world is becoming functionally smaller. It will never physically change in size, but functionally, the tyranny of distance is being eradicated.

Most great-grandparents would have never traveled internationally in their lifetime. Most grandparents might have traveled once or twice in their life. While our generation may travel annually or monthly, in the future, our children's children might be taking the hyperloop daily to cross a continent in getting to school. Or maybe we would have all migrated to Mars by then.

Information Flow

Communication is also a big reason for travel, and if you can communicate without traveling, in some cases, it makes the distance irrelevant. Again, most great-grandparents would never have experienced an international phone call. Local telephone networks were still rare and limited to the rich as recently as the 1940s. Today, everyone is regularly calling, e-mailing, texting, and video conferencing—sometimes to people across town, across the globe, or across the same room.

The barriers of distance, physical travel, and communication are being broken down. Soon, supersonic flights, sub-orbital rockets, and hyperloops might allow us to traverse the globe in one to two hours instead of the current 12 to 20 hours. This is yet another step-change improvement, and even more incredible when you consider that only two to three generations ago, it would have taken the wealthiest and most resource-rich person in the world many months, and much toil, to cross the globe.

Not only are people communicating quicker and more easily, but the capacity of communication itself has vastly improved. In the past, information was communicated slowly, from one person to another—in real-time, in real life.

Before written language, the preliterae cultures could only communicate information to a very limited audience. It was literally confined to the people that shared a space at that moment. Any part of any communication that wasn't memorized would disappear.

This is why history is filled with stories, myths, and legends. Though simple in nature, a story can convey rather elaborate information, lessons, or messages with it. And since they are effortlessly remembered, they can be passed along to new audiences with ease. In contrast, you only have to hear 20 phone numbers in a row to realize that raw data has little emotional impact, and is very hard to recall.

As a result, the impact and reach of spoken language were very limited. Other than talking to those around you, there was no way of scaling or amplifying what you said. The message could never really reach beyond the four corners of the room from which it was spoken. And it was immediately perishable. As soon as your message had been said, it would disappear forever—except for whatever remnants were left in someone's head. This starkly contrasts to today, where almost anything you say, type, or text, is forever immutable and can potentially be broadcast—and repeatedly so—to millions, if not billions of people.

Once civilization could write, it meant that information could be saved, iterated, refined, and distributed. This heralded another step-change in the development of humanity. Writing allowed humans to record and store messages, thoughts, and concepts for the first time. The storage of that information, on paper, meant that it could be instantly recalled, and also iterated. Having ideas in a written form also allowed concepts to be distributed to other people, without the author needing to be present to re-speak it themselves. This allowed for the dissemination and scaling of ideas like never before.

The next quantum leap forward happened around 1440 with the invention of Johannes Gutenberg's printing press. This technology meant that information could be replicated much faster, easier, and cheaper than before, allowing the transmission to many people, in different places, all at the same time. For the first time, there was mass distribution of communication, information, and ideas, which meant that people could enhance connections and build alignment between communities that didn't necessarily share the same geographic location.

Again, it is amazing that people have been around for 300,000 years, yet all these advances have been made in a very recent span of that time. Humans have had some form of writing for just 5,000 of the last 300,000 years. But it is only in the last 500 years that any significant number of people could actually read or write, or even had access to anything that was written. It is really only in the most recent 100 years where a majority of people have been able to read.

Previously, information and knowledge were in scarce supply. And access to it was both limited and guarded. Only the rich and powerful could access universities, libraries, books, and newspapers. They were the only portals that represented the world's accumulated knowledge. Access to information was costly, reserved for the elite, and heavily guarded. The standard population was locked out. There was a huge asymmetry in the access of information. And for good reason. It meant that those with the information had power and advantage over their peers.

However, civilization continued to evolve, and eventually, things really started to speed up. Radio, television, telephones, and the Internet have all exponentially enhanced this progression —enabling increasingly more complex information to be communicated increasingly faster, in higher fidelity, at a lower cost of production, and at a lower cost of communication.

Before, you were considered elite if you were able to read,

and even better if you had access to books. Now, most people on the planet take literacy for granted and walk around with a supercomputer in their pocket.

Now, access to every book, movie, photo, interview, song, and sonnet that has ever been produced—representing almost infinite information and knowledge—can be transferred from one person to another in an instant, at practically no cost.

Today, the average phone is many millions of times more powerful than the computer system responsible for the world's first moon landing. Apollo 11 traveled 356,000 kilometers across space to land Neil Armstrong on the moon in 1969. Its guidance computer was, now, laughably limited with just 64 kilobytes of memory and a 0.043 MHz processor. A toaster now has a more powerful computer than that.

Not only is the gadget in your pocket enormously powerful, but it is directly connected to some of the world's most potent supercomputers. If you access Google Translate, Earth, Maps, or even do a search, your browser is actually tapping into an Artificial Intelligence mainframe. By texting a simple query, you are, by extension, leveraging some of the world's most powerful raw processing power, all within milliseconds, probably without knowing—and all for free!

Communication today, has evolved from merely relaying the content of a conversation to the transfer of information. There is a very finite 'capacity' to an oral conversation. However, there is virtually infinite value and potential productive capacity with the communication of information. This information has never been so freely available, so readily transferrable, and so easily consumable.

A while ago, information transfer was limited to talking, then it could be written down, and copied. Then came scratchy telephone calls, followed by cheap international calls and the Internet. Now, we have free video calls, social media broadcasting to millions, and AI in our pocket. Soon, holograms and Augmented Reality will be accessible to all.

The capacity of communication is now almost infinite. And the value that can be contained and transferred through communication is now almost limitless. The entire code-base of Google's secret algorithm could be transferred to someone across the Internet in just a second for little or no cost. It has no physical presence and just a small digital footprint, yet its value is arguably priceless. If someone had inside information on the next big stock market winner, the value of that knowledge could be worth millions. Yet, it could be transferred in a single sentence, consisting of no more than a few bytes of data. It could be done in milliseconds, and synchronously sent across the globe to dozens of people—for free. The ease with which these things can happen speaks to the complete lack of friction in the new information economy, and also the difficulty for any of this to be tracked, policed, or regulated.

Now that much of the world's work and value is in bits and bytes—virtually anyone can do it from almost anywhere. As digital work dominates, and communication technology improves, the old geographical and national borders that have determined so much of our destiny for so long are becoming increasingly irrelevant.

So much work and information can now be done and distributed completely unchecked over the Internet. Previously, governments would control the workforce through migration restrictions, and geographical distance would naturally limit movement and opportunity anyway. As the world's economies move online, and information, data, and IP become king, people can meaningfully contribute to the global economy from wherever they are sitting.

Workforce Mobility

Globalization of Services

Matt Mullenweg is a quiet, humble, and unassuming guy. He has a slight frame, bedhead red hair and the beginnings of a beard. He's a digital nomad, living a simple life, traveling a lot, and working from his laptop from wherever takes his fancy. He can spend as many as 300 days a year on the road, traveling to meet with colleagues, friends, family, or just traveling for the sake of travel. You might see him in a coffee shop working from his laptop and think nothing of it. But Matt is no ordinary nomad. At just 19 years of age, he created WordPress, which is now the world's most widely used website builder, powering an incredible 37% of the world's nearly 2 billion websites. Matt still runs WordPress, and also heads Automattic, the commercial entity connected to the WordPress open source movement. WordPress is now the world's ubiquitous backend platform from which websites are built and managed. Automattic meanwhile generates hundreds of millions of dollars in revenue and employs nearly two thousand staff. The entire company is distributed. They have no office.

It is incredible to think that Matt is in some way one of the most powerful people in the world. He has enormous control and influence over the entire web and internet ecosystem, and also happens to be working in one of the most technologically advanced commercial fields of today's world.

Yet, he has no fixed location, can work from wherever he wants, and needs no tools or interfaces other than a simple MacBook Air. He doesn't even need a top-of-the-range computer—the entry-level model will do just fine. He can manage his multibillion-dollar empire, hundreds of millions of websites, an entire global workforce of thousands of people, and in some ways the future of the Internet, from a $1,500 mass-produced laptop. And he can do it all from a coffee shop sofa on public wifi. This is an incredible testament to the power of technology and how it can enable incredible value creation and transfer. And also how that, in turn, can empower and liberate the world's workforce.

Previously, the economic opportunity of the world's workforces were mostly governed by the country that they lived in and their location in the world. This has been the case for most of our time on the planet, but recently, this has started to change.

The world's people, and in the same respect, the world's labor forces, are highly geographically restricted. This is in most part, for the simple reason that large numbers of people cannot easily move or be moved. Most people are born into communities and settle into those communities, or similar ones nearby, along with their family, friends and familiar surroundings. There are very few people that can, or are inclined to, live a successful nomadic lifestyle. There are rare examples of this, where adventurous individuals follow their wanderlust, but it is almost never seen across an entire community —with the exception of course of the old migratory tribes.

But even if people were inclined to move, there are numerous logistical and legal restrictions in place that make it far from a free-flowing exercise. Significantly, tight border controls are in place, which limits the egress and entry from one country to another. Generally, countries have always strictly controlled their borders, and the free movement of their people and products.

As a result of all these social, logistical, and constitutional factors, people have always been very limited in their inclination and ability to move around—and governments in many respects, do their best to ensure that this is the case. One of the primary functions of a government, in fact, is to maintain the security, well-being, and status quo of its citizens, and much of this is manifested through the control of its borders.

However, it is for these reasons that limited migrational movement has kept economies relatively confined and static until now. There is no issue with this per se; people want and need a stable legal and economic system, and a secure environment that can ensure their welfare.

This siloed approach to work and opportunity is fine as long as you are from an affluent country, have jobs nearby, and are happy with your surroundings. But if you grow up in poverty, live in a country that's collapsing, or there's no work in your area—then it's not such a good deal.

If you zoom out, stable populations and migration control broadly make sense, as no nation can realistically accommodate big swings in population size. For example, if millions of people were able to relocate to a different country on a whim, it would cause massive strain on infrastructure. It could easily overload otherwise stable and functional systems. No nation could tolerate hosting 1 million people one day, 10 million the next day, and 3 million the day after. You only have to watch the news to see frequent examples of the enormous duress created by immigration and refugee flows on everyone involved.

Due to all these geographical and sovereign constraints, it

meant that people were largely stuck in the location and economic class in which they were born, for better, or worse. However, today, while it is not yet possible, or even maybe desirable, for people to move around freely, at least they are now able to work, produce, trade, and consume on an increasingly frictionless and global scale.

Global industry and production is increasingly moving away from physical products towards services, information, software, the Internet, and Intellectual Property. In other words, from brick-and-mortar to bits and bytes. Across the globe, trade, brands, products, entertainment, systems, art, and cultural norms are becoming increasingly homogenized and 'globalized.'

As a result of this trend, and with rapid advancements in technology and communications, the relevance of location and distance is quickly being eroded. Among many other benefits, the global economy allows the world's labor forces to amalgamate and eventually form one single pool of nearly 8 billion workers. This reconfiguration of the workforce infrastructure and labor norms will have a profound impact—both positive and negative—on employment; something that has traditionally been a rock-solid and carefully controlled bedrock of society.

Much is written about the emerging global marketplace, but it generally refers to the trade and consumption side of the equation. Relatively, very little of this globalization conversation has referred to the workforce—the people—which constitute the production side of the marketplace equation. This is because the globalization of the workforce has not really happened yet.

People collectively form the workforce, which is the principal input of any production and economy. And as discussed, the workforce has traditionally been very static and sticky. Populations don't have the inclination to mass-migrate, and stringent border controls carefully regulate their movement. Previously, for the workforce to be productive, they had to attend a physical 'place of production' like a farm, factory, or warehouse. The world's initial industrialization period funneled workforces into organized farmland. The second industrialization funneled them into bustling factories, and the third into high-rise city offices.

Today, as the world moves increasingly into the digital age, the physical presence of the workforce has become almost optional. The workforce of the fourth industrialization requires only a laptop, and they can mostly work from wherever they please.

So while globalization of the consumption-side of the marketplace has been happening for decades, globalization of the production-side has only just begun. The production side is basically employment itself, which means that the collective size of the global market is enormous—and the impact of its fusion will be felt by all. Eventually, the single market will expand to include the full population of the globe—that's 8 billion people collaborating within one single market.

To give the size of this some context, we can look at the approximate production value of the world's population as it stands now. The gross domestic product (GDP) metric for all countries is a useful proxy for its size. Since people are both the drivers and beneficiaries of global production, it's a relevant metric for the production contribution of each person. At the time of writing, some of the world's economic luminaries and laggards look like this. Liechtenstein is at the top of the pyramid with an annual GDP per person of $139,000, the US in 15th place has a GDP per person of $62,000, and at the bottom of the pyramid, Malawi, Niger, and DR Congo have a GDP per person of around $1,000. In aggregate, the world's GDP per capita is $18,381. When combined, the world's GDP, which is in some way a proxy for everybody's production contribution, is about $144 trillion annually.[1]

---

1   IMF. (2021). World Economic Outlook.
     Retrieved from https://www.imf.org/external/datamapper/datasets/WEO

As technology advances, unifying the global workforce in its wake, it's incredible to think that we could soon have the entire global population possibly working within—and towards—one global workforce.

Cooperation & Collaboration

Catallaxy

In 1958, the economist Leonard Read published an essay about a simple pencil, which caught the world's attention. His purpose was to illustrate the extraordinary complexities of the economy, the free market, and capitalism. And so, he chose something as simple as a pencil to do so. A pencil is extremely basic in nature. Yet, as Read went on to explain, the production of a pencil requires the coordinated collaboration of thousands of people, using a wide range of specialized resources, sourced from across the globe.

The wood for the pencil comes from a tree that was cut down using a saw. To make the saw, it needed steel. To make the steel, it required iron ore. The pencil's lead—made from graphite—involves the contribution of a mine in South America. The red eraser on top came from a rubber tree in Malaysia. He noted that the rubber tree wasn't even native to Malaysia—and had been sent there from South America by a British businessman many years earlier. He tells us that the paint on the pencil, the metal clasp fixing, the eraser, and the black brand name stamped onto the side, all come from different and complex origins. He illustrated that making a single pencil each involved hundreds, or thousands, of people all contributing in some way big or small, right down to the sweeper in the factory, and the lighthouse keeper that guided the shipment into port.

Yet, the pencil costs only such a small amount of money, and it takes almost no time, hardship, or consideration for you to buy one from a shop. He goes on to explain that the construction, packaging, transportation, and marketing of the pencil took enormous collaboration from thousands of people, all contributing fractions of seconds each. However, these people weren't centrally coordinated, and they all acted with little or no awareness of anyone else within the chain of events. Despite the collaboration, the people came from dozens of different countries, had never met, and, as he suggested, probably wouldn't have liked each other if they did.

The article's main point was to demonstrate the efficacy of the free market's invisible hand and that economies are so complex that they cannot possibly be planned. Yet, they work.

It's such a wonderful and powerful observation that even something as simple as a pencil requires the specialized knowledge and contribution of many thousands of people from all corners of the planet. We might feel independent and self-sufficient in our lives, but if you tried to make something in complete isolation—even something as simple as a pencil—you would quickly realize how interconnected and codependent we all are. If you did try to make a pencil yourself, you would probably give up as soon as you had to go and find a rubber tree to make the eraser.

I would go so far as to say that it isn't even possible for one person to make a pencil. And even if it were, it would take an extraordinary amount of time, and I'm sure the quality would be questionable. So, it's incredible to think that you can buy one for just a few cents.

The construction of a pencil illustrates the interconnectivity of the world of trade and the value of specialization. Making a pencil requires thousands of specialists from dozens of countries to collaborate. When you consider how difficult it is to create a pencil, just take a moment to think about the incredible specialization and collaboration it takes to build a computer, airplane, or hospital. We believe that we act in some kind of autonomy and independence, but actually, we have become inextricably linked and reliant on every other member of the planet.

This concept of cooperation and specialization has been understood, or at least acknowledged, as far back as 350 B.C. when Aristotle set about describing the commercial interactions between people, their community, and state. He coined the terms 'economy' and 'catallaxy' to explain the complex phenomena of market forces, including prices, division of labor, and growth. The term was later revived by Austrian-British economist Friedrich Hayek who defines it as "the order brought about by the mutual adjustment of many individual economies in a market." Unfortunately, catallaxy as a word never really caught on in modern dialogue—maybe because it sounds all a bit too 'intergalactic,' but the concept is so accurate for describing the invaluable impact of humanity's ability to cooperate.

The basic concept of catallaxy—generally referred to as trade— is that people are motivated to exchange with other people to benefit themselves. When free trade occurs, in serving their own needs, the other party also benefits. This concept, despite its simplicity, is the underlying currency of our society, and unlocks specialization, which is credited for nothing less than the evolution of humanity.

One of the early instances of trade and cooperation began hundreds of thousands of years ago when tribes first split their routines into specialized functions. For example, instead of everyone going out and hunting for food, the group would split up. Some, particularly those that were more capable, would go out hunting for animals, others would go foraging for plants, while others would stay back at home to prepare the food.

This little observation of an early tribal behavior might seem obvious and drearily uneventful to us now, but that early glimmer of coordinated cooperation is like the 'Big Bang' moment of human evolution. It was the seminal moment of what is now referred to as 'division of labor.' Cooperation of this kind has certainly not been the case for much of our existence. After millions of years of evolution, humans have only been doing this relatively recently, and are still the only species on the planet to do it in any meaningful way. It is, in fact, this ability to cooperate that has excelled our species beyond that of others.

For any other animal, without cooperation from others, its capabilities, wisdom, and resources are limited to, its own individual effort. Even if one day, the evolutionary lottery produced an outlier of freakish intelligence—if it is acting alone, its capabilities will still be severely limited. In contrast, in the case of early humans, as soon as they were able to cooperate with others, each individual's intelligence and capability were immediately multiplied. When a tribe of 10 humans collaborate, they effectively combine their collective intelligence and capability. With this, the group's capacity jumps an order of magnitude beyond any other individual animal. When a group acts as 'one,' they instantly become the most intelligent and capable being on the planet. Importantly, this holds true even if the individuals within the group aren't necessarily anything special, and might even be significantly weaker than others when alone.

Two hundred thousand years ago, in the Middle Stone Age, people were able to make a small array of reasonably sophisticated tools.[2]

They had discovered that early stone tools made into the shape of blades allowed people to go out and hunt for animals more efficiently. If the hunters had to make their own tools instead of hunting, then both the blade making would be rushed, and the hunting time would be restricted. However, with the division of labor, if one person concentrated on making blades, while the others spent more time hunting, then both the quality of the blades improved, and hunting time increased. Having one person concentrate on manufacturing tools allowed them to get better at their work and continually incorporate small process and design improvements.

Fast forward a few hundred thousand years, and now everything we do is so highly specialized, that each of our own contributions is really just a small fiber in an enormous patchwork quilt of humanity. We can now not survive more than a few days, certainly not in the lifestyle that we are accustomed to, without the cooperation and support of our community.

In a modern business setting, it is simply obvious to have specialized roles, in fact, you couldn't run a company any other way. It would not be possible for Elon Musk to build an autonomous Tesla if the scientists not only had to do their share of science, but also equal parts of engineering, accounting, plus some of the marketing, customer service, sales, law, as well as cleaning the factory. The scientists simply wouldn't have any time left to progress in their field, or develop their product.

It is this task specialization that catalyzed the sudden jump in the evolution of humanity. Once people elected to specialize, they could do things better and more efficiently. These roles would be done for the greater good of the overall tribe, which also benefited

---

2   Smithsonian National Museum of Natural History. (2021).What does it mean to be human? Retrieved from https://humanorigins.si.edu/evidence/behavior/stone-tools

everyone individually. Each tribe member was able to use the fruits of their labor, or instead, they could trade their product or contribution for the contributions or products of others.

Specialization is great in theory. But its impact is limited by the number of participants in the network, whether that's a tribe, village, company, or group. If your network is small, then you have a very limited opportunity to specialize. And so, the rocket fuel for specialization is increasing the size of the cooperative network in which it exists.

To illustrate this point, if there is a tribe of just 10 people, then the extent to which they can specialize is minimal. Each person can possibly focus on one, two, or three things each, meaning that a tribe of 10 can generate around 30 unique activities. This is a great start, as each tribe member can directly benefit from, and utilize 30 functions—many of which would be beyond the capacity of each individual to produce. This is already significantly more powerful than just a single person's capacity, but it is still very limited.

If you expand this specialization multiplication to a city like London today, with nearly nine million people in participation, you can start to understand the benefit of being a part of a larger network. If each Londoner specializes in three things, then there are 27 million unique activities on offer for each individual to use, experience, leverage, or benefit from. This is infinitely more powerful than what a tribe of just 10 people can produce.

This illustration might sound impressive, but the full extent of the trade and specialization network effect is even more powerful than that.

In a given group, within an efficient market, each participant can, in theory, trade directly with each of the other participants. An effective system of trade creates a potent network with a formidable power law. In the tribe of 10 people, efficient trade creates potentially 100 exchange opportunities. For London, 9 million people all trading with each other, dramatically expands the chance to exchange specialties to 81 trillion.

The explosion in innovation and development that humanity has seen in the past 500 years is, in most part, due to this powerful network effect and catallaxy, the same concept that Aristotle described nearly 2,500 years earlier. Simple trade generates more specialization, which generates more trade, which in turn generates more specialization. The combination of deeper specialization, with the added rocket fuel of increasingly larger, more networked communities, creates ever larger leaps in progress and improvement for all.

Through ever larger circles of coordinated cooperation, the human species can tackle even bigger challenges with even more profound collective intelligence and capability. In some respects, through collaboration, the city of London is acting as one 'being,' which is collectively 81 trillion times more powerful than any individual acting alone. It's compelling stuff.

City Walls

Back in 200 A.D., the City of London was a thriving metropolis, similar to today. Although it was called Londinium, the country was called Brittanica, and it was ruled by the Romans. The city had a population of about 60,000 people and boasted major public buildings and infrastructure, extravagant basilicas, a range of impressive temples, bathhouses, and a towering amphitheater.

Londinium was a highly sophisticated city, and supremely technologically advanced compared to the almost prehistoric people that lived just beyond its defenses. For this reason, it was always under attack from various marauding factions, like the

Celts, Gauls, Vikings, Picts, Franks, and Saxons. To protect the city and its people, the Roman engineers built a vast fortified and turreted wall. It was two miles long, and along with the Thames River on the Southern side, enclosed about 330 acres of land in total.

Back then, cities really acted as countries do now. Londinium was basically a nation-state—and outside of the city was a completely different world. The London Wall survived for another 1,600 years, still exists in part today, and now broadly defines the perimeter of the Square Mile, and marks the modern City of London.

Much later, in about 1,100 AD, the city was experiencing unrest from within its walls. After centuries of cohabitation, London's city members fought for a right to have a say in the governance of their city. In another fine display of advanced human cooperation, the City of London made a deal—or a trade—with its people. They agreed to provide the infrastructure, the rule of law and security, and in return, they would generate revenues by taxing their residents. For the people, they could leverage the infrastructure, take advantage of the thriving economy, and could vote for its leadership to keep them in check. It was from this development that the city residents became 'citizens,' and also the concept of a 'citizen' was born.

Being a citizen of London, was a lofty position indeed. If you happened to have been born outside of the city, the fact that you were British, living in Britain, and that London was in Britain, would have had no bearing. If you were born outside of the city walls, you were all out of luck. You were most likely a peasant and would have had no access to the city or its facilities and could only enter its walls for limited purposes and special trade.

It's fascinating to see that the word 'citizen,' which today is synonymous with a national identity, emerged from city residents gaining rights to their city. This seems to demonstrate the expansion of the concept of community as communication and society develops.

Hundreds of years ago, people would rarely leave their village, and they would almost certainly never travel around the country, or go overseas. As well as limited travel, there was no communication technology, and so any communication was limited to basic unassisted speech. Before enhanced communications, the size of any network was limited to a relatively small community. This meant that a network could only expand to the point at which functional communication could be maintained between them. With these barriers in place, you can see why someone's participation in their tribe, village, town, or city was far more relevant to them than their participation as a citizen of their country. You might have been told that you belong to a certain country, but functionally, you would have really only felt a part of, and connected to, your local community and surroundings.

As technology develops, and communication improves, the community size can expand. As cooperation between bigger groups of people can happen, the groups will expand from tribes to villages, to towns, cities, countries, continents, and eventually, the planet. It wasn't until the modern age, with improved communications, Internet and online tools, that we began to really collaborate on a mass scale.

Yuval Harari, the acclaimed author of *Sapiens* and *Homo Deus*, clearly demonstrates that larger groups of 'networked humans' are a positive force. His books describe how networked communities generate far more creativity and productivity than isolated, smaller groups of humans. This is why you would generally see an accumulation of better skills, services, and opportunities in bigger cities compared to small country towns.

It's a truism that big cities like New York, London and Paris are home to the finest institutions and educational facilities, alongside the biggest companies offering some of the highest salaries and best opportunities, as well as some of the largest stadiums, groundbreaking hospitals, leading universities, and most acclaimed restaurants. Cities get all the good stuff. This is, without exception, never the case in small towns or villages.

As we have seen, larger networked groups allow for the greater specialization of tasks, and cities are a great illustration of this. The ability for people to specialize is probably the single biggest catalyst for the human race moving from cave dwellers to sophisticated beings.

We can only go to work and 'write code,' to build the next big startup, because someone else has already taken care of building us a house, creating public transport, manufacturing our laptop, and farming our food. If we had to farm our own food and sew our clothes before we went to work, we would never actually get to work—farming and sewing would be our work.

The network effect means that individuals connect with other individuals to collaborate and create, which can be illustrated as an exponential power law. As seen, a small network of just 10 people has a minimal opportunity for multiplication of its capacity. It has a maximum potential of 100 (10 x 10 = 100). A slightly larger network of 100 people has a significantly higher cumulation of collaborative properties (100 x 100 = 10,000), and a city like London has an incredible collaborative multiplication (9 million x 9 million = 81 trillion).

This reality can be seen in small country towns that offer only a limited range of rudimentary services. Their hospitals, libraries, employment opportunities, sports teams, and stadiums are all a shadow of bigger city counterparts. This is because, by virtue of their smaller size, their budgets are limited, and can only cover the basics such as roads, telecoms, and policing.

Geoffrey West, a British theoretical physicist, distinguished professor, and former president of the Santa Fe Institute, has spent his life studying cities. As adaptive systems of interactions among people, he discovered that a city follows the same scaling law that applies to living organisms.

West found that a city's infrastructure, amenities, and urban systems are subject to a sublinear scaling law of 0.85. In contrast, socioeconomic quantities like income, crime, innovation, and GDP, scale superlinearly with the exponent 1.15. This means that every time a city's population doubles, there is a 15% increase in income, wealth, and innovation, and a corresponding 15% drop in infrastructure demand.

Understanding this scientific model means West can predict a city's crime rates, prosperity, GDP, and even how many gas stations and hospitals they have with an 85% accuracy. He just needs to know the population size.

In short, West's scaling law—customarily applied to living organisms—illustrates that a city's network size creates exponentially more output, for exponentially less input as it grows.

So London might have it pretty good when it comes to interconnectivity. But imagine the step-change in opportunity when we have the entire globe of 8 billion people interacting, trading, collaborating, and creating with each other.

Before the Internet, it wasn't physically possible to network and communicate with the entire planet. There were numerous barriers like time, cost, distance, borders, and language. But with today's technology—the world can now participate in an ever-growing network. The entire world is not yet directly connected to one single network, but it is quickly heading in the right direction.

Today, with 2.9 billion people sharing one single platform like Facebook, the reach of communication and its resulting cooperation, collaboration, trade, and catallaxy are far exceeding levels ever thought possible. Just a few years ago, it would have been a fanciful ambition to have the entire world functionally cooperating—or at least communicating—together. There simply wasn't the technology in place to support this notion. Now there is.

If you put a drop of blue ink into a glass of water, or cream into coffee, the two liquids will quickly blend until the color becomes uniform. In some respects, it is the natural result of entropy. Things start separate and eventually blend. In this same respect, humans naturally interact with each other. They share and interchange foods, music, languages, products, skills, culture, inventions, ideas, and values. And once a connection is made, it is hard to reverse.

Humanity has always demonstrated an urge to expand its territories, face the unknown, and go off and explore. That means that people will inevitably intermingle with other new and different people, and as a result, blend. In its early stage, it would have been called exploration. But in its more mature form, we call it globalization. Globalization refers to the blending of our planet's people, cultures and trade. When you put cream in coffee, it will immediately blend. You cannot stop it, and you certainly can't reverse it once it's happened.

Now that countries are a normalized unit of coordination, and communication flows freely amongst its people, we see a proliferation of ever-widening alliances. Prominent examples are the likes of the European Union for Europe, NAFTA for the Americas, and ASEAN for Asia. The inevitable expansion of networks are demonstrated by the G6, a forum of the world's wealthiest nations forming in 1975, expanding to G7 in the 1980s, and then G20 taking flight in 1999. Equally, the European Union started with just six states in 1993 and expanded to 28—before England ran for the doors.

As existing networks become established, they will inevitably expand beyond their old perimeters, and into new territories. It's human nature to do this. This amalgamation will create a profound step-change in progress, innovation, and growth for everyone, as we all participate and benefit from the worldwide economy.

As demonstrated by Brittan's Brexit, the path towards unification won't always be linear or easy. With 8 billion people and 190 nations, there are many different perspectives, needs, and priorities to assimilate. Some might be concerned by the ebb and flow of political tensions. Whether it's the Middle East, China, Afganistan, Communism, Trumpism, Terrorism, or North Korea testing missiles, progress is far from linear. There are wins and losses, gains and then regression. But as we find more ways to interconnect and network, we are inevitably becoming closer as a human race.

It will not be easy to reach complete unity when trying to align a global population, and in some respects, it will never completely happen. The world will always have cultural, political, ideological, and religious differences, and actually, this diversity should be celebrated and preserved.

The blending of humanity's people, countries, cultures, and companies is a positive and powerful force. It creates cooperation, exchange, trade, and collaboration, leading to innovation, specialization, improvement, and evolution. And once this engine of collaboration is turning, it creates a flywheel effect which generates even more collaboration.

Cooperation at Work

Companies today rely on a complex ecosystem of specialist service providers that enable, power, or protect their business. From electricity, to the Internet, education, supply chain, marketing channels, public transport and roads, and a functional legal system to name a few. In most cases, the interruption of just one or two of these things could easily harm, or kill, the company.

It has been a long time since companies were in any way entirely independent. One or two centuries ago, companies used to keep a lot more of the process in-house because the common infrastructure was not yet available in many cases. For example, when electrification was first invented, there was no central supply of electricity, like we take for granted today. Individual businesses would have to invest in their own generators to produce their own electricity, to power their own factories. Thankfully now, we can simply plug in our computer and rely on someone somewhere to sort out the electricity we need to get it charged.

There are some famous examples of extensively vertically integrated companies, but they are very much the exception rather than the rule.

In producing the world's first mass-production car in 1908, the Ford Motor Company was renowned for making everything in-house for its groundbreaking product. They reportedly sourced everything in its raw form—blocks of steel, rubber, wood, and glass—and made every component of the Model T Ford from its wheels to doors, seats, steering wheel, and dials—from scratch.

Cadbury, the chocolate company, was possibly the first to embrace 'bean to bar' manufacturing. They not only controlled the entire process, making their chocolates from raw materials, but they also provided housing for all their employees. In line with their Quaker traditions, Cadbury built an entire township surrounding their factory, so that everything, including the lodging, food, culture, and behavior of its workforce, was provided for—and controlled.

Alas, these 'all-in-one' practices are now, like Cadbury's charming old chocolate boxes, quaint relics of the past, with only rare examples remaining.

Today, car companies are renowned for producing their parts through a dizzying network of thousands of individual specialized external suppliers. This leaves the core company just to design the cars, set specifications for each partner-built component, order the parts, and assemble them. In fact, in some countries, the assembly is also contracted out, or licensed, to partners—leaving the car brand essentially just designing, marketing, and coordinating its concept. Some companies might even outsource parts of their design and marketing roles to consultants, agencies, or domain experts.

Elon Musk's Tesla and SpaceX are known for going back to first principles and making everything in-house. But they aren't quite going all the way back to basic raw materials. Elon is not making the paint for the cars, the tires for the wheels, the LCD screens, or the computer chips. He also relies on external expertise to build his buildings and fund his projects. Plus, I assume that he is probably working from an externally sourced Apple Mac and sending emails from Gmail. In addition, his companies exist within the American market and legal system—from which the corporate entities can trade, raise funding, and enforce contracts securely. All of these things rely on the existence of complex ecosystems and are the result of immense interdependence. Despite being lauded for first principles manufacturing, he is very much dependent on an incredible network of brilliant tools, products and skills to get his creations out the door—and onto the moon.

Today, after centuries of deepening cooperation and trade, the world is interconnected like never before. When two parties trade, it creates a complex relationship of codependency. Usually, one person is the client and the other the supplier, but both stand to win from the interaction, and equally, both stand to lose, if it doesn't go to plan. And so trade creates this curiously compelling bond that is equal parts risk and reward, dominance and subjugation, controller and controlled.

No one knows this better than Apple—the world's pre-eminent king of luxury technology. The tech giant maintains a complex web of partnerships to develop, supply, make, and ship its popular products. Among thousands of others, it partners with Chinese specialists to manufacture its iPhone, and its semiconductors—the mechanical brains behind any kind of computing—are mainly sourced from Taiwan's TSMC. In the beginning, Apple was very much in control of the manufacturing relationship, but after partnering for years, it is now very much dependent on both China and Taiwan's ability to produce the world's cutting-edge technology. Despite Apple becoming the world's first trillion-dollar company, it cannot call the shots on its own process and supply chain. It can influence, but it cannot control. Even if Apple tried to bring their production in-house or back to America—they simply couldn't. America can simply not compete against the technological capabilities of China, and even if it did, the product would cost ten times the price.

The reality is that neither Apple, China, nor TSMC, have the upper hand in any of these relationships. These companies and the entire global economy are now all inextricably intertwined. They are completely codependent on each other. Not only does Apple rely on its intricate supply chain to build the product, but it also needs the smooth coordination and cooperation of the shipping and freight industry, the retail stores and shopping malls, the media, and marketing channels, as well as the ongoing affluence and stability of society so that consumers can actually purchase their products. If just one of these pieces in the puzzle stopped working for any period of time, Apple would face severe interruptions and even complete failure. This entire ecosystem mimics a complex living organism where each of the individual parts has incredible autonomy, capability, and complexity, but needs the other parts' presence to survive. Despite Apple's domination, it is in some respects no more than a participant, or even a servant, to the ecosystem in which it exists.

Smaller businesses are even more dependent on their network environment. For example, a little coffee shop would rely on external partners for almost everything. They would rarely produce their own coffee beans or bake their own bread. Instead, they buy products from wholesalers, who in turn buy their raw components from a range of other suppliers—each of them specializing specifically in just a few things. They buy or lease their coffee machine from a manufacturer, have their shop fitted out by specialists, and likely their store signage, taxes, and marketing are done by others.

When you break everything down to its constitutional parts, you might wonder if any of it needs to be, or should, be done in-house at all. Surely, there are better, more specialized experts out there for every part of any production, marketing, distribution, and organizational puzzle? Maybe there is.

As this chapter highlights, despite strong notions of autonomy and individuality, we have never really acted independently. It would be impossible to even write with a pencil if it was not for the support of an entire global community. We are just a tiny node within an enormous network of interlinked communities and infrastructure. Far from being a bad thing, it is an incredible, almost miraculous thing, that has come out of only the last few thousand years of human evolution—and we are the only species to do it.

As technology improves, we will see further step changes in our ability to connect, collaborate, and work with anyone else on the planet. We are doubtlessly moving towards, and not away from, a progressively homogenized world, culture, and economy. As the web of cooperation expands, we are all moving closer to a functional network of 8 billion people. That's 8 billion people all working together: trading, sharing, competing, collaborating, producing, and consuming.

No man is an island, no business operates in isolation, and no country is independent. Just as it takes a globalized army of people to construct one pencil, the entire world is interconnected on every level for every interaction within it. The nationalists among us might see this as a curse, but it is actually an incredible opportunity. To have 8 billion people working independently and serving their own interests, yet in some way in unison, is a compelling and powerful concept.

We are seeing this happen within the employment market right now, as the world's workforces meld into one. And everyone stands to benefit.

Outsourcing In Concept

Exploring Outsourcing

Many centuries ago, society's early merchants became some of the wealthiest people of their time by sourcing rare and unusual products from the far-flung corners of the then infrequently traversed globe. The basic premise of these merchants was to explore the as yet unchartered world, discover new civilizations, and bring home an exciting array of exotic products from alien cultures. Every culture would have its unique crops, products, and specialties back then, and local producers would gladly trade their unique wares.

The merchants would bring home their discoveries to eagerly awaiting consumers who would excitedly incorporate the new finds into their lifestyles. One of the big hits was peppercorns— otherwise known as black gold. No one gets that excited about pepper these days, but it was an immediate sensation when it was 'discovered' by the Europeans. Peppercorns originated in India, and were initially discovered and traded by the Arabs in the 15th century. They eventually introduced peppercorns to Europe and the Romans, who all went crazy for the spice. The competition got so heated that prices went berserk, with a pound of pepper eventually costing between $5,000 and $40,000 of today's money. Because of the intense popularity and audacious prices, European explorers contrived to cut out the Arab middlemen and source the rare spice for themselves. They eventually did, but it took them 50 years of exploration on fleets of sail ships to eventually find the country of India, and finally the source of the peppercorns.

That all sounds like a lot of work for a bit of pepper on your steak. But this was the nature of the early merchant trade. It all fuelled incredible exploration and dealmaking, and resulted in the discovery and adoption of many of the now-common items that we all take for granted today.

The adventurous merchants sourced an impressive range of specialties like olive oil from Italy, fashion from France, and china —like tableware and vases—from China. They also introduced the world to port from Portugal, Ceylon tea from Ceylon, champagne from Champagne, cologne from Cologne, cognac from Cognac, and...you get the idea.

The global sourcing and trade of physical products used to be a hugely complex affair. The endless logistical challenges such as months of sailing across the treacherous seas, lawless pirates, communication barriers, taxes and tariffs, quality control, and a complete lack of internationalization made it an almost impossible mission. Certainly, at best, it was a highly risky endeavor, with as many as 30% of the ships—along with its crew and cargo—never making it back.

Allowing for a short side story here, it was, in fact, the costly repeated loss of fleets and merchandise that spawned the concept of insurance, and the subsequent global insurance industry that followed. The individual losses from a sunken ship were so big, that an inspired Edward Lloyd came up with the idea of sharing any possible losses between a group of investors. Lloyd reasoned that while the losses from a sunken vessel was catastrophic to one person, if it was shared by many, the impact is minimized. For example, with a shipwreck costing $1 million, when shared between 10,000 people, it costs only $100 each. Instead of facing an unpredictable but ruinous loss of $1 million individually, people now have the option of cooperating together and paying $100 each. They have to pay this all the time, even if there are no wrecks. However, the smaller amount can be factored into the cost of doing business, and is at least tolerable, known, and reliable. Most importantly, it protects them from a $1 million catastrophe. In essence, he created an economic instrument leveraging human cooperation that allowed for the cost and risk of a downed ship and cargo to be shared between a wider group of people. With this ingenious innovation, Lloyd had created what was to become the modern insurance industry of today. It all began from a small coffee house on Tower Street in London, in 1688. It was called Lloyd's of London, and they are still leading maritime insurers today. This little anecdote is yet another powerful example of the value and utility of networked cooperation between humans. Necessity is indeed the mother of invention.

Today, we take for granted how easy it is for us to trade amongst each other. International trade was an enormously complex affair before streamlined technology, communications, marketplaces, and infrastructure. To be an old-world international merchant, you needed extensive global infrastructure and a sophisticated logistics network—all before the days of the Internet, telephone, and electricity. With real-life pirates out to get your stash, it was a challenge, to say the least. However, if you did manage to build and secure a network, the rewards were also huge. Merchants of the old world were commonly richer than the kings and governments of their day. Mastering global trade and solving the associated logistical complexities made these companies the Googles of their time.

Needless to say, international trade is infinitely simpler

today. Helped by sophisticated ecosystems that offer seamless communications, turnkey third-party logistics, and easy travel, payment, contract, legal, and packaging solutions. In addition, the rise of simplistic online 'prosumer' marketplaces like Amazon and Alibaba, among many others, now make international trade as easy as ordering a pizza. With all of these individual services combined, it is now infinitely easier to explore, source, and trade internationally. These are examples of the valuable 'rails,' or ecosystems, that have been laid down ahead of us by others, so that we can now easily participate within a market, without too much thought or difficulty.

Alibaba, of course, did not 'invent' international trade. They just made the interface straightforward, systematized the approach, and added layers of trust and reliability in the form of reviews, recourse, and centralized governance. But these steps all contribute to a significantly easier experience for everyone. Now, if you want some pepper, it is abundant and cheap. You can go to your local market or buy it online in bulk from India directly. You don't need to risk your life to get it anymore, and if you're not happy with what you get, your money will be refunded.

The merchants of old were the first to really leverage offshore services for the benefit of their own home market. By sourcing products internationally, they were able to distribute valuable merchandise locally that created a win-win opportunity for all. Everyone became wealthier as a result of the trade, consumers got what they wanted, and the collaboration resulted in the closer alignment of global participants. Following hundreds of years of this behavior, we can see that the shift from siloed nation-state self-sufficiency to a globally networked economy has created greater abundance and prosperity for all. Just as its a good thing that the cotton looms were eventually mechanized, it seems that it is also a good thing that the once disparate world started trading together. Instead of trying to make port better than the Portuguese, the merchants successfully outsourced that to the experts, and everyone won.

Specialization

Some people are against outsourcing. Others are into it. But in truth, everyone outsources. It's really just another type of trade. In the same way that we rely on other people to make the pencils we write with, outsourcing is just a form of cooperative trade with someone else, who can get a job done better, faster, or cheaper than we could.

In this respect, trade, specialization, and outsourcing are nothing new. It has always played a huge part in our lives. It's just that we don't necessarily notice it. Take, for example, the moment when you finish work late, and you simply don't have the time or the energy to cook. So you call on the trusty services of your local Thai takeaway. With little effort, you have successfully outsourced that part of your daily routine to someone who specializes in making great Thai food, who is happy to cook it for you, and can probably do it much better.

Your reliance on specialists probably doesn't just stop there, though. If you're like 99% of your contemporaries, you also wisely outsource your car repairs to a mechanic, your children's education to a teacher, and your household maintenance to a handyman. In short, we're all familiar with the concept.

In practical terms, 'trade' and 'outsourcing' are analogous. They are essentially referring to the act of getting someone else to do certain jobs or services for you. It happens in both your personal life as well as in business.

One of the primary justifications for outsourcing is that most companies can, and should, only specialize in one or two things. These are referred to as key or core competencies. If a company strays too far away from its core competencies, then they risk inefficiency, distraction, and loss of focus.

For example, an accounting firm, Happy Books, might be great at accounting, but one day they realize that they also need to promote their company, improve their website, get active on social media, and tell the world they exist. Happy Books have all the right accountants in place, because that's what they specialize in, and it's also how they earn their money. But for Happy Books, marketing is just not its thing. They kind of don't get it, and that's okay, because they're an accounting firm after all and not a marketing agency. And even if they did get it, they can't necessarily afford the five full-time specialists to cover the various skill sets needed—including a web developer, copywriter, email marketer, automation specialist, and social media manager—to design and implement a successful strategy. As a result, Happy Books decided to outsource this service to a specialized marketing agency—Happy Sales. Happy Sales has the requisite skills to do the job that Happy Books needs, and already has all the specialized marketing roles in place—because that's what they do. And so they allocate some of their resources to their new client by means of a tailored service or productized offering.

There is really no limit to what can be, and is, outsourced to trade partners. There is a good argument for the lower level and easier activities to be outsourced, since they are less mission-critical and easier to teach. These functions are also more repetitive in nature and so can generally be more easily scaled. Typical examples are bookkeeping, data entry, research, and customer service, but literally any rudimentary role can be outsourced.

Equally, there is a good argument for the most complex roles within a business to be outsourced to specialized firms. Typically you see this with many technical, professional, senior, and advisory requirements. For example, a company might need the occasional legal or tax advice, or technical or branding guidance from experts. However, they don't need these people full time, and they would neither be able to afford them full time, even if they wanted.

If both the top and bottom of the pyramid can, and often is, outsourced, then it also stands to reason that outsourcing can just as easily be applied to the middle of the pyramid. And indeed, it can, and is. The opportunity for specialization to enhance a company's processes is very real.

Technology has helped a lot with this shift towards interdependent trade. Now that people largely work digitally, and can quickly send an email, jump on a Zoom call, or chat over Slack, it allows companies to engage with a wide array of experts and specialized service providers, from across the globe, in an almost instantaneous and frictionless manner.

Typically one of the main constraints of outsourcing to third-party experts though is the additional cost that it incurs. It costs more to partner with third-parties because they also have to provide and cover the costs of the service and generate a profit margin on top of their contribution. This layering of costs and profit margins can quickly erode any profits left over for the principal. However, when you combine the concepts of outsourcing with the globalized workforce, then you can get both the expertise and significant cost savings in the same go.

In most cases, people mistake the offshore staffing industry with outsourcing. While much of this might be semantics, it is valuable to split the two out. We will focus on this topic in the coming chapters, but for now, it will suffice to say that outsourcing and the offshore staffing industry offer two different value propositions. The primary specialization of offshore staffing is not necessarily the provision of business services like accounting and customer service. Instead, the primary specialization is the facilitation of a globalized workforce. It is not to say that these firms don't also provide high-quality business services like accounting, but predominantly, it is the access to the global workforce that is the real differentiating factor.

To lean on an example from above, Alibaba specializes in connecting American merchants with Chinese manufacturers. This is their core value proposition, and they have built a lot of infrastructure around this offering. However, it is also true that Alibaba provides a lot of household decorations on its website. It might even have a section of the website dedicated to these products and offer special services in relation to this segment. Some observers might see and conclude that Alibaba specializes in home decorations, and in some respects, this is true. But it is more accurate to say that they facilitate easy trade with Chinese manufacturers as their specialization, and home decoration is one of the products of this service.

So while the offshore staffing sector does provide business solutions like accounting, customer service, and sales, their main specialization is actually in the facilitation of globalized employment, and is the core offering from which other services are offered. We will dive deeper into this topic in the following chapters.

Towards Digitization

Trade is usually divided into two broad segments in business—products and services.

In the modern world, the specialized sourcing of physically manufactured products has been happening for much longer than service-based outsourcing. For many decades, China, Japan, and Taiwan have been the outsourced manufacturing hubs for the

US and much of the West. This global supply chain is now so normalized, that we all get excited, and brim with pride, when something is actually made locally.

Unlike product outsourcing, the service-side of outsourcing has been much slower to develop, has not yet become universal, nor reached the collective consciousness of society. However, this is now about to change.

As we have discussed, with the relentless digitization of the world, the service sector will continue its trajectory towards prominence and domination. There will always be a need for physical products of course, but much of tomorrow's activity will be in the digital space. The move towards information and knowledge-based services will happen in both a traditional onshore setting, and also in the newer offshore context.

Similar to products, services have also long been supplied by specialists. Companies have been outsourcing aspects of their business to specialized firms as far back as the beginning of commerce. It is common for smaller companies to seek specialists for their accounting, bookkeeping, and web design, for example. They might also outsource their marketing and would most likely have any vehicles maintained by a specialized mechanic and the computers and servers managed by someone else.

The sourcing of services, instead of products, has become far more prevalent today, in step with the overall shift towards digitization and a service-based economy. This is corroborated by the fact that most new startups and businesses today are service- and information-based solutions. Think, SaaS and marketplaces, cybersecurity and AI, web services and digital agencies, lawyers and accountants, and even 'influencers,' gamers, and YouTubers, to name a few. This is a massive shift away from the economies-of-old where physical manufacturing was the mainstay.

As things continue to move toward a digital economy, thousands of new jobs are being created to support the new activity. For example, nascent broad sectors like 'YouTube' will be broken down from one big broad category into a multitude of new subsectors, careers, jobs, and functions. As other new categories mature and expand, they will also be broken down into their constitutional parts. Entire new categories of careers, jobs, and experts will emerge for people who specialize in getting them done. In focusing on a narrow capability, these specialists of tomorrow will do their jobs better, cheaper, and more efficiently than others.

If you think about it, the Internet, and everything on it, simply didn't exist 30 years ago. From YouTube, to Facebook, Twitch, Amazon, e-commerce, blogging, influencers, and TikTok, it has all appeared out of nowhere. At the beginning of the Internet, there were obviously very few jobs in the sector. Now, the online economy has grown so large that it has created, and supports, dozens of industries, hundreds of sub-sectors, and thousands of complex, specialized roles within it. It now collectively employs tens of millions of people, across an endless array of jobs, covering every country on the planet. Email automation, SEOers, frontend and backend developers, UI/UX designers, database engineers, conversion specialists, content writers, funnel designers, network engineers, data security, hackers, and backlinkers—all these jobs have seemingly popped out of the ground, virtually overnight, like mushrooms. None of that existed just three decades ago.

With the emergence of this new digitized economy, the geographical relevance of its production and consumption is also becoming immaterial. This means that with the digitization of the 'product,' the roles making the product are also being digitized. With such a high velocity of change and the birth of new sectors, jobs and expertise seemingly overnight, the people that do these jobs and the way in which these jobs are done, will also quickly change. The digitization of work and its workers also means that access to the global workforce is being unlocked. And as the digital world breaks down the friction associated with global employment, then the international labor force will start to gain prominence. The new global workers will have to compete at an international level of competency and quality, but their significantly lower salaries will undoubtedly help their adoption by the market.

As previously mentioned, the more common examples of outsourced services are accounting and marketing, but it can just as easily extend to any role that can be done on a computer or from in front of a monitor—which is virtually anything and everything these days. While there are many cutting-edge roles like AI, big data and animation, to use as interesting examples, there are many more standard ones that are more applicable to the average business. Some examples include business development, digital marketing, strategy consulting, content writing, design, developers, appointment setters, customer service, HR, recruitment, and the list goes on. All of these are now readily available in the new offshore global economy.

If you are reading this, and your business is within the physical economy, and you're feeling a bit left out, don't be concerned. You might be a plumber or electrician, or even make drones or space rockets—and wondering how all of this applies to you. As the world's economy continually expands outward, any business can tap into and benefit from digitization, the global workforce, and the migration towards service-based solutions. In fact, it's almost impossible for you not to be swept along by it.

When considering digital and offshore services for physical businesses, it is valuable to clearly identify which parts of the company are well and truly in the physical domain, and which crossover into the digital. For example, an electrician has a very physical business, with the core activity requiring a person to visit a physical location. However, there are still many digital and knowledge-based activities that are an integral part of the business. Marketing, customer service, scheduling, recruitment, finance, and web development are all critical elements, and can all be plugged into and benefit from the global digital economy.

We can't all be good at everything. This is especially the case as the world continues to expand rapidly in all directions, and as all products, services, and sectors continually increase in complexity and specialization.

The world—and your business—will continue to see more and more specialization of roles. As the world gets more complex and more closely networked, it is inevitable. More job requirements will necessarily be outsourced to specialists as the world moves into a more service- and information-based global economy. We will continue to see a rise in the prevalence of outsourcing in business —and also in our personal lives.

The result of this exponentially expanding economy means that more people are becoming increasingly networked, engaged in cross-trade, and offering wider access to more specialized services. This enhances innovation, efficiency and growth, which in turn generates even more trade and collaboration.

Luckily, we don't actually need to be good at everything. In fact, the economic model of catallaxy demonstrates that it is actually better for everyone if you specialize in just a limited range of core competencies, and then cooperate with others to get the rest of the work done. It benefits you, it benefits them, and it creates a self-perpetuating cycle that ultimately benefits everyone.

For those who are worried about job destruction as a result of outsourcing—fear not. The world has a fantastic ability to exponentially expand, adding dozens of new jobs every second onto the 'to-do list of life.' The growth of innovation and specialization is limited only to the imagination of society's brightest minds, and its wildest dreamers.

Global Workforce

You Versus the Globe

A global economy and a globally-sourced workforce is the future, and it is not going away.

Just as it is impossible to separate coffee and cream once mixed, and the Internet can never be turned off once turned on, globalization cannot be undone.

Rather than being an end product in itself, the inevitable blending and ultimate globalization of the world is really just a by-product of the continued cooperation between humans that we have seen for thousands of years. As technology improves, interactions increase, and the economy progresses, globalization— barring any major interruptions like war—will march onward.

Globalization may create new challenges for companies, but it also offers a raft of compelling opportunities for development and growth.

In today's world, a traditional shop is no longer confined to its local geography. Now, it can expand its customer base well beyond the physical constraints of its physical retail space. Thanks to e-commerce platforms, easy third-party logistics, cheap offshore manufacturing, and a hungry global audience, someone's market size is now only limited by their appetite to compete.

In the past, for most traditional businesses, its Total Addressable Market (TAM) was determined by the catchment of its local village, town, or suburb. Even if the company was in downtown Manhattan, despite being in a city of 8 million people, the physical catchment area would mostly limit it to the local residents that lived or worked around it. So a high-density suburb in New York might expose a business to 100,000 or even 200,000 people at most. Not bad, but it's certainly limited. Most other businesses across most standard towns would be left with a catchment of maybe just 20,000 people.

Now, businesses have the opportunity to market and sell globally. That's 8 billion potential customers—and a 4 million percent increase compared to the Manhattan shopfront. And you don't even have to pay rent!

As consumers, most of us are happy to buy a sweater made in China, Turkey, or Pakistan because it costs so much less than one made in our home country. Even the world's most reputable brands selling luxurious products have their items made from these countries, mostly using the same manufacturers. Global sourcing and sales is now an utterly normalized phenomenon.

A natural extension of globalization is that the world's workforces will amalgamate into one. As the notion of work moves from physical labor, to a digital contribution, people can now collaborate together, seamlessly from all corners of the globe. As remote work becomes normalized, it highlights the opportunity to source staff from a deeper pool of candidates. Businesses are continually facing constraints on resources, and hiring people is one of the most expensive activities that a business must do. Having access to the global workforce offers a huge pool of highly qualified candidates at a fraction of the cost. As these trend lines continue to converge, we will eventually be left with one single seamless market, from which we can buy, sell, work, trade, experience, and consume.

Staff outsourcing is a direct product of globalization and technology. With communication technology, and a connected world, it's now possible to build a team of people, for your business, that is spread across the globe.

The outsourcing industry has been working for 30 years to make this a reality, and to make it accessible, flexible, affordable and reliable for the masses. The outsourcing industry has long been exclusively available to big businesses only—but recently, this has changed. Offshore staffing is now within easy reach of small and medium-sized companies of the world.

Does this mean you, as a business owner, entrepreneur, or hiring manager, have to outsource in today's global marketplace? Absolutely not. But it should compel you to seriously investigate whether some degree of offshoring can positively impact your business.

If, for example, offshoring means that you were able to produce a better service at a cheaper cost for your clients, you would be remiss if you didn't at least explore this opportunity.

Offshoring is changing the rules of the game. People haven't invited these changes—but they are happening regardless. But change in the workplace, and the world, has, and will always, occur. And this is no different.

You may choose not to ride this wave; it is your prerogative. But it would be foolhardy to simply ignore it. Businesses that embrace and evolve with the times tend to be more resilient than those inflexible to change.

Lee Kuan Yew, Singapore's founding father, and former Prime Minister, probably said it best: "If you deprive yourself of outsourcing and your competitors do not, you're putting yourself out of business."

Companies generally cannot afford to ignore the progress that comes with globalization. To thrive in the 21st century, today's businesses, whether large or small, must accept that they are now competing on the world's stage and not merely on their local Main Street.

8 Billion Employees

Globalization has had a profound impact on how we trade with each other—both from the consumption and production side of things. As the relevance of location and distance continues to diminish, increased cooperation and interconnectivity will result.

Globalization will continue to broaden the workforce we come into contact with and enhance the 'pool' from which we hire. Eventually, there will be one giant employment pool, and one single workforce, instead of the current geographically fractured markets that we have in place today.

As more people enter the single market, the opportunity for trade, and especially employment, will exponentially expand. Currently, only 63% of the world's population—5 billion people— have access to the Internet. Though this is quickly changing.

The early users of the Internet—i.e. wealthy countries—mostly participated as 'consumers.' They consumed content, games, and products through the Internet. In contrast, the later entrants to the Internet age—those from the developing economies—will predominantly be the 'producers.' They will be the workers of the Internet era—in the beginning at least.

Most of the 3 billion people that aren't online yet, commonly earn less than $5 per day. They are starting right from the bottom of the pyramid—at the moment. But as they become more educated and culturally aligned, they will become more relevant, eligible, and valuable to the market. Previously there were a lot of hurdles that prevented people from getting an education. Slowly but surely, those barriers are dropping. Now, those with the Internet can access for free, endless content, and some of the best knowledge, learning systems and education in the world. Khan Academy, MOOCs, Duolingo, YouTube, Coursera, and many hundreds more—enable the world's less fortunate to upskill and enter the global economy.

Over the coming generations, there will be another 3 billion people entering the global employment market. There is an enormous disparity in global earning potential right now. Market forces will eventually cause salaries to reach a better balance, although we will likely never see a 'true' parity, whatever that really means. Even in an efficient market like the US, for example, we see the spread between its highest earners and the lowest earners widen, so it isn't likely that we will ever see complete congruence across an entire market of 8 billion people. However, a single efficient marketplace will create a better balancing of salaries, and a pricing system that is guided more by competency and meritocracy, rather than the country that you happen to be born in.

There are already many millions of online, well educated, and culturally-aligned people that will happily work for significantly lower salaries than their Western counterparts. Previously these people were not viable candidates for the typical Western employer, because they were stuck in a different country. But this is all changing.

As more of the world moves online, and technology offers seamless communication and remote-enabled tools as standard, and remote-work becomes normalized, these lower-cost candidates are suddenly an enticing alternative.

Many people in society see this shift as a huge threat to their own employment stability and prospects. This global market will indeed create a readjustment, and the relative prosperity will drop for some. But the network effect of a larger, more efficient market, will doubtlessly create exponentially more opportunities and wealth for the globe and its people over the medium term.

While it is likely that eventually, a new global equilibrium will be reached, it is unlikely that it will happen too quickly. There will be a steady stream of 3 billion new participants entering the new world market over the coming years. Since there is a large supply of people, who are happy to earn a relatively cheap salary, then it stands to reason that the low-end of salaries would remain modest for a long time to come.

However, the ever-expanding market and increased prosperity across the board will probably offset any softening on prices. After all, modern outsourcing and globalization have been happening in earnest for the last 30 years and we haven't yet seen a softening in salaries or a spike in unemployment as a result. This globalization phenomenon is really just a ramping continuation of the trade, cooperation, specialization, and catallaxy that we have seen over the last few hundred years. This interaction generated enormous opportunity and prosperity for the globe and its people over that time, and there is no reason to think that that would change.

Different Types of Outsourcing

Globalization is happening all around us. Relative to the offshoring of physical product manufacturing, the offshoring of staffing has been relatively slow to start and catch on. But this is about to change. Now, more than any other sector, there's a perfect storm forming around the globalization of employment. In short, this means that offshore staffing will eventually become the norm, and pervasive across the western world of business. I have outlined some of the reasoning for this below.

Knowledge-Based Work

The currencies of the 4th revolution are information, data, software, and knowledge. This work can be done from anywhere using very standardized tools. This is highlighted by the example that Matt Mullenweg can grow one of the world's most influential companies, using a standard laptop and a distributed workforce that work from anywhere.

Converging Cultural Alignment

The younger generations of the world are all inevitably converging. Kids across the globe all learn, communicate, and evolve—for better or worse—using online platforms like YouTube, TikTok, Facebook, Instagram, Twitch, Discord, and others. Regardless of where these kids come from, they are all mingling on the same platforms. The world of tomorrow is already infinitely more intermingled than our generation is today. Additionally, most of these platforms are free to use, so they are equally accessible to emerging populations.

Alignment of Tools and Communications

The dramatic improvement and adoption of software—such as Slack, Skype, Zoom, Trello, and Asana, among many others—means that the methods by which remote work is done are becoming increasingly normalized. It was not so long ago that the concept of paperless offices was a hopeful but challenging proposition. Now it is the default, and anything other than paperless seems weird. As it becomes normal to work with the tools mentioned above, remote work becomes a natural and easy step.

Technological Enhancement

As predicted by Moore's Law, computer processing speed has, quite incredibly, doubled every 18 months for the last 55 years.

With it, almost every other aspect of communication technology has improved instep. Computers are cheaper, lighter and more powerful than ever. The Internet has gotten faster and cheaper, and software, apps, and tools continually improve. And the cutting edge of algorithms, AI, big data, virtual reality, wearables, and quantum computing are all relentlessly progressing. As every day goes by, the technology that enables the global workforce gets increasingly powerful, cheaper, and more accessible. This, in turn, enables the workforce to do more, more efficiently.

Affinity to the Online World

The youth of today demonstrate with their actions that they enjoy, and even prefer, online and technology-enhanced communications. We see this with the millennials spending all day texting each other, interacting in Facebook communities, and the massive rise in virtual gaming worlds, as well as the darker side of gaming addiction, and the toxic effects of Instagram on our youth.

Remote Work

The COVID pandemic quickly forced the world to go remote. They say that one year of COVID has advanced many industries by 10 years—and remote work is certainly one of these. The pandemic has forcibly introduced a lot of companies and workers to the remote work paradigm. Some love it, others hate it, but it has at least brought the concept, tools, and habits of location-independent work to the forefront of the collective consciousness.

Many employers have now realized that it is an option. They have also realized that if their staff are working online and from some other location in their city, they could just as easily be working from another country altogether. If there was nothing to be gained by this, then it would be a moot point. But if there was the possibility of saving 70% on costs, it becomes something worth exploring.

Removal of Borders and Government Controls

Governments and their border controls have strictly controlled the flow of physical products and labor migration. However, knowledge work, information technology, and its workforce cannot be tracked or managed in the same way. The creation and transfer of production and value, in the form of information, is virtually impossible to police. As of yet, there has been no regulation put in place to control what is effectively 'virtual worker migration,' and it seems that it would be very difficult to do.

Growing Awareness and Acceptance

Part of the challenge with any emerging industry, trend, or product is the awareness and adoption curve of the future users of that market. According to Innovation Theory, the adoption of a new innovative market is characterized by five different avatars: the innovators, early adopters, early majority, late majority, and laggards. It takes the innovators and early adopters to first try the new product, before eventually, the early majority participate. Finally, the late majority and laggards will follow. Every industry follows these stages, and offshore staffing is no different. Incorporating offshore staffing into a business, like anything else, requires the formation of new habits, and the dissolution of old ones. So it takes time, and in this regard, change is slow.

Emergence of Platforms

Online platforms and marketplaces help build a market. Before Uber, there were taxis, but Uber made it so much easier and more enjoyable that usage skyrocketed. Alibaba makes it safe and easy to connect and communicate with Chinese manufacturers. This opened the once complex market up to a legion of new e-commerce entrepreneurs. And marketplaces for hotels, flights, credit cards, restaurants, and home buying are all taken for granted.

We see a slow but sure rise in marketplaces representing the various offshoots of globalized employment. Upwork and Fiver are now well-known examples of the part-time, amateur, and project end of the freelance market. TopTal and Lemon.io offer remote-based contractors from a global pool. And recent startups like Deel and Remote provide global payroll and EOR (Employer of Record) solutions. And of course, Outsource Accelerator marketplace aggregates and represents the 3,500 outsourcing firms that make up the 30-year-old offshore industry. These platforms all contribute to the awareness and understanding of global sourcing and make it easier for businesses to participate.

Progress is Everywhere

Hopefully, the earlier chapters of this book have demonstrated that progress is relentless and certain. We are on a trajectory of globalized employment, and it will only speed up.

All these factors are individually and collectively contributing to an increasingly online world and a unified global workforce. Technology is quickly changing the way we both live and work. The only things that are relatively slow to change are our own habits and routines. This means that it can take a few years to make meaningful changes to the traditional organizational structures that we have grown accustomed to. However, as we have seen with paperless offices, it does eventually happen. The recent pandemic has certainly helped with the awareness and adoption of remote work, which for many, could be a stepping stone toward global work. And just like coffee and cream, once the two have been introduced, there's no going back.

As globalization and technology reduce the relevance of location-based employment, global employment will not only become a good option, it will become the default. Global employment simply means sourcing your next employees from a global pool of unlimited candidates. Simple. Compared to traditional employment, which restricts you to a local and limited pool of candidates, the benefits seem obvious. When you combine this, with the added bonus that you can save 70% on your staffing costs, then offshoring becomes an increasingly compelling choice.

Part 2

About Outsourcing

2.1

Employment

What is Employment?

Employment, in its simplest form, is traded labor. And the trade of labor, which has effectively derived from the earliest division of labor and specialization, has been happening in some form or another since basically the beginning of time. It forms the foundation of our economy, and is a fundamental part of our society—and way of life. In fact, it is so fundamental to who we are as people and what we do in our daily lives that we mostly wouldn't know what to do with ourselves if we didn't have it. We all know what employment is, in concept, but it's so foundational that most don't think about it in any depth, and rarely, if ever, explore its traits, routines, and traditions.

As David Foster Wallace observes in his speech "This is Water," fish mostly don't realize that they exist within water and are surrounded by water. It is so ubiquitous that they don't even notice it. Employment is a little bit like that for us in our society.

We all expect to be employed in some capacity within our lifetime, and we spend much of our earlier years preparing ourselves for the system that will eventually employ us. It's so universal that it's by-product, money, provides the essential means with which we feed and clothe ourselves and provide warmth and shelter for our family. The justification for working is so deeply intertwined with so many of our core human philosophies of contribution, selflessness, sacrifice, and being part of a bigger purpose.

Not only is it central to the way we live our lives, but labor itself is really the fundamental core resource of our economy. Nothing would get done, produced, shipped, invented, or iterated without labor.

Modern work and employment is an incredibly broad term, covering everything from full-time employees, part-timers, students, interns, apprentices, and everything in between. It also includes contractors, volunteers, temps, gig-workers, as well as consultants, agencies, and advisers. A relatively small number of the population will venture to the other side of the fence and do the employing. But it's all employment.

If you zoom in, the employment of people is an enormously complex affair. There are endless rules and regulations to stay compliant, and millions of books written on how to manage people properly, build effective organizations, and get the best out of your workforce. But if you zoom out, then the concept is straightforward. It's something that we all know, understand, and need no introduction.

The nature of work has, of course evolved, over the decades, centuries, and millennia. Though it has remained fairly stable for the last few hundred years, it is always evolving. However, in the last few years, the employment landscape has seen some dramatic changes, and the rate of change is accelerating.

The shift from the industrial revolution to the now 4th revolution has progressively decreased the significance of our physical contributions and emphasized our conceptual, creative, and intellectual contributions. It has removed the relevance of physical location and changed 'work' from being a place that you go to, to a thing that you do. And from a timeframe in which you do something, to an output that you deliver.

Before, work would likely be a factory or office job, or a professional career in academia, law, or medicine. There wasn't a lot of choice. People largely dedicated their careers to one line of work, and would only switch jobs once or twice in their lives.

As the world becomes more sophisticated, the diversity of roles and depth of specializations seems to expand infinitely. People are now working more freely than ever. They jump from job to job like stepping stones and criss-cross careers as they please. Most work and jobs are now done through the familiar and increasingly universal interface of your own personal laptop. As the modern worker switches jobs, they could be working for a different employer, from a different country, in a different sector, doing a different role, and using a different skillset, but it will be done from the same laptop and likely the same set of software. So now, instead of needing access to a farm, factory, or office for a living, a simple laptop becomes a universal interface plugging its user directly into the entire global economy.

The move from an economy based on physical production, to one based on bits and bytes, has meant that the workforce and its output is increasingly cerebral and decreasingly physical. In order to get the best out of employees, the work environment is being continually improved and made increasingly social, lenient, and pleasant. The once opposing polarities of work, life, and holidays are all melding into one. Sometimes work can feel more like a holiday, and a holiday—more like work. Certainly, it's a far cry from the mostly back-breaking and physically demanding work that humanity has had to endure for the previous 150,000 years.

Global Employment

The concepts of outsourcing, offshoring, call centers, virtual assistants, and remote workers might seem foreign to you, but it is really just a slightly different take on employment. It is no more different, no less simple, or no more complex than just employment itself.

The only significant differentiator is that instead of working locally, which means physically in the same office as you, these people are now working in a different location. That's it.

The type of work is not necessarily any different. The way that they work is not necessarily any different. The only differentiating factor is that it's done in a different location.

The concept is so simple, yet the world largely hasn't yet caught onto it yet. This is mostly because global employment has only existed for the last 20 to 30 years, which is only very recent when you consider that traditional work has been happening in some form for millennia.

Globalized employment is now only possible because of the recent meteoric advances in technology, communications, the Internet, and the general trend towards digital work and globalization. With all of this infrastructure now in place, and as work becomes increasingly information-based, remote work is moving from a theoretical concept to a realistic and even popular choice.

So while work and standard employment has been happening in some form or another for millennia, the concept of remote work and globalized employment has only been with us for a fraction of that time. This is why it is a very recent and often misunderstood concept. It is also why many people are as yet unaware of its existence, or at least unfamiliar with how it works.

But the thing is, if you zoom out, it is exactly the same as standard employment. It is actually so similar, that if you just thought about it as employment, you would be 99% of the way there. Globalized employment is simply the employment of people from a globalized pool of candidates instead of a limited localized one.

When globalized employment began—just 30 years ago— it was very much a nascent industry. Obviously, technology was nowhere as advanced as it is now. For global employment to work seamlessly, it relies on very powerful technology rails and as a result, the earlier generations of the industry were rudimentary, expensive, and accessible only to highly sophisticated international corporations. It also meant that intermediaries, in the form of call centers and outsourcing firms, played an important role in its facilitation.

However, as technology has advanced, people's access to global staffing has become simpler and cheaper. And as the common acceptance of remote work increases, and the understanding and adoption of its tools grow, then the reliance on outsourcing intermediaries will diminish. Until now, the main facilitators of globalized work are referred to as the outsourcing, offshoring, or IT-BPM industry.

The firms within this industry are typically referred to as call centers, outsourcing suppliers, or BPOs. Also, people can increasingly access global staff directly via popular prosumer marketplaces such as Upwork, Fiver, and Freelancer. In the earlier days, offshore staffing was all part of an obscure B2B subsector. However, as the concept of globalized employment becomes more normalized, the entire industry by association will move out of the shadows and into the mainstream.

There is no reason why any company today should limit their hiring to a local and very finite talent pool from their immediate geographical market. The reason why this remains a dominant approach in most cases is simply because it is traditional, routine, and the standard approach. But as people become more aware of globalized employment, and doing it becomes easier and cheaper, then the move toward an expanded model of global employment from an otherwise more limited pool is somewhat inevitable.

Eventually, it just makes sense that there will be one single global workforce, where sourcing the best people, regardless of their location, will become the default choice, instead of an avant-garde outlier. Just as companies have long since sourced their software, manufacturing, and raw materials globally, and consumers now shop for their entertainment, cars, and fashion globally—all businesses will soon be sourcing their staff from an equivalent global source.

What is Outsourcing?

The first obstacle of this book is to establish what offshoring and outsourcing actually is. In its most basic form, as mentioned, outsourcing is simply, employment. The only variance is that the staff are sitting in a different location.

Unfortunately, the word 'outsourcing' in itself doesn't really accurately portray the industry that it covers. It's a big umbrella term, and one that isn't really representative of what it does…so that's not a great start. On top of that, the outsourcing industry broadly covers a wide and disparate range of varied employment options and business solutions. In short, there is no 'one' type of outsourcing, and there is no one standard approach, nor price.

Remote and distributed employment, offshore employment,

staff augmentation, staff leasing, Employer of Record (EOR), and Professional Employer Organizations (PEO) all fit somewhere within the sector. As do the sub-sectors of virtual assistants, call centers, Business Process Outsourcing (BPO), as well as specialist verticals like offshore accounting, legal, sales, and customer service. Also, the increasingly visible and popular freelancer, gig-work, and project platforms like Upwork, Fiver, and Freelancer are more recent participants of the outsourcing phenomenon.

To add to the milieu, the common moniker for an outsourcing firm is a 'BPO'—which is a functional abbreviation referring to a firm that does 'business process outsourcing.' While not all offshore staffing firms do BPO-type work, for simplicity, they are generally colloquially all clumped together and referred to as BPOs.

The outsourcing sector has exploded recently—in step with the rise of digitization, remote work, distributed teams, and alongside the liberalization and expansion of the concept of work itself. This was helped along, in part, by the recent COVID outbreak. In many ways, the pandemic has been brutal, but it has had the inadvertent benefit of pushing everyone toward a digital-first reality. Businesses were quickly forced to adapt and adopt a remote-friendly, and digital native, environment for their staff and operations, wherever possible. Whether you liked the concept of remote work or not, the whole world has had to embrace it—for a short time at least.

This started a cascading set of events which led to a progressively immersive way of working, and an increasingly flexible workforce. The confluence of technology, globalization, digitization, and this changing trend towards remote-enabled work means that offshoring and outsourcing are becoming more pertinent every day. What started out as a fanciful concept only 30 years ago will soon become a default instead of an unusual exception.

In some corners of the business world, outsourcing is best known for Upwork, the freelancer platforms, and the Virtual

Assistants as popularized by Tim Ferriss. At the other end of the spectrum, most people are aware of the giant offshore call centers that manage much of the world's banking, flight, and billing inquiries, and service the majority of the world's mega-corporations. Unfortunately, both of these attract a disproportionate amount of attention, as well as negative press, with the freelancers often responsible for disappointing work quality and the call centers also derided for their poor service and capabilities.

These are all a part of the recent trend towards global staffing —and cousins, if you like, within the broader outsourcing family. However, the offshore staffing that I am referring to in this book, is a little different to all of these. It emerged 10 to 15 years ago, evolving from the bigger call centers, and was built to specifically address the offshoring needs of the world's small and medium-sized businesses.

Offshore staffing covers a broad spectrum of services, with endless types, suppliers, pricing structures, and methodologies on offer. Usually, firms are generalist in nature, catering to a range of different options, but they can, and do, also specialize in certain approaches, sectors, or verticals.

With an enormous patchwork of loosely connected services, sectors, and naming conventions to navigate, no wonder the average business owner is a little bewildered.

But I don't want this wall of jargon to discourage or confuse you. If you start to feel yourself getting a bit lost in a sea of semantics, I encourage you to bring yourself back to the core definition of offshoring. In its most basic form, it is almost identical to 'traditional employment,' except that the people are sitting somewhere else. These employees are sourced globally, instead of locally. That's it.

The offshore industry really focuses on the facilitation of staffing solutions. They might also add other services or bundle it together and offer certain outcomes, but at the core, the main value proposition is the access that they provide to the global employment market.

The emphasis is really on the facilitation of global employment. The outsourcing industry is just the conduit that enables 'globalized employment' for your business. From another reductionist perspective, they are an employment agency that unlocks the world's workforce. For the purposes of this book—we are referring to 'offshore,' 'nearshore,' or 'global' solutions. This means, significantly, that the staff are sourced from a different country than your own.

In the following chapters, I focus on the benefits of globalized employment, and how you can leverage that opportunity as a business owner, entrepreneur, or hiring manager for your company.

Quick Benefits

I will go deeper into the benefits of offshore staffing, and also how to use it later in this book. For now, I want to provide a brief outline of the core benefits, as they provide some focus, and at the same time, help to explain the concept of outsourcing, and why it's so effective.

- Offshore staffing can save you 70% on staffing costs.
- Offshore staffing is just like traditional employment, in that you manage and treat them like your own people—except that they are sitting in a different location.
- Offshore staffing leverages the global workforce—an incredible 8 billion prospective employees.
- Offshore staffing allows you to source and hire a wide range of highly qualified dedicated staff. It is not just limited to basic roles. Literally, any job, profession, qualification or role is available, as is the case with traditional employment.
- Offshore staffing can assist you with the backend functions

of workforce employment, compliance, administration, and infrastructure as standard.

- Offshore staffing reduces the need for capital investment and gives you access to a highly flexible and scalable team, and facilities.
- Offshore staffing can assist you with designing, building, running, and optimizing your processes and operations.
- Offshore staffing is not always about savings. Instead, it's about the exciting operational upside of being able to triple your workforce for no extra cost.
- Offshore staffing can help you build the sophistication of your company, through process mapping and improvement, and operational enhancement.
- Offshore staffing can assist with a wide range of associated activities related to your staffing needs and daily operations.
- Offshore staffing can offer specialized services, and significant domain expertise, in addition to fulfilling the basic staffing needs—i.e., call centers, accounting, Cx (customer experience), and data.

2.2

Constant Change

Change is Inevitable

Ned Ludd was getting increasingly concerned about his job prospects. He had never been a star performer, but that's okay. A lot of people thought he could have worked a bit harder sometimes, while others outright accused him of being idle. But Ned was committed to his trade, and as far as he was concerned, he was doing a good job. However, the world was quickly changing around him. Emerging technology was beginning to threaten his line of work, and his future prospects were starting to look bleak.

He wasn't quite sure if he was concerned for the industry, or the quality of the product, or maybe it was his livelihood and paycheck. Perhaps all of the above. Or, maybe it didn't matter. Ned's normally a passive guy, but when his back is up against a wall, he's not going to just roll over. He was a craftsman and took pride in his work and product. Yet, he was seeing a worrying trend towards automation. Machines were being installed and started to perform his job. He lamented that these things were no match for his workmanship, and would readily rattle off a list of other shortcomings—if ever invited. But technology seemed to march on, and workers were being replaced.

So he started to speak out. He shared his unease with his workmates and others in the industry, and found that the same issues also resonated with them—the loss of jobs, the compromise of quality, and the obvious ineptitude of the machines. One thing led to another, his issues led to meetings, meetings led to protests, the protests led to a movement, and the movement led to a protracted battle ending in riots and shootings.

Except for the shootings, maybe, the story is not at all unique. We have seen millions of workers collectively displaced as a result of technological progress. Detroit car plants have had their workers replaced by machines, robots operate Amazon warehouses, bank tellers have been swapped for ATMs, supermarkets have installed self-checkouts, and autonomous cars, trains, and airplanes are all on their way. People are continually being threatened and displaced by technological advancement, and Ned was no different.

Ned's plight, is sadly not uncommon, and something that we can all relate to. However, the year was 1779. All of this happened over 200 years ago. Ned Ludd was from a small town near Leicester, in England, which back in the 18th century, was renowned for its world-class textile industry.

For decades, the textile industry used manual wooden looms to weave fabric by hand from cotton and wool. However, with the advent of efficient steam-powered engines, modern mechanized looms emerged. These new machines promised to produce fabric faster than the human craftsmen. They weren't yet able to produce the same quality, and they were not proficient with finer tasks, but the speed and volume were there, which was a good start. Factory owners were beginning to experiment with the machines, and the rest, as they say…is history.

Reading this today, you might think how crazy it is to fear the rise of mechanical cotton looms. In fact, taken from a modern perspective, it might seem frankly ridiculous to think that fabric would be manufactured by anything other than a machine. However, back in 1779, the proposition of mechanical weaving was considered to be, quote: "a fraudulent and deceitful manner."

At the time, the Northern England hand weavers were so enraged that they rose up in protest. With Ned Ludd leading the efforts, the 'Luddite' movement was born. The radical faction gathered momentum and set about destroying textile machinery in protest. The Luddite mutiny raged on, lasting five years, and ultimately to the loss of lives as mill owners and protestors began all-out fighting. According to the now immortalized fable, the dispute was eventually quelled, but only after significant legal and military force.

The moral of this story is either very hard, or very easy to find —depending on your position. I hope I'm not spoiling the story by telling you that...the Luddites were right. Machines did eventually replace the historic hand-weaving techniques. But looking back, would any modern clothes-wearing person ever consider any other alternative?

Now, sewing machines have all but replaced hand sewing. Washing machines have replaced hand washing. Trains replaced the canal boatmen, and basic computers now quickly do the job of a thousand typists, accountants, and mathematicians. For that matter, most processes within motor car plants, and manufacturing facilities, are now done by machines and robots.

Soon, driverless cars may wipe out millions of driving jobs globally—with estimates of 4.5 million jobs in the US alone. Meanwhile, Amazon is fast replacing its warehouse staff with robots and its retail staff with automated self-serve checkout counters. Other estimates suggest that automated checkouts could wipe out yet another 3.5 million jobs in the US alone.

If that wasn't enough, there is fear that offshoring will eradicate what's left of Western jobs, and send them overseas.

The world is full of threats. We take what we have in life for granted, and see it as being largely static and stable. But the reality is that the world is quickly moving beneath us like quicksand. The status quo is continually under threat from technology, innovation, globalization, and maybe also the rising lower classes from developing economies.

The obligatory search for efficiency is relentless, and progress is unforgiving in keeping processes efficient and honest. Less efficient processes will not last long in the face of challengers who have a more efficient approach. Milton Friedman, the Nobel economist, once recounted a trip he had made to Asia in the 1960s, to a worksite where a new canal was being built. He was shocked to see, that instead of using the readily available modern tractors and earth movers, they were lying idle on the side, and the workers were left to use their shovels instead. He asked why the machines weren't being used, to which a government bureaucrat explained: "You don't understand. This is a jobs program." And went on to describe that while the machinery would certainly help get the job done, it would undermine the work of the people. Milton, standing there aghast, considered the options for a minute, and replied, "Oh, I thought you were trying to build a canal. If it's jobs you want, then you should give these workers spoons, not shovels."

They say that "no man can serve two masters." If you are motivated to run an efficient business, but are also conscious of saving jobs—how do you know where to draw the line? I would suggest that you will only be able to pursue just one of those realities properly. If it is your mission to save jobs, why use any tools? If you are using a shovel instead of a machine, because it saves jobs, then with that same logic you should be using a spoon. Or better yet, maybe the men should be using their bare hands. This would certainly slow them down. Similarly, in business today—if you refuse to automate processes, hire cheaper offshore staffing, or oppose more efficient means of working, then where do you draw the line? Maybe you should also stop people from using their computers? Instead, offer them a ream of paper, pencil, and an old-school calculator to do what they need to do. Maybe that would slow your staff just enough to preserve their jobs. And if they get too efficient at that, perhaps you could confiscate their calculator and give them an abacus.

Even if you did manage to find a balance between efficiency and job preservation that you were happy with, you, unfortunately, don't exist within a vacuum. Your competitors are probably working hard to improve their processes, efficiency, and output while you sleep. If you're standing still in a competitive landscape, you're actually going backward.

We are all fearful of change, but few people in this world would opt to revert back to hand weaving their own fabrics or washing their clothes on a rock in a stream. The future might be uncertain, but you only have to look to the past to realize the incredible progress that has been made, and that generally the net result of change is the raising of the standards of living and a better outcome for all.

Sometimes, when you're dragged into a disruption or change that you didn't sign up for, the incessant march towards greater efficiency can seem ill-considered or wrong, most especially if you are one of the ones that are negatively impacted. But in hindsight, people would rarely opt to go back to an older, less efficient way of living.

Despite the positive outcomes of progress, it is the furthest thing from a 'black and white' or linear exercise. Any progress is usually the result of a complex mosaic of successes and failures, characterized by a few steps forwards and then a few steps backward. You only have to have a ratio of 51% successes to 49% failures, and you are by definition progressing towards a better reality. Yet, for those who experience any amount of the 49% of deleterious effects, then the progress will appear misguided, chaotic, slow, wrong—or anything but progress. But overall, and eventually, the net benefits appear.

Maybe a natural tenet exists that humanity must advance. It must evolve. Nothing stands still. If it doesn't progress, it will only regress. For society to advance, it must move towards an output, a life, and world, of greater efficiency and evolution. Perhaps we are all on a Darwinian conveyor belt of development, hoping that we all fall on the ride side of natural selection.

Today, the city of Leicester has no remaining textile manufacturing at all. The only looms you'll see are those sitting in museums. None of us want the jobs of our countrymen to be lost. People rightly fight to preserve the jobs and welfare of people in the car industry, the train drivers, the pilots, checkout staff, and truck drivers. They might lament the loss of these jobs and the cruel march of change. But they do not lament the loss of handmade fabric, nor the loss of handwashing clothes, blacksmiths, or canal systems.

The Luddite movement left an indelible mark on society. The term Luddite is still used in conversational language today, referring —disparagingly—to people who are opposed to new technology or ways of working. It reminds us of the dilemma that society, and all of us, face on nearly a daily basis: the internal tussle between the destructive properties of change, yet the inevitability and benefits of progression. How do we balance these two interests?

Our feelings on the issue don't much matter, though. Irrespective of our intentions or perspectives, technology and innovation will march on. If capitalism is described as the invisible hand, then innovation could be described as the invisible army—as it relentlessly wipes out old processes and heralds in the new. As Heraclitus, one of the world's early philosophers, noted over 2,500 years ago: "The only constant is change," and the times have indeed been changing.

Poverty

The world has an enormous disparity in salaries and personal incomes. At this time, there are still about 690 million people in the world living in extreme poverty[3], which the World Bank defines as those surviving on less than $1.90 a day. In the Philippines alone, with its 110 million population, there are 6.6 million surviving on just $1.90 per day, and 52 million living on just $5.50 a day.[4]

It's a humanitarian disgrace that with today's modern technology and general 'first-world' affluence that there are still so many people existing without life's barest essentials.

However, progress is being made on this front. There are legions of well-meaning nations, organizations, philanthropists, and people around the world that are tirelessly working on every aspect of the struggle to alleviate poverty and its associated calamities.

For the first time ever though, with the rise of globalized employment, we see a real win-win opportunity for the world to become more balanced with its wealth, opportunity, and income distribution. Technology is fast-breaking down borders and geographical relevance.

As more of the world's 'work' becomes an information-based transaction and more of the world's workplaces are defined by an Internet connection instead of a location, then employment prospects will increasingly open up to everyone.

Currently, most people owe their situational success to a lot of luck—they're lucky to be born in the right town, in the right country, to the right parents, with access to the right universities, internships, and employers. As the relevance of borders and

3   World Bank. (2021). Poverty Overview. Retrieved from https://www.worldbank.org/en/topic/poverty/overview#1

4   The World Bank. (2018). Philippines Poverty Headcount. Retrieved from https://data.worldbank.org/indicator/SI.POV.UMIC?locations=PH

geography disperse, the barriers-to-entry will dissolve, then all inhabitants of this world can begin to compete on a level playing field. Skills will continue to be important, likely more important than ever, but there is an increasing opportunity to 'win work' on the basis of skill and an output-based meritocracy instead of the lottery of life.

Some are worried about this dramatic change in the employment landscape, but I believe this is an exciting prospect for all. World innovation and growth will boom once we have everyone in the world playing the same 'game' on the same 'playing field.'

There is a fear from many in the West that outsourcing will take the jobs and destroy the careers of those from the West. To a degree, this is true. There isn't a direct 'taking of jobs,' but there will, most definitely, be a disruption to the current employment traditions.

However, humanity has never stood still. There have been many significant evolutions before. Like the printing press, steam trains, electrification, motor cars, computers, and the Internet—among many others—where the world has had to—and did—evolve. Things will change. They always have. Progress is as essential as it is inevitable. But society will evolve and a stronger humanity will emerge.

For employment, there is a definite win for the West in having access to cheaper, more abundant staffing solutions. If a company can get cheaper high-caliber employees, then it can do so much more with its limited resources. It can increase innovation, grow faster, and be stronger. The key core competencies and highly specialized tasks of any company will likely stay in-house, as do the profits and growth of that company. If the company flourishes, the benefits are shared by all—its employees, the community, the country, and any stakeholder. A stronger company means a healthier, more profitable, and affluent economy— and happier people.

While the shift towards globalized employment can seem

scary, it's worth considering that job migration is nothing to be concerned about when compared to the transformational effects that machines, computers, and robotics have had—and will continue to have—on jobs. As I've mentioned before, hundreds of millions of jobs have been replaced by computers, machines, automation, and robots.

Science fiction author, Edmund Cooper, was intrigued by Ned Ludd's plight. His book, *The Cloud Walker*, contemplates an alternative world that, based on Luddite principles, chose to reject progress and technology in favor of certainty and stability. Cooper explores a dystopian future that is governed by the Luddite Church and a belief that all machines are evil. In efforts to protect the present, they expelled machines and set carefully prescribed limits on technology. It does not take too much imagination to see that a future without innovation and machines is not a great idea. Needless to say of course, the story doesn't end well.

We can all relate to Ned's predicament in some way. Progress can be painful. But just imagine if Ned had won his fight. Would our development be frozen? Would we all be left in some parallel universe putting up with 19th-century technology? None of us want to see our jobs disappear and our livelihoods lost, but equally, none of us would want to be stuck still sewing our clothes.

Maybe then, progress represents the best worst option that we have.

Outsourcing is a People Business

Outsourcing is a people business. It is powered by people, for companies run and owned by people, and for clients and consumers who are also people.

Silicon Valley's VC technologists can sometimes rate the efficiency and scalability of a business by a revenue per employee ratio. The purpose of this ratio is to see how much productivity can be generated per employee. The implication is that the more revenues you can generate for each employee of a business, then the more efficient and scalable that business is. In theory, if you could generate a $1 billion business with just one employee, then you're leveraging exceptionally effective software and tools. Ultimately, you're generating enormous value for each human input, and no doubt, some exceptional shareholder returns.

Silicon Valley is, by its nature, looking for ways to optimize software and technology. The intended consequence of this is that they are able to do more and more with less and less human input. Offshore staffing as an industry is, in stark contrast, a people-intensive and lowly scalable business. Silicon Valley would not be impressed. This contrast can easily be illustrated by looking at some of the large publicly-traded outsourcing firms of the world. As the following examples show, they all have relatively high employee numbers for relatively low revenues per employee.

For the tech world, Google's parent company Alphabet generates $1.4 million for each of its 119,000 employees. Facebook generates $1.6 million for each of its 44,000 employees, and Netflix generates a staggering $2.3 million in revenues for each of its 12,000 employees. In comparison to some of the outsourcing industry's leading players, Concentrix generates $21,000 for each of its 250,000 employees, Teleperformance generates $17,000 for each of its 383,000 employees, and Wipro generates just $12,000 for each of its 221,000 employees.

This analysis shows that Netflix is able to generate nearly 200 times more revenue for each of its employees compared to Wipro. Seen another way, for every 40-hour week that a Wipro employee works, someone at Netflix can generate the same productivity, denoted by top-line revenue, in just 12 minutes. This is a testament to the scalability of tech, the incredibly low marginal cost of information-based products, and the comparative cost of mobilizing people en masse.

The tech titans might have you believe that the optimal number of humans in a business is zero, but it's certainly not the case with most companies. At the end of the day, humans are actually really good at creating things for, and servicing the needs of, other humans.

People are complicated though. And ironically, it is maybe the human element of the outsourcing industry that can make it such a controversial topic.

When a company installs new software or machinery to improve processes, then it is hailed as a success and celebrated as another step towards technological advancement. In contrast, if a company employs someone better, for cheaper, from overseas, it is considered treachery and an attack on the people. The common concern is that 'those' people are taking jobs from 'our' people— and outrage ensues. Yet, overall, software, machinery, and robotics have collectively wiped tens of millions of jobs from the planet— and very few think to complain about this.

There are very many passionate nationalists who staunchly stand for local employment. Yet, they use a Chinese-built laptop and a Korean mobile phone, powered by Taiwanese semiconductors. They drive a German car, wear a Swiss watch, clothes made in Turkey, and listen to music performed by artists worldwide, from an app engineered in Sweden.

As humans, we pay enormous attention to other humans doing other human stuff. We all innately prefer people that belong to the same group as us, and are conversely dubious of people outside of our group. So, otherwise sensible discussions on global trade, international cooperation, or globalization can quickly degrade into an 'us against them' predicament.

This is very different from inanimate objects, like computers, technology, and software. Single pieces of software can wipe out hundreds or thousands of jobs in one installation. Telephones and computers have wiped out millions of jobs—all without one complaint. And robotics in manufacturing plants have reduced previously bustling factories into virtually human-free ghost towns.

These changes happen incrementally, so it is difficult to see. And even when it is noticed, it is mostly hailed as 'progress' and celebrated. Software and technology are seldom shunned. Most people are excited by it, and are proud to be a part of its implementation. Whereas if a business hires a foreign offshore worker in an effort to leverage a global talent pool, it will generally always be met with resistance and derision. When people see another worker introduced to their community who is 'not like us,' they are immediately shaken to attention. It seems to trigger an innate tribalism that is quickly awoken and riled. All the emotions of distrust, jealousy, and dread come rushing to the surface.

People will quickly point out the incompetencies of their foreign counterparts, lament for the old days when everyone came from the same town and supported the same sports team, and suddenly start caring a lot more about their office mates down the hall.

People will hastily reprimand a foreign worker when making a mistake, but they overlook the time and training they would naturally invest into any of their normal colleagues, and ignore the enormous engineering, installation, and setup costs required by any new software integration. They lament for jobs lost, but overlook that their company is actually giving a great opportunity to other people, sitting somewhere else on the planet.

We are all humans, and the displacement of one human for another human is not actually displacement at all.

Too Few Humans

It is a commonly held assumption that there are too many people on the planet. Maybe this is because, for most of our time on this planet, humanity has had to fight for its existence and whatever meager resources came its way. If you didn't brutally defend your food, clothing, and shelter, an equally callous person, animal, or natural calamity, would mercilessly leave you with nothing. Catastrophe and starvation were only ever one misstep away.

However, things have come a long way in the last few hundred years. Most people on the planet—certainly those reading this book—are now relatively secure from the perspective of basic requirements of food, shelter, and education.

A lot of people worry that the planet will eventually run out of food, water, and resources, as the world's population spirals out of control. In the 1960's, the concern reached a fever pitch when well-meaning futurists predicted a bleak destiny of mass starvation, poverty, and depletion of non-renewable resources. The result was quite different. One paper found that while the world's population increased by 70% in the 50 years from 1960, commodity prices actually fell in price by 70%.[5] The United Nations Food and Agricultural Organization (FAO) data shows that within that same time, calorie production per person has risen from 2,196 kcal to 2,850 kcal[6]—an increase of 30%. Since 1960, the number of people on the planet living in extreme poverty has more than halved—from 1.6 billion people back then to 730 million now. That means that 5,000 people have been lifted from poverty every

---

5   How the World Survived the Population Bomb: Lessons From 50 Years of Extraordinary Demographic History. (2011). Retrieved from National Center for Biotechnology Information https://www.ncbi.nlm.nih.gov/pmc/articles/PMC3777609/

6   Max Roser and Hannah Ritchie (2013). "Food Supply." Published online at OurWorldInData.org. Retrieved from: https://ourworldindata.org/food-supply

single day since 1960—and the rate of improvement is increasing. In 1990, more than 750 million people in China lived below the international poverty line—about two-thirds of the population. Recent World Bank figures show that this number has dropped to just 7.5 million people. A staggering drop of 742 million people in just 20 years.

Despite the common trope of global overpopulation and starvation, the data convincingly points in the other direction. As humanity proceeds, through relentless innovation and technology, it is almost miraculously enhancing life and the availability of necessary resources as it goes. The cost of commodities are dropping, poverty is being eradicated, education levels are rising, and the world's population is richer and living a longer life than ever before.

We are now seeing a dramatic slowdown in the growth of the human population. Experts think that it might peak at 10 billion people, and then start to decline. Already we are seeing significant stagnation or shrinkage of the population in the developed nations, with many of these countries seeing a significantly negative birth rate. If populations don't replenish themselves, then countries can face severe economic challenges. Without a young population to work, pay taxes, reproduce, and care for the elderly, countries can very quickly go into the red.

Elon Musk, in typical contrarian fashion, tackles this issue head-on. Aside from populating Mars, building spaceships, hyperloops, Neuralinks and cars, he is also setting an ambitious target to build robots. He also takes the view that there is a growing shortage of humans. He goes on to say, quote:

"The foundation of the economy is labor, the primary resource constraint is labor. I can't emphasize this enough—there are not enough people. One of the biggest risks to the population is the low growth rate and the rapidly declining growth rate. And yet so many people, including smart people, think that there are too many people in the world and think that the population is growing out of control. It's completely the opposite. Please look at the numbers. If people don't have more children, civilization is going to crumble."

Elon's contention is that there are too few people on the planet. He believes that humans are in fact the bottleneck for getting things done. With more people, there would be more innovation, output and progress, which would lead to a brighter future and better life for all.

This can be corroborated in part by the observation that people are so extremely expensive to employ. In line with supply and demand— human labor costs so much simply because of the scarcity of productive people in the world. Instead, imagine a scenario where people were super cheap to hire. This would catalyze a boom in productivity and development and significantly drop the prices of the resultant products and services.

In most cases, the major cost component of any product or service is the cost of the human contribution that goes into its production. If humans did not cost so much, then things would be a lot cheaper, and growth would soar.

The argument is that humans would need significantly less money to live a great life. The difficulty with this argument is that it is circular in nature, and so it is hard to disentangle and test. People are the primary contributor to output, and they are also the primary consumer and beneficiaries of that output. So if input costs go up, then also the output costs rise too—and a circular inflationary spiral ensues.

People always fear the replacement of human labor by cheaper forms of labor and machines. Instead of being the existential threat that it's made out to be, maybe it's actually the solution. Whatever the case, salaries in the West are enormously expensive. Every business owner would agree that high salary costs and labor shortages are a common challenge for companies. Access to affordable Human Resources would be a golden ticket for most—especially for smaller, growing, and resource-constrained businesses.

Elon's solution is robots. Instead, I suggest offshoring.

Why go to the trouble of building a robot, when there are 8 billion highly capable candidates in the world already. For employers in the West, they have an unfair advantage over the rest of the developing world. They can take advantage of global cost structures and access competent offshore staff today—for a fraction of the cost. And the batteries are included.

AI and Automation

With the rise of digital technology, life and work as we know it is quickly evolving. As Marc Andreessen of A16Z puts it: "Software is eating the world."

As we speak, AI, automation, machine learning, and robotics are being developed at breakneck speed. Some believe that sooner or later, AI might take over the vast majority of frontline jobs, perform them better, at an infinitely cheaper cost, with better results—and the machines don't take sick days.

Some suggest that the 'birth' of a broad Artificial Super Intelligence (ASI)—defined as, quote: "an intellect that is much smarter than the best human brains in practically every field, including scientific creativity, general wisdom, and social skills"[7]— could be as little as 20 years away.

As technology phases out more and more of the world's entry- and mid-level jobs, there's reasonable concern that robots and AI might soon replace the entire working class. Roles across academia,

---

7   Bostrom, N. (1997). How Long Before Superintelligence?
      Retrieved from https://www.nickbostrom.com/superintelligence.html

technology, physical, and service sectors are all under threat. And it's not just in the basic functions. Computers can now compose a better opus than Mozart, beat humans at chess, and diagnose better than doctors. Soon, driverless cars and drones will be commonplace on and above our streets.

This means that many—if not 95%—of jobs could disappear from the face of the earth. People have always been disrupted by the march of technology, as were the canal boat makers, Luddites, and candlestick makers. But so far, they have always found new ways to contribute and evolve. Despite 500 years of rampant technological innovation, employment levels are still at all-time highs. However, there is an argument that this time might be different. Some argue that soon, there might not be any new jobs to turn to.

As technology becomes more pervasive and the world becomes digitized, then much of the work becomes increasingly information-based and the need for human contribution is usurped. Through technological advancements, we have already seen that geographical distance plays less of a part in our lives, and physical presence and production is becoming almost optional.

Physical products and manufacturing are in some respects slower to change, but robotics and automation are fast encroaching this space. Platforms like Amazon and Alibaba allow you to access, and instantaneously buy, almost any product, from practically any country in the world, from the comfort of your own sofa. The world's factories are increasingly populated by robots, and deliveries will be made by autonomous vehicles. The continued development of 3D printers, might soon mean that your physical goods—from frying pan to television—can be printed locally— even from your own home.

There are now even rudimentary versions of 3D printers that can, amongst other things, print… 3D printers. This means that they can reproduce and replicate themselves—something that is pure science fiction.

Imagine a day where your AI assistant buys you a Hermes bag from France, using Alibaba from China, paid for with Stripe from America, using your Lloyds bank account from England, which is then 'printed' for you using your Korean 3D printer. You're doing all of this from a sunny beach in the Bahamas during your lunch break from your remote Ukrainian job.

Things could certainly get crazy.

But before we get carried away, let's get back to reality. You only have to look around to realize that most things are still the same. And in that respect, for most of us, it is still business as usual. Certainly, if you are running a company, and avoiding distraction, then the next five to 10 years are all that we should be focusing on right now. And based on a 10-year horizon, all indicators suggest that most fundamentals will remain the same.

◇◇◇◇◇◇◇◇◇◇◇◇

Much has been written on Artificial Intelligence, machine learning, automation, and robotics. Some fear that AI could take over the world. It certainly is possible. It is viable that this fast progressing technology reaches the unnerving level of Artificial Super Intelligence, and gain a human-like broad intelligence. If this actually happens, then the rules of the game will almost certainly change. The experts estimate that it will happen, in some form, between 20 and 70 years from now.

People often put these concerns to me, as a quick challenge, like a kick of the tires, to see if outsourcing is up for the fight ahead of it. For some reason, people see the outsourcing industry as the 'first to go,' when the robots come knocking. Most assume that the bigger call centers, that handle a lot of high-repetition functions, are trembling in their boots.

While a lot of automation is already happening, any greater

concerns for an AI domination seem to be overblown—right now at least. Certainly, I have never heard or seen of a situation where an AI robot walks in, sits down, and takes over a job. Thankfully, this is fanciful science fiction, but we are certainly seeing change underway.

If you look around the Main Street business world, it is commonplace to see various technologies shave off tiny aspects of functions, across a broad range of basic, mundane, and repetitive 'white-collar' roles. The progress comes not from a single headline-grabbing momentous event, but a subtle, imperceptible creep of minor version updates. The single 'automation' event that we're all keenly looking out for is instead actually happening all around us every day. We see it in the proliferation of common software tools that are all incrementally making human jobs a tiny bit more efficient.

Even something as simple as a basic CRM (customer relationship management)—in offering a range of useful analytics, process efficiencies and shortcuts—contributes to this gradual but certain sea-change. As the CRM evolves, it continues to enhance processes, and with each iteration, shaves off more tiny fractions of time. Maybe, after years of development, the software will yield a 5% gain in productivity for its users overall.

However, a 5% efficiency gain is not profound for a single role. For example, the 5% win, that was painstakingly made possible, by CRM innovators, engineers, and coders, will have little effect on the daily routine of a typical employee. These hard-fought gains could be easily wiped away by that person adapting to a new process, checking Facebook, or chatting with the boss. In this respect, employees within smaller and fast-growing businesses—due to their low scale and ever-changing environment—are relatively protected from and resilient to automation.

Small businesses and their staff typically have very variable dynamic needs. Their operations, processes, and roles are continually in flux and evolving. Few processes are set in stone or even set. Everything can, and usually does, change from one quarter to the next. They are far more immune to the threat of AI and automation, simply because it's very hard to automate small, unique, and fluid processes that are changing all the time.

For automation to be effective, it requires a lot of upfront programming, very stable processes, and sturdy rails from where it can do its thing. These programs are a bit like a train running along its tracks. If you have time to lay down rails, have a reliable path, and need to carry heavy loads, then trains can be very efficient at their job. However, if you only need to transport something very light, along ever-changing new pathways and dusty tracks, then a train and its rails are completely useless. Unless a broad superintelligence comes along, most AI and automation are too rigid and require too much upfront programming to be efficient for a small and fast-changing business.

In contrast, if a bigger business has 100 staff doing the same function day in day out, then a 5% gain in productivity is very powerful indeed. It essentially means that five jobs can be cut. This is where automation will be felt.

However, this is not new for the outsourcing industry. The industry is called Business Process Outsourcing, exactly because its core remit is to optimize processes. So improving processes and shaving off 5% or 10% from operation is de rigueur for this sector.

Most improvement is not seen or noticed, though. It is slow and gradual, like a massive glacier imperceptibly inching across the sea. And this kind of improvement, as we have seen, has been happening since the dawn of modern humankind.

If AI and automation do progress quickly, and serious gains are made, then many of these jobs could be lost to computers. It would start with the simple repetitive jobs, but would inevitably progress to the middle and higher complexity roles.

As jobs are eroded and eventually wiped away, there have always been a high flow of new jobs and needs coming along to replace them. It turns out that there are always other new roles to work on, new ideas to be launched, and ambitious plans to be supported. And so when an old job is eradicated, there are 10 new jobs to take its place. This has always been the case so far, but we can't be certain that this replenishment of jobs will be sustained.

While people are concerned about the prospects of outsourcing amidst these looming technological threats, I really have little concern. For one, if jobs will be lost en masse to a hyper-intelligent successor, or even slowly through insidious automation, then all jobs will be universally impacted. This issue is of equal threat to the outsourcing sector as it is to the West. If anything, I would suggest that offshore staffing is possibly in a slightly better position. If jobs are going to be removed, then logic would suggest that the higher paid roles—specifically those from the West—will go first.

In some respects, outsourcing is at the forefront of this evolution —as globalization forces local businesses to reconfigure their approach to an increasingly internationalized and digitized world. However, even outsourcing—which is currently best served by this seismic shift and technological enablement—might even fall prey to the very technology that supports it.

The potential disruption is huge, but it's all just conjecture at this stage. All of these possibilities are still well beyond the horizon, and so for now, as company owners and employees alike, I feel that the best approach is to continue with business as usual.

Regardless of specific timelines, a huge change—in the form of slow, but certain progress—is on the way. As much as change is disruptive, it likewise creates exciting opportunities. The question is, are you taking advantage of the changing times, or will you be part of those swept under the rug? You can choose to take advantage of this opportunity, or get left behind, but change is inevitable.

If any of the larger concerns are valid, we are all in this together. In the extreme case, if a form of Artificial Super Intelligence is actually created, then the entire world as we know it will be forever changed. All poverty would be eliminated, cancer would be cured, global warming solved, and food, water, and resources would all be in endless supply—oh, and none of us would need to work. That is, of course, if it doesn't first blow us all up.

But one thing is certain, if Super Intelligence happens, then the question of who does your bookkeeping will no longer matter.

SMEs and Business

All the Big Boys Outsource

It's a common myth that Henry Ford invented the automobile. It's not true. What he actually built was an efficient process for building the motor cars. The motor car had already been long since invented. He was not an inventor. Instead, Ford was an innovator, and it was his keen eye for efficiency and process improvement that enabled him to first commercialize the car. As a result of fanatical attention to process and process improvement, he was the first to make affordable cars that were adopted by the masses.

As discussed previously, there is enormous value in specialization and gradual process improvement, and the nascent Ford Motors, in building its first run of Model T Fords, is a perennial textbook example of this. Back then, Ford Motors was renowned for building its cars from the ground up. They would source raw materials, like chunks of steel, rubber, and wood, and fashioned a car from these. This is how they could control costs, as well as the entire design and production process. In some ways, Tesla's first principles approach to ground-up manufacturing resembles this methodology.

Surprisingly, Ford's biggest innovation was not the motor car, but the moving assembly line and conveyor belt system that built them. He believed that the more clearly delineated and specialized a task was, the more efficient that task could become. They would break apart a process into multiple sub-processes, and then break those sub-processes down even further. Eventually, they were left with a set of isolated simple tasks that could be repeated with speed and accuracy, which were easily monitored and optimized.

Ford's efforts to break processes down into the core tasks was the beginning of large-scale process specialization. While this concept was first applied en masse to manufacturing, it is now equally applied to the services sector, and business generally. It is also the kernel concept of Business Process Outsourcing. It is this concept of process isolation, specialization, and optimization that gave first flight to the offshore outsourcing industry three decades ago. Now, big businesses all work on the basis of process building, analysis, and optimization—and inevitably reap the benefits of efficiency through specialization.

Smaller businesses typically specialize a lot less than their bigger counterparts. When business functions and roles are all clumped together, as they commonly are in smaller businesses, it is harder to untangle, analyze, or improve them. As a business grows in scale, the processes within them become bigger, and so naturally become more delineated and standalone. Smaller businesses can also accelerate this process by consciously unbundling functions, mapping processes, and building Standard Operating Procedures (SOPs).

Bigger businesses have all the advantages of size and specialization that small businesses do not. Just as a large city can outcompete a small town, bigger companies are able to outspend, specialize, and out-compete their smaller counterparts.

Big businesses specialize more and go deeper in sophistication. Their size also typically affords them exclusive access to specialized tools and services—like offshore outsourcing, tax loopholes, cheaper funding, and hedges. Previously these were out of reach of smaller players. However, more recently, access to these things has been increasingly democratized.

Eventually, as Ford developed their processes, it realized that each task could be just as easily be done by other people from outside the company. This created an opportunity where one company could just focus on the innovation, production, and optimization of just one single part—instead of an entire car. This intense specialization enabled them to get extremely good at one particular task, and hyper cost-efficient. This resulted in an external company that was able to produce a part on behalf of Ford, that was able to build it better, faster, and cheaper than Ford itself.

Today, Ford outsources virtually all of its manufacturing process—spreading the sourcing of its products across hundreds, if not thousands, of separate specialized suppliers distributed across the globe. And Ford is not alone, now most other companies across most other industries also follow suit.

Despite becoming the world's most valuable company, on the basis of luxury cutting edge products no less, Apple offshores practically all of its manufacturing production to external partners. The first trillion-dollar company is by any measure a highly successful company, so maybe there is something to learn from its methods. Their actions clearly demonstrate that the offshore specialists that they partner with can deliver these products better and cheaper than they are able to do themselves. And this is Apple that we are talking about—they have almost unlimited resources and are renowned for producing the highest quality products, yet they choose to go offshore and partner with third parties.

This is not uncommon for most of the 'big boys' of business. In fact, offshoring, outsourcing, and specialized partnerships are the default for most. It is almost taken for granted that big businesses tap into the global supply chain and are able to generate better prices, scale and outcomes as a result. All the airlines, carmakers, tech giants, banks, consumer goods conglomerates, and the fashion, sportswear and shoe brands all rely on offshore staffing solutions and manufacturing.

Yet, in contrast, the typical small and medium-sized business is hyper-local in every respect. They live locally, they employ locally, they produce locally, and they sell locally. Why? And why is it that bigger businesses specialize more, optimize their products, tap into global efficiencies, and partner with specialists more than their smaller counterparts?

Maybe there's a lesson here.

Big Versus Small

For the purposes of this book, I focus on the needs of the small and medium-sized enterprises (SMEs) of the Western World. There isn't actually any categorical definition for an SME, and classification can vary from country to country, but for the sake of clarity, let's assume the following parameters: An SME can range from an early stage and small company of maybe just a small handful of staff, and extend right the way up to businesses that employ as many as 500 people and generate hundreds of millions of dollars in annual revenues. It's quite a big range.

For the sake of this book, and due to its prevalence, we also consider startups and very small or micro-businesses—referred to as MSMEs—to be great candidates for outsourcing. However, outsourcing is fundamentally about the employment of full-time staff, and so if your business isn't quite at that stage yet, then many of the following principles won't apply. To get the best out of offshoring, you have to hire ongoing staff on a full-time basis and ideally—or as quickly as possible—build a team of more than one person.

More specifically, I focus on the SMEs from the main high-cost English-speaking economies of the world, which can be loosely referred to as the Anglosphere, or more colloquially, 'the West.' United States, Canada, UK, Ireland, New Zealand, and Australia as well as Singapore, Netherlands, Norway, and Denmark are examples. Given their relatively high labor costs, these advanced economies have the greatest potential in cost savings from offshore staffing. And also, their large English-speaking populations minimize the language barriers.

There are over 35 million SMEs and startups between these countries, and they constitute 99% of all businesses across the region and collectively employ a staggering 64% of its workforce.[8]

While the world's SMEs are regularly credited as a primary employer and catalyst for global economic growth and resilience, it's not an easy ride. Collectively, they are a dominant economic force, however individually, they are far more fragile than their bigger counterparts. They typically make less profit, have limited reserves and access to capital, and face a legion of tougher commercial hurdles, costs, and charges. SMEs are regularly excluded from most of the opportunities for cost savings and operational efficiencies that are enjoyed by their larger counterparts. Equally, they have limited access to skills and labor, and tight budgets prevent them from better specializing.

Small businesses face a lot of adversity in their fight for survival and growth. The punishing impact of these headwinds can be seen in the disturbingly high stagnation, distress, and failure rates amongst SMEs. Running and growing a small business clearly isn't easy.

---

8   SMEs expected to provide bright future for Philippine outsourcing. (2019). Retrieved from https://www.outsourceaccelerator.com/articles/smes-expected-to-provide-bright-future-for-philippine-outsourcing/

However, few SMEs actually take advantage of many of the tools that are at their disposal. Tools that would allow them to better optimize, save, specialize, and grow. Or maybe they simply aren't aware of them. The very tools that allow bigger businesses to thrive, like specialization, process design, and offshoring are, in many cases, left on the shelf.

Smaller businesses argue that it is good to be free and creative and to 'let good people do good work.' Big companies instead build structure and processes. They still allow for freedom, innovation, creativity and autonomy, but it is allowed for from within certain constraints. With complete freedom, there is chaos. But with a structured framework, great things can emerge. Ironically, it is structure and a framework that brings freedom.

Many small companies claim to value staff autonomy and celebrate free-wheeling entrepreneurial initiative over structure, protocols, and process. I sometimes wonder if this is a fully conscious decision based on objective analysis, or just a reactive defense of haphazard operations. In many cases, SMEs rely on intuition and creativity, simply because they have not yet matured to a point where better structures were necessary or afforded. Businesses don't just magically inherit systems. They have to be built. And they take a lot of work and a long time to do. So it is not unusual for systems and structure to significantly lag behind the development of a company—especially if it is early stage, fast-growing, or under-resourced.

But it is possible for small companies to emulate the bigger companies. If so inclined, they can build better systems and tap into the benefits of specialization and many of the sophisticated solutions that the bigger businesses take for granted.

There is good reason why the 'big boys' outsource. Outsourcing and offshoring are some of those unfair advantages that big businesses have had over their smaller rivals now for decades. It's like a secret superpower that they've been keeping all to themselves.

So why don't more smaller businesses follow suit? After all, SMEs, startups, and even solopreneurs, all have tighter resource constraints than their bigger counterparts. In this respect, all of them have more of a need to offshore compared to the big ones— yet very few do.

Generally speaking, almost any product, service, or role can be offshored—and it is now available to any business. Imagine the benefits it could bring to your own business, whether you're a startup needing support, a small business cutting costs, or a growing enterprise looking to scale.

Even the average consumer outsources most activities in their life. They outsource their plumbing problems, car maintenance, and even washing and cleaning to others. They mostly do this because they either lack the expertise to do it themselves or have other better things to do with their time. The average consumer clearly understands the value of outsourcing and specialization.

So why do small businesses not better specialize, not offshore, and not run a company based on building, mapping, and optimizing their processes? Why is there one way for the big boys, and one way for the small? Outsourcing is probably the single most potent business tool in existence—but it is being overlooked by the vast majority of small and medium-sized businesses. This trend is slowly starting to change—with the emergence of more online, tech, and e-commerce companies—but on the whole, small businesses stay local.

There is no need for this. It is hard enough being a small business.

Offshoring for SMEs

Thirty years ago, access to offshore staffing was strictly limited to the Fortune 500 companies of the world. This was not through any collusion, but simply the setup, infrastructure, communication and technology costs were so great, that companies needed a massive scale to justify the daunting upfront and ongoing costs. Outsourcing clients back then would typically have a minimum of 500 to 1,000 people performing one business function.

Now, as servers, software, and everything is in the cloud and IT, technology and communications are a fraction of the price, outsourcing has become infinitely more advanced, flexible and affordable. As the industry has matured, there is a new breed of outsourcing firm, that focuses on the needs of the small and mid-size clients, offering a wide range of turnkey and done-for-you solutions. They offer enterprise-grade solutions, but are equally happy to start with teams of just one or two people, with no setup costs and flexible contracts.

The $273 billion outsourcing sector[9] has never been more primed, or accessible, for the world's small and medium-sized businesses. However, access does not mean adoption. Despite the fact that the world's major corporations have all been outsourcing for decades, it seems that the SMEs are yet to catch on. Estimates show that a whopping 95% to 97% of the world's big companies outsource. There is almost complete penetration amongst big enterprise. In stark contrast, only 0.5% of the world's SMEs have tried it.[10]

The adoption of outsourcing in the SME sector is obviously still very much in its early stages. The fact that the purpose of this book is to explain what outsourcing is illustrates that the awareness, understanding, and adoption of the offshore industry is still very nascent. In contrast, when people first described Uber, they didn't have to first explain what taxis were and why people use them. Everyone

---

9   Fact. MR. (2022). Business Process Outsourcing (BPO) Market to be Valued at US$ 620 Bn by
     2032. Retrieved from https://www.factmr.com/report/4599/business-process-outsourcing-market

10   www.outsourceaccelerator.com/articles/smes-expected-to-provide-bright-future-for-philippine-out-
     sourcing/

knows what a taxi is, but very few really understand offshoring.

Outsourcing is beset by people not really understanding what it is, mistaking it for 'side-hustle freelancers,' enterprise call centers, or just generally dismissing its efficacy. This is similar to the early doubters and opponents of mechanized fabric looms, motor cars, e-commerce and technology. When a market is nascent, it simply means that the customers need a lot of education and nurturing. I hope that this book will help you understand outsourcing much better and show you the great opportunities for helping your business thrive.

The West has about 35 million SMEs. If just 50% of these businesses eventually outsource just one role, then that's another 17 million jobs on the way. However, I believe that that number will be much higher. With work, technology, and globalization trends all heading in one direction, it's apparent that globalized employment will eventually become the norm instead of the exception. It might take 10, 20, or 40 years, but it will eventually become ubiquitous.

Changing Tides

Bigger companies are usually more sophisticated in nature, but paradoxically, their outsourcing requirements are often less complex. They would typically offshore a large number of people, but have them focus on a small number of lower-value higher-repetition functions. In contrast, the offshore staffing needs of an SME will usually require a small number of highly-skilled, but broadly capable experts—as is usually the case with smaller companies and startups. They usually need a small number of highly capable generalists to cover a wide range of activities, who can work with minimal supervision and guidance.

To illustrate this point with an example, a large multinational might need 500 mid-to-low level administrative staff to manage one single client-billing process. The process would be very stable and change very little over time. In contrast, a fast-growing SME might need just five staff consisting of a digital marketer, an SEO expert, a sales executive, a social media manager, and a developer. All of these roles need to be senior, independent, and capable of managing their own workflows. And since the business is fast evolving, the roles and job requirements will also be quickly changing. As you can see, there are a lot more complexities with the smaller requirement.

The incumbent outsourcing firms were slow to adjust to the needs of the SME and this newer highly-skilled dynamic. As a result, the last decade has seen a proliferation of new innovative offshore firms that cater specifically to this market.

Ironically, the big end of the outsourcing sector, which previously saw enormous growth due to the almost complete utilization by the world's multinationals, is now starting to see a significant slowdown. With 95% of the world's big conglomerates already outsourcing, and automation and machine learning putting downward pressure on the industry's basic roles, there is simply not much more growth to be found in the enterprise space. Until recently, the incumbents that have enjoyed a golden run, have shown little interest in the SME market. Since they are used to catering to the mammoth-sized single clients that contract thousands of staff each, the smaller minnows of the market have failed to pique their interest.

Instead, it took the emergence of new, more nimble, outsourcing firms to provide flexible services that meet the needs of the SME market and the growing offshoring demand. Now, as the BPO market matures, it realizes that despite five staff being less impressive than 500, the five staff are more highly skilled and offer more value. In addition, the industry is attracted to the blue ocean opportunity of there being tens of millions of Western-based SME's, who collectively employ 60% of the workforce—and are all about to start offshoring.

In response to the needs of dynamic smaller companies, the outsourcing sector is working hard to keep pace with the educational requirements of the workforce. They are quickly upskilling to ensure an adequate supply of higher-skilled roles and deeper more specialized pools of talent. This is an exciting development for the industry and clients alike, as it can offer increasingly higher-value services.

Staying Small

Small businesses are staying flat, unstructured, simple, and local— and it is to their detriment. Yet, they tell themselves that these are endearing or positive attributes of their company and an intentional part of their values and purpose. Instead, in many cases, I believe that these things are more of a bug than a feature, and a product of the status quo, instead of deliberate engineering.

It is not necessarily any harder to be structured, to specialize, and to develop your processes. It is not any harder to utilize the tools and methodologies that the bigger boys take as a given. And it is certainly not any harder to tap into the global workforce and take advantage of outsourcing's superpowers.

I would argue that things can actually be easier if you harness these tools—in particular, outsourcing. There is good reason why the big boys do it.

Staff outsourcing can save small businesses as much as 70 percent on overhead costs. Outsourcing firms can also provide the solution to many common issues that SMEs face, such as attracting and retaining talent, capital constraints, limited infrastructure, prohibitively expensive salaries and high cost of employment. Outsourcing part of their operations can allow SMEs to focus more on their core functions and hire more skilled staff to help them with their growth.

Many SMEs subscribe to the mantra of staying local—to support the community. This is nice, but is this mantra based on any sensible analysis or deliberate strategy? Or is it really just a defensive rhetoric that allows them to stick with traditional methods they are most familiar with?

Many people all too quickly dismiss the opportunities of outsourcing, without first properly examining it. It's a common trope that 'they won't be able to do it properly,' or 'the quality will suffer,' or 'the clients will complain.' But is this really the case? It certainly isn't with Apple, Canva, or Zoom. I sometimes feel that the mantra of 'stay local' is more of a martyrdom than a business strategy. It serves nobody—indeed, not the company or its stakeholders.

Previously it was not possible for SMEs to access the global employment market. Now it is not only possible; it's easy. Despite being around for 30 years, SMEs were mostly locked out for the first 20. It is only in the last 10 years that offshoring has been accessible, cost-effective, and flexible enough for the SME market. Now, 10 years on, and it is easier than ever to hire staff offshore. In fact, it is even easier than hiring people locally. This is because you have a specialist partner helping you, and an entire $273 billion industry in support. Plus—you get to save 70% on staff costs. How could you say no?

The Outsourcing Firms

Outsourcing Firms and Facilitators

The type of outsourcing that you might engage with can vary dramatically depending on your needs, business sector, and niche, as well as the size, maturity, and growth trajectory of your company. The big end of the outsourcing market has existed for over 30 years and has a very different structure and value proposition to the other parts of the industry. Upwork, freelancers, and VAs equally offer different solutions for different parts of the market. The professional outsourcing sector catering to startups and small and midsize businesses has really only existed for 10 to 15 years, and offers a very different range of services and options yet again.

So what is the outsourcing industry? And who are the firms behind it?

As discussed in the last chapter, outsourcing provides a range of valuable services to its clients. However, its distinctive and single most valuable contribution is access to the global workforce. Which, in short, means easy access to significantly cheaper staffing.

As mentioned many times already, you can generally save

around 50% to 70% of your staff costs if you source globally. On top of this, offshore firms can offer a range of specialized knowledge and services to help you setup, manage, and optimize your team, processes and operations.

Not all outsourcing firms are built the same. Far from it. Like employment in your own country, there are many different approaches to offshore staffing. In the following chapter, I will do my best to condense these services down into their simplest concepts and most actionable benefits. For clarity, in this chapter, I will generally refer to offshore staffing, outsourcing, and call center firms as BPOs.

For simplicity, an easy way to conceptualize a BPO is to think of it as a co-working space or serviced-office provider. Major global players in the serviced-office space are Regus, Servcorp, and of course, the now somewhat infamous WeWork. You likely have one or many branches of these serviced offices in your own hometown.

If you're familiar with this business model, then you're halfway there. However, outsourcing firms provide many more powerful benefits on top—as standard. I often suggest that clients think of outsourcing firms like a WeWork—on steroids.

If you are looking to offshore, then there are four primary components to consider. Most firms will usually offer a range of services in respect to each of these components. Sometimes they are all packaged together and presented as a bundle, and other times they are separate. Regardless, as an employer, I believe that these four items are the primary things to consider to ensure a successful offshoring experience.

Of the four items, there are two first-order or foundational services and a further two that I consider being second-order services.

The two foundational core components are:

1. Office and facilities
2. Staffing and employment

The two second-order components are:

1. Operations and oversight
2. Auxiliary services

I would encourage everyone to assess the suitability of their BPO and outsourcing needs on the basis of each of these four component parts. Certainly, a team's facilities, employment, and operations are all constitutional parts of building a successful organization. This is true in your own country and is no different overseas.

I would encourage people to see these parts as separate from each other yet interlinking. The offshore industry has now reached a level of maturity and flexibility where each of these component parts can generally be sourced, or at least priced, separately. It is usually the most convenient and standard to take a bundle of services from the same supplier. This is especially true if you have a small or fast-growing team or are new to outsourcing. However, it is valuable to know that these components are interchangeable and can be sourced somewhat independently of each other.

I will run through each of these now, and then dive into other relevant details for each afterward. First, let's begin with the employment and facilities.

1. Employment and Compliance

It might sound obvious, but the primary foundational requirement of employing a team is—believe it or not—employment.

Employing someone properly, legally, and compliantly is a complex and expensive undertaking. It is hard to do in your own home country, and it is many times harder to do offshore, in a developing nation, that is many thousands of miles away.

Employment in any country is complex. Not only are there costs and administrative burden, it also exposes you and your company to an untold number of potential liabilities and downsides. And it is expensive. Despite employment being an essential catalyst for the economy, governments tend to heap a lot of costly obligations and responsibilities onto the companies doing the employment. Most countries require a certain amount of employer contributions, taxes, healthcare payments and insurance.

On top of all that, there is generally the cost of an HR consultant, person or department to manage all the administrative work and ensure that the employer is compliant and that the staff are safe, happy, and will hang around. It's complicated stuff.

Plus, there is always the looming specter that things could go wrong. Maybe, one day, someone in your company might have an accident at work, leave on bad terms, or offends, harms, or abuses another employee. This is all on you as an employer, and it could cost you dearly. And you don't know what you don't know. The rules are constantly evolving. Especially now, with the 'new normal,' and the ever-changing landscape of woke, politically sensitive workplaces and the post-COVID work environments.

Sometimes it's a wonder that you are ever able to get on with the job of building a business when you have so much to manage when employing someone.

With outsourcing—this core element of employment is managed for you. Your offshore staff will be employed on your behalf.

It is important here to highlight exactly what part of employment we are talking about. When we talk about a team being outsourced, it does not necessarily mean that an external company does the work, knowledge, or production. In this scenario, it simply means that an external offshore company manages the legal and administrative aspects of employment.

The outsourcing firm, in this case, officially employs your staff, but for all intents and purposes, they still remain your staff. They are your team and will have been sourced and selected by you. This team, just like your own internal staff, will be trained by you, aspire for growth within your company, work beside you operationally— and be onboard with your mission, vision, and values.

In this respect, the outsourcing firm just facilitates your remote team's international employment on your behalf. They will manage all of the formal employment of each individual as well as the paperwork, compliance, and payroll. And importantly, the BPOs inherently take on the legal responsibility and liability if anything untoward happens.

They act as what is referred to in the US as an EOR—which is Employer of Record —or a POE—a Professional Employment Organization. In some ways, the thinner and more invisible that this service layer is, the more effective they are at doing their job. Outsourcing firms are specialists in the legal employment of people and teams. This enables overseas client companies to source and hire people in countries like the Philippines without the complex legal or administrative burden of hiring people internationally themselves. Importantly, it allows the client companies to sidestep all the bureaucratic red tape, complexities, and legal exposure synonymous with developing nations.

With offshoring, many people have the impression that these outsourcing destinations are completely lawless renegade countries that allow for the under-payment and ill-treatment of staff—quite the contrary. Certainly, for the Philippines and India—the two primary outsourcing destinations—both countries have incredibly extensive and strict labor laws that oversee their workforce. Generally, they are very protective of their people, and are usually highly pro-labor and conservative in their approaches.

When you add that these countries are also insanely bureaucratic with a high predilection for red tape and corruption, employment compliance can be a particularly gnarly topic.

In fact, foreign people or entities are not allowed to employ staff in the Philippines directly. It has to be a local incorporated entity that does the hiring. It is possible for external foreign companies to incorporate in the country, but the process is long and arduous, typically taking around six to nine months to arrange. Plus it is highly bureaucratic to stay incorporated, and most companies need to have a minimum interest of 60% Filipino ownership.[11] So employment in these emerging economies is an absolute hornets' nest—at best.

If you are looking to remain in the Philippines over the long term and expect to be employing more than 50 to 100 people for an extended period of time, then local incorporation and direct employment is certainly an option, but it should not be taken lightly. Also, if you do ever incorporate in the country, you— as either owners or directors—become personally liable for any happenings within that jurisdiction.

So there is a lot of value in using an external company for the legal and administrative aspects of employment. And there is even more value in this assistance, when you build an international team from within a developing nation.

In many respects, the cost and complexity of employment is all too often undervalued and overlooked. When working with an offshore company, it is a win-win for all. The employee gets long-term, stable, and compliant employment as well as all of the commensurate benefits. Meanwhile, the client has all the convenience of a traditional full-time employee, with most of the hassle of employment removed—and none of the liability. If employees need to be terminated for any reason, then the BPO would manage the release and redundancy of any employees. All

---

11   Philippine Constitution, art. 11, 12

of this is offered to the client with typically flexible terms, allowing them to rapidly expand if needed or walk away if plans change or it does not work out.

2. Office and Facilities

Just five to 10 years ago, an office was a standard requirement for all employees, anywhere. It was a given. This is becoming less the case now, and certainly, the requirement for an office has been tested since COVID. However, I would suggest that if you are a company of any size, appreciate things done properly, want a scalable, reliable, repeatable outcome, and want to minimize chances of failure, then using an office is still a good option for an offshore team. I will discuss the reasons below.

For those of you that are anti-office and pro-work-from-home, this next section might have me come across as dreadfully traditional. Before you burn this book, please keep reading, and I will later explain the reasons for my support of the office in the offshore context.

For this section, when thinking about office facilities, if you still have the WeWork office analogy in your head, that's a great place to start. Outsourcing firms, alongside the staff, typically provide the office space and all facilities from which your team would work.

Contrary to outsourcing's detractors, these offices are generally nicely decorated, well-appointed, and have a comfortable, cheery and safe atmosphere. The BPOs have long since realized that if they invest a little more money into nice work environments, then they will get more out of their employees, their employees will get more from their jobs and stay longer, and the clients will be happier.

As a result, and after 30 years of progressive development, you now see some pretty awe-inspiring workplaces. In fact, many BPOs offer fantastic work environments that would equal the fabled workplaces of Google, Facebook, and the best that Silicon Valley might offer. It is not uncommon to see table tennis tables, gyms, reading nooks, coffee bars, lounges, canteens, sleeping pods, and sofas in some. Just as you would imagine a WeWork—but better. Some might even offer beer and karaoke.

For some BPOs, their offices are absolutely world-class and are run with all the energy of a holiday camp. They offer before- and after-shift activities, fitness and social clubs, and site-wide Christmas, summer, and Halloween parties. However, beyond the fancy space and social club vibe—BPOs offer so much more. This is where they far exceed the WeWork analogy.

To start, the BPOs offer dedicated desk space, as well as the computer, hardware, chair, and accessories for each of the staff. Typically, most employees would now have two 24-inch dual-monitors, modern desks, ergonomic chairs, air-conditioned offices, and a great corporate environment.

Beyond the standard hardware, the BPOs manage all of the infrastructure including the Internet, security, IT, firewalls, and of course, the AC, electricity, and water. They also generally ensure zero-downtime and manage redundancy and backups.

Having someone manage all of these backend aspects for your business in itself offers an exceptional value proposition. After all, you are in business to do business—not run an office.

In the real world, offices can be enormously expensive things to set up and run. Generally, they require a lot of upfront capital to cover deposit, decoration, fit-out, furniture, IT, and hardware. Then, you are locked into a long-term lease and an office that typically offers little flexibility in terms of expansion or contraction. These things not only take a lot of cash and upfront investment, but they also take a lot of time and focus away from the management team.

Managing facilities such as the Internet, communications, hardware, IT, desks, chairs, and air-conditioning is a pain at best. The management team will either be wrongly consumed by these things or have a department or team of people—at a high cost—to manage them for them. Regardless, someone has to do it, and it usually costs a lot of money.

When placing staff overseas or offshore, it becomes not just a luxury to have someone else manage the office and facilities, but a standard requirement. If it is hard to set up and run an office in your own hometown—then it is exceptionally difficult to do this internationally—certainly with any level of efficiency.

The property management side of the outsourcing industry is now inextricably linked to the offshoring of teams. In the Philippines, the outsourcing sector accounts for a vast majority of the country's A-grade office occupancy, demand, and growth. Also, after 30 years of leasing, constructing, and managing office space at an enormous scale, you can be assured that the industry has got all of this down to a fine art. For general businesses, office and facilities management is either an afterthought, or an annoying distraction. In either case, it is highly expensive, capital intensive, and a distraction from the core business. For BPOs, facilities are the core business—certainly a major part of the core business—so they can set up and run them extremely well and efficiently. Again, this is the benefit of specialization that I have touched on previously.

BPOs are now experts in managing facilities and providing environments that positively impact employees' welfare, retention, and motivation. The good thing here is that this sector is highly commoditized, and BPOs really see the facilities just as an essential part of doing business with their clients. As a result, office pricing is highly competitive, margins are low, and so the client gets a great deal.

Bringing Them Together

Your team's need for proper employment and facilities is often an overlooked and undervalued aspect of running a business. Yet, it is a basic constitutional part of building a workforce. It is possible to get by without these things, but I would argue that if you are focused on building a reliable, repeatable, scalable, and productive team—then ensuring that they have proper employment and facilities is a baseline requirement. This is especially the case when you plan to build a team from a developing nation.

Paradoxically, facilities and employment are a foundational first-order requirement of a team, but they are far from a core activity of your business. So they should not command much of your attention or energy. But it is essential that it is done properly, and that someone does it.

Normally, they are expensive and time-consuming things for any business to manage. However, a BPO—through specialization—is able to manage them better and cheaper than you could. In addition, through managing the team and facilities, the BPO is providing easy turnkey and assisted access to the global talent pool—where you can access great staff at significantly discounted salaries. Without a BPO, it is significantly harder to source, employ, and manage an international team—so they are very much the gatekeepers and facilitators of this opportunity.

These services offer so much value, at such a low cost, they can only be done for so cheap—exactly because they are done from a developing country. To provide some perspective on the pricing, generally, these all-inclusive services of office, facilities, computer, hardware, employment, HR, and client account management come in at a lower monthly price than a standard WeWork co-working subscription in your local market.

To summarize so far, I want to come back to the core concept of outsourcing, which is the facilitation of global employment. The core components of this provision is the formal employment of the staff and the management of the facilities from which they work. If you understand this core value-proposition, then you understand the concept of outsourcing.

However, this is only the beginning of what outsourcing is. It expands well beyond this core and can offer so much more value to your company. After 30 years of evolution, the outsourcing industry has developed incredible collective expertise in helping your business setup and run more efficient operations.

I feel it is important to separate out the functional aspect of outsourcing—i.e., the employment and facilities—from its production, output, or operational aspects. For example, a rocket scientist, accountant, developer, architect, or writer all have very different operational outputs, workflows, and routines. However, functionally, their employment is very similar and homogenized. They all want proper employment, benefits, and security, and they need a functional, warm, and happy place to work from. They also want a job they can be proud of, a career that allows them to grow, and some colleagues to bond with. These are now basic fundamentals of any productive work arrangement—irrespective of the actual job that they are doing.

Because of the homogeneity of these basic needs, BPOs can offer an extensive range of roles and professional services. This is why and how they can be generalists in nature. Just as any kind of role or professional can work from WeWork with equal efficacy, a BPO can also help and support an offshoring client in virtually any role that they need.

Outsourcing can certainly help with operations and process improvement, but they should be regarded as separate 'second-order' services. Let's take a look at these second-order services now.

3. Operational Oversight

It is certainly possible for BPOs to offer operational assistance and oversight. And many of them can generate enormous value in doing so. It is even an option for BPOs to have complete oversight and control of entire processes on your behalf.

In the latter case, a client is really engaging a BPO, not for a staffing requirement (i.e., two staff doing 'x' role, working 'y' hours), but instead on the basis of an agreed output or outcome (i.e., production of 'x' results, within 'y' time frame). There is a significant difference between these two services if you think about it.

On one end of the spectrum, you have a company providing you with staff—meaning they supply you the employees and facilities—according to your requirements. But what you do with those people is up to you—just like a standard employment arrangement. An example of this might be a client hiring two full-time full-stack developers.

On the other end of the spectrum, the facilities and employees are almost irrelevant. Instead, you are paying for an agreed output, deliverable or outcome, and it is the BPO that will make sure that they get this done. In this case, it is more of an agency or consultancy arrangement than staff augmentation. An example of this might be the same client instead contracting an agency to build and maintain a website.

Both arrangements have their benefits and drawbacks—but it is valuable to know the difference between the two.

We spoke previously about a gray area and crossover of responsibility in operations when outsourcing. This possible gray area of accountability is markedly heightened when you work with a firm based on a proposed operational deliverable.

For example, if a client engages a BPO to sell $1 million worth of widgets, and the BPO is unable to achieve this—then who—or what part of the system—is to blame. For example, it might have been the sales staff that were unqualified for the job. It could be the training that they received. It could have been the script or the process that they were following. But equally, they could have been the best staff in the world, but the product was no good, the pricing was too high, the training was insufficient, or maybe the client could not properly complete the sale.

The more the lines of responsibility blend, accountability becomes increasingly uncertain, and the more problems can arise. This is why I think it is best to separate out all of the constitutional parts of an operation.

First, work on the first-order components of a team. Ensure that you hire the right staff, have them working from good facilities, and give them the right tools to get the job done. This part is at least quite a black and white exercise. If you can first set up and confirm that these first-order factors are all in place, then at least you know that you have the right foundations. This is the foundation of your team. Ensure that you get this right.

Then, on top of the foundational team comes the operational layers. These include onboarding, training, processes, quality control, support systems, and SOPs. These things are equally crucial to running a successful operation, but they are completely different to the aforementioned foundational aspects.

If you want help to build the processes that your team will follow, you can likely engage the BPO to assist you with this. BPOs are, by nature, longstanding experts in building processes, and managing, analyzing and optimizing them. The BPO industry has been doing this collectively for the last 30 years, so they can be a fantastic resource to help you build your processes, especially if the processes require a team of people that are following limited set processes with repetitive functions.

However, bear in mind that running a business is hard. And running a successful business is even harder! Just because you are hiring a BPO to run a process for you, does not necessarily mean that the process will be a success. For example, I could hire a BPO to create a competitor to Uber or build a rocket to fly to Mars. A BPO can certainly assist with the staff and process of working towards these objectives, but they are intrinsically difficult to do, and so nothing is certain. Successful and thriving businesses are continually testing, iterating, and failing. Testing and failing is a huge part of any growing and evolving business. And so, by using a BPO, it does not necessarily underwrite your endeavor, guarantee success or prevent failure.

This is why it can become complicated if you completely abdicate the responsibility of outcomes to a BPO partner. Instead, I would suggest that a BPO can assist in optimizing certain processes, but it is still very much a partnership, and it is ultimately up to the client to stay close to the operation, guide the progress, and continually optimize for success.

Think of it a little bit like a gym membership. The membership gets you access to the gym, facilities, and the general assistance of the staff. For many people, this is all they need. However, you can add personal training services on top of the basic subscription. You might use a personal trainer every day, or just for the first month and then never again. Even if you use them every day, they can still not 100% guarantee your desired outcome. Ultimately, the results will rest on your own contribution and effort, but the personal trainer would at least improve your technique, optimize your routines, and increase your chances of success. Later, you can assess if you still need the trainer, but regardless of your decision, you will still have access to the gym and can exercise independently.

If you are building a team for sales, customer support, debt collection, appointment setting, client management, or have a consistent content, design, or technical production requirement; then you are in luck. A BPO can assist in setting up these teams and the processes they follow to get the work done.

However, if you are just hiring one developer, accountant, manager, designer, or small team of different roles doing disparate activities, then a centralized process design and management is probably less applicable.

You might still want to draw on the expertise and experience of the BPO to help run that team though—whatever their size or function. The truth is that BPOs know how to build a successful local team. They are far more conversant with the subtleties of motivating their people, and using the right levers to get the best results. There are a lot of nuances to this, that we will be discussing later. Needless to say, if you yourself aren't an expert in building and running teams—and in particular Filipino or offshore teams—then a BPO can offer you a lot of help with this.

For a BPO to be involved in your operations, they will very much need to be a partner alongside you—not just a vendor. They will need to get intimately involved with your business, systems, tools, and processes. Ideally, the people running these processes will have a seat at the table alongside the business leaders to work from a high level and contribute to organizational design.

I hope that once you start outsourcing, you will never go back. Like a gym, once you start, I would hope you would maintain a gym routine forever. Over time, you might want to change the gym you go to, the trainer, or methods, but the underlying foundation of a gym and exercise should remain fairly consistent throughout.

The same principles apply to outsourcing. The foundations are important. Ensure that you get those right. The operational oversight and assistance can certainly add value, but it should be treated as separate from the core fundamentals. Because of these crossovers, I often refer to outsourcing as a kind of co-parenting—

which I will discuss in greater depth below. The BPO will manage one aspect of the team, while the client manages another. These aspects will often overlap, and each will be dependent on the other.

4. Auxiliary and Support Services

There is a range of additional ad hoc, infrastructure or system requirements that you will likely need when setting up and running your team. Because you are physically separated from your staff by thousands of miles, the BPO provides an important and necessary resource. For this reason, most BPOs offer a range of auxiliary and support services that attend to these needs.

The main one is the recruitment and sourcing of staff for your account. Because the nature, frequency, and process of recruitment can be very specific to each client need, this service is commonly charged separately. This is the correct approach. Recruitment needs can vary dramatically. Hiring 100 junior sales agents and replacing them if they churn is a very different requirement to sourcing one key executive, CTO, or product designer. Recruitment is a big process, and it is important that it is done right—so it is sensible that it is a separate service, and one that is paid for—as and when needed.

Generally, BPOs will offer these recruitment services, but there is always the option to use third-party recruiters, have your team do it, or do it yourself.

On the Bench

If you are just starting with a BPO, you should expect people to be recruited from scratch, specifically for your particular role requirement. I would be wary of any BPO that tells you that they already have a person sitting on the bench that is perfect for your role. It is highly unlikely that a BPO has the resources available to keep great staff just sitting on a bench waiting for you to appear. If they offer this, I would be suspicious and ask why they are sitting on the bench, how long they have been on the bench, why they aren't working on an account already, and what happened to their last account?

Instead, you should expect that you will go through a recruitment process specifically for your requirement, according to your job description.

The downside to this is that the recruitment process will take time. It is not easy or quick to find the perfect employee for your roles. It would, of course, be nicer if you could just select the perfect employee off the shelf, but generally, this opportunity does not exist. Recruitment is an essential part of building a successful team, and there isn't really a reliable hack to avoid it. However, there might be a few exceptions to this.

If a BPO has a lot of staff, such as a company size of 5,000 to 20,000 people, they will be recruiting all of the time. As a result, they will have a pretty significant flow of available candidates—certainly for the more standardized roles—all the time. They will naturally have a big database of applicants and a very effective recruitment team. In fact, many of the bigger BPOs have continuous marketing programs to attract candidates and extensive dedicated screening and testing facilities to manage the flow. They have gotten the whole process down to a fine art. It is not unusual for these bigger organizations to be recruiting 1,000 or 2,000 people every month.

Or if you are working with a call center that specializes in sales, and you need a small team of just two people, then possibly they might have two candidates 'on the bench' somewhere, or somewhere in their recruitment funnel at least.

So if you are dealing with a big BPO and require only a small team of very standard roles, then it is possible for the process to be sped up. However, if you are looking for very specific roles that are in high demand, then the search and selection will still take some time. However, it is better to go through a standard recruitment, sourcing, and selection process outside of these sorts of exceptional examples.

Generally, there is a cost for this recruitment service, but again, it is far less than what you would pay for recruitment or headhunting in your own country—typically 70% to 80% less. The recruitment fees might be 5% to 20% of the annual base salary as a guide.

When recruiting, if you have the perception that there will be endless queues of poor people from the third world lining up to take your job offer, think again. Offshore staffing is highly competitive. Sure, they earn less money than in the West, but it is still a red hot market. And great employees are in peak demand.

Also, bear in mind that the Philippines has many masthead employers such as P&G, Google, Facebook, JP Morgan, and Citibank to name a few. If you want to attract and retain good staff, you have to offer a good job, competitive salary, career progression, and a nice environment to work from.

Recruitment should be taken as seriously with your offshore team as with your traditional onshore staff. The BPOs can provide invaluable assistance in this process. They will know the peculiarities of their market—you will not. They will be conversant with the standard protocols, application and notice periods, candidate behavior and expectations. They will guide you with salary ranges and help you navigate the market. Recruiting, interviews, and the selection process is very different in a foreign market compared to your own, so lean on the support and experience of your recruitment team to help you through this process.

Additional Services

The BPO will typically act as a concierge service if you want anything done to support your team and their workflows. Typically this centers around the IT and facilities, but it could also extend to ad hoc solutions such as training, HR services, facilitation of social events, special support for staff, extra hardware requirements, merchandise, or gift buying.

BPOs can typically configure their IT infrastructure for whatever setup is needed. Or you might have certain security requirements such as HIPAA or PCI compliance, ISO standards, or similar. You might want dummy servers, firewalls, or dedicated lines, or you might need assistance with auto-dialers, VOIP systems, headsets, or special configurations on the computer, or access to certain software or tools.

All of these are possible. Most of these things would come with an additional cost, but typically they are charged only at-cost or with a small margin on top. Most BPOs wouldn't aim to make any money on these additional services; they are usually seen as essential requirements that ensure that the client can get the work done that they need to get done. So you should not have any issues getting the setup you need.

Other Considerations

First-World Services

It is worth mentioning here that while you take reliable electricity, Internet, and infrastructure for granted in your home country, the same cannot be said about many of the outsourcing destinations.

These things are generally more challenging to bring to a world-class standard in emerging countries, and as a result, they cost more to create and more to maintain.

The Big Mac Index illustrates this point well. In 1986, The Economist started tracking the cost of a McDonald's Big Mac burger across a range of countries. They made the counter-intuitive finding that a Big Mac costs more money in a developing country than it does in a wealthy country. This is because it costs a lot more to set up a clean, reliable restaurant and source quality and safe ingredients in underdeveloped nations. This is because infrastructure and supply chains are more efficient in a wealthy country. Emerging countries often have to pay considerably more if they want to set up and operate at Western standards, mostly because they are more chaotic and don't have the basic infrastructure that Western countries take for granted.

Outsourcing is most typically done in developing economies. That is why the costs, salaries, and living expenses are cheaper. But there is a downside to this. It is much harder to build and maintain the infrastructure required to run a modern office in these places.

For example, in the Philippines, its Internet and electricity can be unreliable, slow, and expensive. The electricity can suffer from seasonal brownouts and random blackouts, and ranks as one of the most expensive in the world. Whereas the Internet, until recently, was painfully slow, unreliable, and insanely expensive. BPOs spend a lot of money on multiple systems to ensure continuity, redundancy, load balancing, and backup, to ensure zero downtime for operations. It is not uncommon for them to have generators on site, multiple internet cables, water purification, sleeping quarters —and other equipment that is usually more suited to doomsday preppers than businesses.

This is one of the reasons why outsourcing was so expensive and exclusively available to big companies 20 to 30 years ago. It took enormous investment to set up facilities that were commensurate with Western IT and communication requirements of the time.

Thankfully, technology has progressed at breakneck speed, and it is all becoming exponentially cheaper and more reliable as a result. Also, through the success of the offshore industry, many of the outsourcing destinations are now becoming relatively affluent, and so they can build better, more reliable infrastructure that continues to drop in price.

Corruption

The developing nations are generally characterized by corruption, red tape, bureaucracy and inefficiency. I would love to say that this isn't the case, but unfortunately it is—for most of the outsourcing destinations at least.

However, it is important to point out that the outsourcing industry itself is not corrupt and has very little red tape and bureaucracy. Of course, there can be bad actors, but generally, 99.9% of the proper professional outsourcing industry is legitimate and conducts itself extremely well.

In fact, this is maybe one of the biggest and most underappreciated value propositions of the outsourcing industry. Collectively, it does a brilliant job of protecting its clients from the corruption, red tape, bureaucracy, and infrastructure issues that commonly plague these countries.

Clients are, in most cases, blissfully unaware of many issues and threats that crop up on a daily basis just outside of their operational bubble. It is actually one of the major benefits for a client to be shielded from the corruption and mind-blowing inefficiencies that are prevalent in these places.

Because clients are largely uninvolved in all of this, the value of this is so easily overlooked. But actually it takes a lot of work from the BPOs to operate from a developing nation at first-world performance levels. They are doing a lot of work behind the scenes to ensure that everything is calm and orderly, clean and straightforward for their clients.

Office Versus Home

Prior to the pandemic, for the outsourcing industry, it was almost a given that people would work from an office. But now, many outsourcing firms are offering work-from-home arrangements, as well as fully remote options.

The cheaper Virtual Assistant and freelancer markets have always offered home-based solutions, using their own computers and Internet, mainly as default. They are very much the 'cottage industry' corner of the outsourcing sector, but ironically, as the world now adopts home-based work, maybe they were ahead of the curve. I will share my thoughts on VAs in greater depth in a later chapter.

Prior to COVID, you would have had very few professional outsourcing firms supporting or offering home-based services. Of course, since COVID, everyone has had to reconsider work, and the context in which it is done.

Many clients will opt for the work-from-home option when deciding between an office or home-based team. This is mainly because of four common factors:

1. The staff are working remotely from the client's own office anyway,
2. The client will likely never visit the offshore office themselves,
3. The staff might prefer to work from home, and
4. It is cheaper.

These factors are all relevant, but at the risk of sounding old-school, I would strongly suggest that clients have their staff working from an office. At least in the beginning.

While working from home is now becoming a thing in the West, many clients aren't aware of the typical conditions that Philippine-based staff would work from. People might casually assume that a cheap home in the Philippines is equivalent to a cheap home in their home country. But this is not the case. Many Philippine homes are extremely basic, more akin to a shanty than a home, and are usually small, overpopulated, and cramped. They can commonly suffer from poor lighting, unstable electricity, unreliable Internet, disruptions from weather, and would rarely have a proper place to work from, never mind a designated desk or workspace. These factors can have a dramatic effect on the quality of work produced.

Office facilities in the Philippines mean that the staff have a proper workplace. It means that they have the proper equipment and a suitable environment that allows them to concentrate on the work in front of them.

Also, the office environment, professional dress code, and city centers attract a certain class of people for the reasons mentioned above. It is likely that more professionally inclined candidates will be attracted to jobs, that work from offices and commensurately offer more career cache and opportunity.

Generally, if you are a professional organization, and you are expecting to employ more than one or two staff, then I would strongly encourage you to set yourself up for success, and make sure that you use proper office facilities. This is certainly the case in the beginning, when you are onboarding a team, learning how to offshore, and setting expectations and routines.

It is also easy to eventually convert over to a home-based team later, if you choose. However, it is much harder to go the other way. In the short term, and certainly, when you start, you should do everything within your power to reduce uncertainty and chances of failure when you start offshoring. This is why we recommend that prospective employers opt to pay a little extra and have their staff work from a professional office environment.

Overall, it will cost you a little more, but quality and productivity will be higher, reliability will be improved, you will attract a better quality candidate – and…you will still save 50% to 70% on your all-in employment costs.

Co-Parenting

I refer to the co-management of facilities, employment, staff, and operations as a form of co-parenting.

The BPO is the official employer of the staff. It also manages all of the fundamentals of employment, the payroll, the compliance, and take on the liabilities. They would also provide HR support and ensure the general welfare of the staff, including their safety and comfort at work, monitor their attendance, punctuality, and manage any grievances, concerns, complaints or queries.

The client would typically then manage everything to do with the operations, including their daily activities and deliverables. They would oversee the actual work that each staff member does. This would include the training and orientation, management of the output and quality of the work, as well as the employee's engagement. In this respect, it is just like traditional employment.

In its simplest form, the client would treat the staff as their own. They would train, and work with them, encourage them to do their best, and reward them accordingly when they succeed. Like any kind of traditional employment, it is a two-way street. The employees are obligated to do their best work, and the employer is obliged to treat the staff well, and do what they can to keep them engaged and excited to come to work in the morning.

In every respect, this relationship is identical to how employees are hopefully treated in the client's own home environment.

It is very much the furthest thing from any kind of sweatshop or coerced labor. The straightforward reason why coercion doesn't work is simply because it works like any other market. If you want great staff to work for you and want them to be inspired to do great work, you have to treat them well.

So there is a co-parenting kind of arrangement between the staff, the BPO, and client. There are times when there will be a considerable crossover of the employment and operational aspects of the team. For example, if the employee is not performing, then the BPO will need to assist the client in following the due process. The due process will either seek improvement, or the person will be managed out. This has to be done lawfully, professionally, and sensitively. Just as you would do this for anyone anywhere. The BPO would typically manage this entire process, but they would still need input from the client regarding the specific details of the grievance.

Since the BPO is the legal employer, it is also within their interests to see that the staff are being treated well—or at least properly. If a client is inconsiderate or abusive to staff, and the BPO does not seek to stop this behavior, then it is the BPO that will get in trouble with the labor courts. And so, it is important that a BPO ensures that the staff are treated properly and fairly.

Sometimes this co-parenting can create some awkward crossover of responsibility. Some gray areas may arise where it is unclear whose responsibility it is for some unintended occurrences. It can possibly get complicated. However, it is not complicated 99% of the time, and it works well.

Easy Scaling Up and Down

Having these done-for-you services at your disposal allows you to focus on the core functions of your business. All administrative activities, employment compliance, payroll, and facilities are taken care of. Equally, no capital investment is required, and there is no setup time or distraction. You can also have them help set up and manage your systems and processes.

For the last 30 years, the outsourcing industry has specialized in quick, reliable, and scalable solutions. Some of the bigger clients might respond to peak season requirements by adding thousands of staff for a Christmas rush. All of this is managed by the BPO partner. Literally, thousands of people might be recruited, trained, and managed for a short 6 to 10 week period, and then dismantled again after the rush.

You can tap into all of this infrastructure, support, and expertise for no significant cost. In fact, the total cost is generally a lot less than what a standard employee's base salary would cost you in your own home city. The industry has now adapted to the needs of startup and smaller businesses. They offer all of this on highly flexible terms, easy pricing, and little or no notice period if you need to terminate.

It is only because these things are being provided from a significantly cheaper developing nation that any of these incredible services are actually affordable.

2.5

How Much Should I Pay?

Putting It in Context

Many people inquire with Outsource Accelerator asking simply: "How much does a salesperson cost?" I wish we could give an equally simple answer. But unfortunately, there isn't one. If I'm feeling particularly cantankerous at the time, I might push their question back to them by asking: "How much does a salesperson cost in your country?" The reality is that salaries, and costs, can vary dramatically.

For example, I would guess that a cheap salesperson in the US costs about $30,000 per year, while an expensive one is about $3 million per year. But where does that get us? Nowhere. And does that mean that an average salesperson costs $1.5 million per year? Absolutely not.

Below, I will try to provide a framework to think about Philippine salary and outsourcing costs. I don't want to spend too much time talking about specific numbers because salaries are changing all the time, and in 10 years, the number I propose will look preposterous. But hopefully, the considerations offered here will provide valuable guide rails.

Basic Rule of Thumb

Before we go into costs, it's essential to frame the topic by saying there is so much more to employing someone than just their base salary. Some costs are obvious and visible—like employer contributions and taxes, insurance and healthcare. But many others are far less apparent—things like office space, hardware, training and retention, sick leave, holidays, and transport costs. Plus, all of the other operational costs like the HR advisor or department, recruitment, admin, and compliance are all in place to keep the human resource component of a company ticking along.

When considering all of these things, it is easily possible for the all-in cost of an employee to rise 50% to 100% above their base salary. This is important to bear in mind when assessing like-for-like costs.

In short, someone earning a $100,000 salary in the US is likely to cost $150,000 to $200,000 per year, when considering all overhead.

With outsourcing, I would suggest that you should look to save somewhere between 50%-70% on your entire staffing based on like-for-like all-in costs. Importantly, this assumes that you will achieve a similar level of output and quality, with only a fractional increase in friction—a concept that I will discuss a little later.

Using the example above, for a $100,000 base salary, if you can properly utilize offshore employment, it means that you stand to save somewhere between $75,000 to $140,000 per year. That's impressive. And that's for just one employee!

I want to repeat the basic rule of thumb: you can save 50%-70% of all-in staffing costs with offshore staffing. That's huge.

Complex Picture

To dive deeper into the numbers, we first have to explore the Philippine economy, employment landscape, and some typical salaries more fully.

In the West, most companies hire average staff at average salaries. This is a truism; otherwise, the average—or certainly the median—wouldn't be the median. This is also why the distribution curve of salaries within each country follows the familiar bell curve-shaped pattern. Some people earn very low, and some earn very high, but the vast majority of people are grouped together and earn within a fairly uniform bandwidth.

When it comes to offshore staffing, you will be disappointed if you use this same approach. And this, in part, is why so many people do get disappointed when outsourcing.

As the first point of reference, it's good to know the typical range of salaries for the Philippines. As with any country, you will find an enormous range of possible salaries, from very low, right up to eye-wateringly high. At a casual glance, Philippine salaries may generally appear 60%-80% cheaper than a comparable US salary, but it has a far far wider distribution. This enormous 'spread' between the high and low salaries can get Western employers trapped into paying too little for offshore staff that is simply not capable enough. Navigating this spread can be a big determinant of the success of your outsourcing journey.

In the Philippines, the vast majority of well-paid professional salaries would range between $4,800 and $12,000 per year.

However, this does not paint anywhere near the full picture of the economy or the workforce. The Philippines has 52 million people earning less than $5.50 per day[12], 37 million people without a bank account[13], and only 22% of the population are registered tax payers.[14] Most of these people exist within either the gray economy, or a form of rural subsistence living. On this basis, there are about 60 million people in the country that would absolutely jump at the chance to earn $10 per day. So if you are simply after people, for cheap, then there is an awful lot available.

However, those people generally have very low levels of education, and a lot would be illiterate and certainly have never used a computer. As a result, they would not be able to contribute meaningfully to your company's requirements.

Please note: From a social and ethical point of view, this is not a great situation, but it is a reality. It is not nice, and it is not a good thing that the world's people are not yet all economically secure. But outsourcing did not create this situation—though outsourcing can certainly contribute to fixing it. Eventually, as the world globalizes, I believe that severe disparity will flatten out. The world has and should continue to dramatically improve the global population's access to education and opportunity. While the current situation is not great, it is certainly improving and heading in the right direction.

So as you can see from the numbers, those that have proper employment, with a reasonable wage and benefits in the Philippines, are in the minority. Many people working basic jobs would get the government-mandated minimum wage. This is about $10 per day

12   The World Bank.(2018).Philippines Poverty Headcount.Retrieved from https://data.worldbank. org/indicator/SI.POV.UMIC?locations=PH

13   Bangkok Sentral ng Pilipinas.(2020).Financial Inclusion Survey.Retrieved from https://www. bsp.gov.ph/Media_And_Research/Financial%20Inclusion%20Dashboard/2020/FIDash- board_4Q2020.pdf

14   Number of registered taxpayers in the Philippines.(2020).Individual taxpayers.Retrieved from https://www.statista.com/statistics/1018465/registered-taxpayers-philippines-by-type/

in the major cities and about $6 to $8 per day in the provinces. This is what most factory workers, farmers, supermarket, fast food, and basic retail staff would earn. In comparison, nurses and teachers mostly earn between $650 to $1,000 per month. So a large proportion of the formal workforce would also earn between these figures. And bear in mind that tens of millions of more people don't even make it into the workforce.

So there is a very low 'price floor' for employees in the Philippines.

Meanwhile, a young college graduate in one of the main cities with limited work experience can earn as much as $400 to $500 per month. And there are entry level administrative or call center roles in outsourcing that are paying up to $500 to $600 per month. If you move into the higher-demand technical jobs like developers, data scientists and engineers, then they might be earning $1,000 to $3,000 per month—depending on their skill level and niche attributes. For the majority of Filipinos, these are highly enviable salaries and career opportunities.

While the picture I have painted so far might seem a little bleak, please don't think that the country is short of highly sophisticated people, roles, talents, and companies. The Philippines, despite being a developing economy, has an impressive array of highly advanced multibillion-dollar conglomerates. They are competing at a global level and are doing this with world-class Filipino staff. As a result, senior executives at these companies would be earning globally-competitive salaries—otherwise, they would simply go elsewhere. Metro Manila is also home to many of the world's major companies, from Facebook to Deutsche Bank—with all of their senior executive staff earning competitive global salaries. There are also many tens of thousands of expatriates working in the country—certainly before the pandemic—that have relocated with their families. These people would typically be earning a high Western salary, plus compensation for their relocation and many extra perks, including private education for the kids, housing, cars, maids, drivers, and flights.

So at the top end of the market, there is a significant contingent of people that are earning the big-hitting international salaries. They might be discounted by 10% to 20% because of the relatively low cost of living in the Philippines, but they would very much be at international levels. I would guess at maybe $10,000 to $30,000 per month for senior executives, and maybe $50,000 and above to the C-Suite. So you have an enormous disparity of roles and salaries within the country and even within a single company. This also means that you have very wide gaps between the various pay levels within a single org chart.

This means that as staff get promoted through the ranks, they will transition quite quickly from very low local starter salaries up and through to the higher levels. Some might eventually work through into the highly paid international-level salaries. When you combine this all together within a Philippine corporate environment, it would not be uncommon for the junior staff to earn $500 per month, mid-managers around $3,000 per month, senior managers around $8,000 per month, and then senior staff execs at $30,000 per month. As you can see, there is a much broader pay span than you would see in most developed countries.

Employee Competence

To some degree, you could employ anyone in the US and you know that they would have a certain base level of competency. Most usually, they would be able to contribute in some way to your business. Unfortunately, this is not the case in the Philippines or across most other developing nations.

In terms of education, quality and price, the market distribution is generally much more compact in the West, providing a far more economically homogenized population. It is one of the crowning achievements of Western society that mostly everyone can read, write, and have completed a basic level of education. This is a great thing and a testament to the public education systems, social safety nets, and technological penetration of developed economies—and cannot be taken for granted. Unfortunately, many of those social systems underperform in the Philippines, and so the distribution of capability, education, and opportunity are far more diverse.

In short, employers can pick from the low, or mid-end of the market much more in the West, because employees from the bottom of the market there are not that low. It is not that much below the top of the market. Economists measure this in terms of either economic disparity or income inequality. The majority of citizens within a wealthy country typically exist within a very narrow distribution band. However, in developing nations, wealth, education, and opportunity distribution are significantly wider. The rich easily equal the best of the West, yet the poor are substantially less lucky.

So it is not surprising then when many people try outsourcing and find that the staff lack in quality and capability. It is not that there aren't brilliant people in the Philippines—there are 750,000 college graduates annually[15] and millions of accomplished professionals—but it's just that the outsourcing clients are looking in the wrong places. They are assuming that the Philippines works something like their own country where they can pick the average worker and they will be alright. It is, unfortunately, simply not the case.

In fact, if you took the median distribution of the Filipino population, then the average person is maybe uneducated, illiterate, speaks no English, and earns less than $5 per day. If you

---

15   Commission of Higher Education.(2019).Higher Education Indicators.Retrieved from https://ched.gov.ph/higher-education-indicators-2019/

are going to successfully offshore, then you must ensure that you employ from the top echelons of society. While this might sound elitist, it will at least ensure a successful and ongoing engagement between your company and your offshore staff. And if you do this, you will have access to an incredible pool of world-class talent at a significant discount to the West.

However, the problem is that people come to the Philippines —virtually, of course—looking for a bargain, and they are scraping around the cheap marketplaces trying to find a great employee for $2 per hour. They try a few people priced at $2 to $3 per hour, and are quickly met with disappointment. After a few letdowns, they conclude that it's not working, not worth the hassle, and that the whole system is broken and a waste of time.

And I don't blame them.

People can become fixated on finding the 'perfect $300 per month employee.' It is possible to find some superstar people at that price, but it's rare and unlikely. For this reason, they're referred to as 'unicorn' employees. Even if you strike it lucky and find a unicorn, it means that they are undervalued for some reason, so they probably won't hang around for long. Plus, if your business relies on finding 'unicorns' at $300 per month, you aren't building something that is sustainable or will scale. You might get lucky with one person, but you will more often than not be disappointed, and quickly become frustrated.

This is where it all starts to unravel.

It's why you hear so many stories of people trying outsourcing and saying, "It doesn't work." Too many people take 'two steps forward, then two steps backward,' and after a while give up.

I have conversations with many people who have been burnt by this type of outsourcing. It is an exhausting process to crawl these freelancer websites, set interviews and tests, onboard staff, invest time and money in training, get back unsatisfactory work, critique the work, get back more unsatisfactory work, realize they aren't great, back out of the arrangement, and then start the whole process over again.

Sometimes the lack of compatibility with the employee is obvious and acute. They are clearly not capable of doing the work required, or they are clearly unreliable, or just disappear after a while. However, sometimes the issues are much more subtle and insidious. Both can be infuriating and a big waste of money and time.

Alternatively, clients might hire someone cheap and expect them to build a website, design graphics, or manage social media accounts to high-level Western standards without any issues. This is the wrong move. People don't realize that most people living in a developing nation will have a degree of, what I call, 'quality blindness.' The standard quality of work that is taken for granted by the client in the West is typically not at the same level in developing countries. Developing countries generally suffer from poor education systems, less mature markets, and lower levels of sophistication. A staggering number of Philippine citizens do not have bank accounts (34%)[16], internet access (53%)[17] or pay taxes (79%)[18]. Many are illiterate and a vast number live in very rudimentary villages and lodgings. So you can't simply expect them to have the same reference points in terms of culture, society, quality, style, and workmanship. If you recruit the 'wrong person,' their interpretation of a 'good website' or a 'great poster design' might be very different from your interpretation.

---

16   Bangkok Sentral ng Pilipinas.(2020).Financial Inclusion Survey.Retrieved from https://www.bsp.gov.ph/Media_And_Research/Financial%20Inclusion%20Dashboard/2020/FIDashboard_4Q2020.pdf

17   Individuals Using the Internet.(2019).Retrieved from https://data.worldbank.org/indicator/IT.NET.USER.ZS?locations=PH

18   Number of registered taxpayers in the Philippines.(2020).Individual taxpayers.Retrieved from https://www.statista.com/statistics/1018465/registered-taxpayers-philippines-by-type/#:~:text=Individual%20taxpayers%20were%20the%20leading,quantity%20of%20approximately%20four%20thousand

There are many very well-educated and capable people doing great work, but it is statistically the exception rather than the rule. This needs to be factored into your pricing, sourcing, and selection strategy. Instead of seeking out the cheap, average, or readily available, you need to hunt down the best of the best that the market has to offer.

If you consider it from this point of view, it also stands to reason that the Philippines' elite employees are likely not working from home, in their pajamas, from freelancer websites doing part-time gigs. It is more likely that they are working for the biggest and best companies, in shiny tall buildings, and earning enviable salaries. This should come as no surprise, though—it's how it works in most countries, and it's no different in the Philippines.

Yet unfortunately, there are far too many Western entrepreneurs that get enormously frustrated by their offshore endeavors. They come out the other side of a failed project, having wasted a lot of time and money, and have convinced themselves that all of outsourcing in its entirety is broken. They are essentially saying that a $273 billion industry, which employs millions of people and successfully powers Citibank, Microsoft, Canva, and Zoom, does not work. From their failed endeavors of a few ill-run tests, they seem to have concluded that no one in a country of 110 million people can do their work properly.

Instead, it is probably more the fact that they have been scraping around the bottom end of the industry, and have been surprised that when they pay peanuts, they get anything other than monkeys…and this is a shame.

Pay More!

So when consulting with clients, I tell them to spend more money. A lot more money. People most often reject this, and bristle against the idea. No one likes to be taken advantage of. Why should they spend more money when there are people out there that will work for $2 per hour? They argue that they are offering $3, or even $4 per hour, which is a 50% or 100% premium on what they see as the established market price. And they will not pay a penny more.

Unfortunately, they are missing the forest for the trees.

I might suggest that people instead look for staff in the Philippines that command—based on market values—a base salary of $750 or even $1,500 per month.

Regardless of the candidate's credentials, the salary is two to five times more than the $300 price tag that they have seen on the Internet. The people looking to pay $300 per month understandably think that I am trying to rip them off. But they are missing the point.

The $1,500 staff member will be a well-educated college graduate with an excellent CV, solid career path, and a good professional pedigree. Sure, they might be earning $1,500 per month—but if you were to hire the equivalent person in the US, they might cost $6,000 or even $10,000 per month.

People are overlooking the fact that you actually stand to save more money and make more money if you hire more senior, more capable staff. If you find someone good in the Philippines for $1,500 per month, then you stand to save $4,500 to $8,500 per month, compared to your home market. That's incredible. Plus, at that price, you know that you will be dealing with a disciplined and dedicated employee who is committed and capable of taking your company to the next level.

If you choose to hire and work with these sorts of professionals, then it is a completely different paradigm to what you will experience when scrapping around for a $300 home-based freelance VA somewhere out in the province. As mentioned, there are tens of millions of uneducated, illiterate people in the Philippines. You could employ legions of these people for $5 per day, and they would eagerly work for you for this. It is not slave labor, it would be an exceptional opportunity for them to earn money. So while you could quickly recruit a virtual army of eager employees for peanuts, bear in mind that they would not be able to contribute to your business in any way meaningfully.

As Warren Buffet says, "Price is what you pay; value is what you get." It's cliche to say it, but it really is pertinent in this situation. When looking to offshore to a developing country, especially if you are new to it, it is important that you are not too fixated on price and stay well away from the bottom of the market.

When offshoring, business owners and small companies from the West—maybe for the first time—have an opportunity to flex their muscles a bit. When tapping the Philippine job market, a Western company has a relatively impressive 'buying power', so you can afford to shop around for the best possible employees for your needs. You can even go to the Philippines' equivalent top schools to hire the most successful Ph.D., MBA, or graduate. Normally, they are snapped up by one of the bigger firms—and smaller companies would not have a chance; however, if you are a foreign company that can pay well and have an interesting angle, you will be a competitive option.

This is an enticing option for your company when hiring in the Philippines. Instead of recruiting ordinary people from the mid-market at home, you now have a rare opportunity to pick and hire from the top of the talent stack in the Philippines. The best candidates in the Western countries can cost hundreds of thousands of dollars per year, if not millions, so are generally too expensive to consider for SMEs, and probably wouldn't work for an average company anyway. In comparison, the best candidates in the Philippines are still surprisingly affordable and would be interested in an opportunity to work for an international employer. It's a win-win—and this is actually where you will see the highest savings and most value.

So before you spend all your time hunting around for a $2 Virtual Assistant instead of a $3 Virtual Assistant, you would be better served to see if you can find a top-level Filipino developer, financial analyst, or architect, for example. Their salary might even be $50,000 per year—which is a whopping salary. But this would mean that you're sourcing from the high-end of the distribution curve, and so you're tapping into a fantastic pool of candidates. Plus, the equivalent person in the US might cost $250,000, or even $500,000 per year—so you're saving, at least, an incredible $200,000 each year, on just one employee.

I am using somewhat extreme examples here to illustrate the point. In reality, you should not need to spend that much money. In principle, the core message is to avoid the $300 employee and instead shoot for someone earning $800, $1,000 or even $1,500 per month. By taking this approach, you stand to save tens or hundreds of thousands of dollars per year per employee and at the same time sidestep all of the low-end frustrations and failures. Also, by hiring someone great, you save money and have more chances of moving the needle, building a better company, and growing your revenues—which has almost infinite upside.

The Best Approach to Outsourcing

If you are building a company based on finding the cheapest people working from the cheapest countries in the cheapest conditions and expecting great things in return, it will not end well.

This strategy would not work particularly well in any country, and it certainly does not work when offshoring to the developing world. In fact, the best approach to offshore staffing is actually the opposite.

Spend big!

Spending big—but properly—will ensure that you get great staff, support, guidance, and results. Do this, and you will get the results you had hoped for, while avoiding the heartache, failure, and hassle, plus you will still be saving inordinate amounts of money compared to your home country.

In terms of individual salaries, you should not actually overpay compared to the person's market value. If you overpay too easily, too often, then you will simply be wasting money and won't necessarily reap any better results. However, make sure that you are shopping around for the stellar candidates that are sitting in the top percentile of their particular market. Ensure that you hire the experts and top performers.

I would also encourage you to source more senior and experienced people first, as they will help you build your processes and require less hand-holding. As your team grows, then you can start to hire more junior staff—as they will then come into an established team and a supported environment. Instead, if you hire junior people too early, you might get frustrated by the amount of training and guidance they will probably need.

Over-pay, hire the best, and seek out the best intermediaries to assist you with your journey.

When you start outsourcing, make sure you are not doing it alone, and make sure that you are using any available training wheels offered by your outsourcing firm. The training wheels mean the intermediary functions, facilities, recruitment services, and operational support. Use all of these things at the beginning. Yes, you will be paying more. You might even be paying more than what you need to pay—but this is only in relation to the Philippine context.

You need to focus on the fact that if you use this strategy of over-paying, and utilize the best staff and services at your disposal, then you will still be saving 50% to 70% compared to the West. I would suggest at the beginning that you pay whatever you need to pay, within reason, so that you can ensure that your outsourcing mission is a success. Once you overcome the initial learning curves and become familiar with your team and the Philippine offshoring environment, you can take off the training wheels and cut away from your support structures.

You won't need to use the training wheels forever. Eventually, you can remove the higher levels of assistance. Ensure that you work this into your contract. Just like when you start going to a gym, using a personal trainer can be wise. Later on, you might not need them. And that's fine. But at the beginning, there is a lot of value in using their services and leveraging their experience.

Work From Home?

As discussed in the chapter above, there is a growing opportunity to have staff work from home. Many prospective employers consider it partly because they aren't physically in the same country to feel the difference and because it saves the employer money. And few people need much of an excuse to save money. But in many cases, saving the $200 to $400 per month for a professional quality office, can be a fool's errand.

Certainly, since COVID, home-based work has become more the norm now, and is becoming an accepted practice worldwide. But most people are not aware of, and do not consider the typical conditions that home-based freelancers would work from.

Many Philippine homes are very basic and often cramped. They can commonly suffer from poor lighting, unstable electricity, unreliable Internet, and have no proper designated workspace. This is especially the case if you are looking for the cheapest Virtual Assistant you can find, working from the provinces. These factors can have a dramatic effect on the quality of work produced.

This is why I strongly recommend that prospective employers should opt to pay a little extra and have their staff work from a professional office environment. It will cost you more, but the quality and productivity will be higher, and you will attract a better quality of candidates.

Freelancing Versus Professionals

There are different ways you can outsource your work to the Philippines. You can either hire a freelancer direct, or work with an outsourcing partner. There's a big difference in terms of quality, scalability, and price between the two.

There is a big world of online freelancers in the Philippines. In fact, they are one of the biggest pools of workers found on international freelance platforms like Upwork, Freelancer, and Fiver. These freelancers can work for you full-time, but most are either project-based or part-time. Prospective employers can find many people here, for very low salaries, who are all eager to get started.

However, the freelancer community can be hit and miss—at best.

Arguably, the other—better—option is to partner with a professional outsourcing firm. The outsourcing industry has existed for 30 years and specialize in facilitating international employment. They have got this service down to a fine art. They know all of the common issues and pitfalls that outsourcing clients typically face, and they know how to source, select, and manage Filipino staff for optimal outcomes.

The type and quality of offshore staffing candidates can vary greatly—just like in any labor market. Many of the stereotypes we take for granted in our own home turf can also be applied to the Philippines. If you are looking for strong employees to drive your company forward, those candidates would typically be living in one of the major cities, have attended prominent universities, and have a stellar CV of working for blue-chip companies in one of the main central business districts. You would expect these staff to have the routine of getting up every morning, going into the city, and working in an office alongside senior professionals and colleagues.

Having your staff work from A-grade office facilities allows an employee to work more efficiently and brings a whole host of side benefits. It creates a professional atmosphere, encourages routine and discipline, and an environment of healthy competition and self-improvement.

When hired, your staff will have a dedicated desk space, within an A-grade office, in one of the major city centers. The BPO will provide a professional work environment and the latest hardware and good Internet, and they will have the proper employment, HR, health insurance, and benefits provided for. The company will also manage attendance and set disciplinary procedures if the staff fail to perform.

They will also provide a professional but friendly environment so that the staff enjoy coming in, work hard, and are able to learn from their colleagues. It's just like a standard professional environment that you would expect in your hometown, or any country in the West.

It should come as no surprise that these services cost more than going it alone—but it should also not come as a surprise that they get better results. These professionally managed services ensure that the results from offshoring are more certain, more reliable, more repeatable, and more scalable.

This is especially important if you aim to build a team of more than one person. It is simply more efficient to have all of your Philippine staff working from one office. There is an enormous benefit in having all your staff turn up to the office at the same time, have morning meetings, have those 'water cooler moments,' and actively share the essence of your company—the mission and values.

Outsourcing Cost

If you use a proper outsourcing firm, you end up paying a little more in a lot of places, which adds up to considerably more money. But you are opting for professional staff, working in a professional environment, that will work to a far higher level. You will also typically be hiring someone living in central Metro Manila or one of the big cities, which naturally commands a premium—just as it does in other big cities.

Too many people get caught up chasing the pennies and not concentrating on building a valuable team. People are especially distracted when they see that they can hire people online for $2 per hour. But as explained, these candidates generally fail to provide long-lasting valuable, sustainable results.

Too many people walk away from offshoring, after being let down by people or disappointed by the work. The industry is littered with unhappy clients, failed projects, and endless frustrations. This is why outsourcing has a bad reputation. But it does not need to be this way. There are millions of people doing incredible work across the globe, and most of the world's top brands successfully use offshore solutions, so it does not have to fail. It should not fail. It is a very viable solution, and it can unlock enormous value and opportunity for businesses—if done correctly.

Instead of saving an extra $1 or $3 per hour, it is much more advantageous to pay $6 or even $15 per hour. Along with a higher caliber of employee, your team will benefit from HR, full employment and benefits, government contributions, office space, hardware, and account management. And you will still be saving 50% to 70%. Be happy with that. There is a significant diminishing return if you try and chase more savings.

The people that chase the 80% to 90% savings often end up shooting themselves in the foot—and usually limp away defeated and disappointed.

If you use a high caliber offshore solution with an equally high caliber staff, you will have a fantastic team, attentive support and guidance, and a significantly reduced risk of failure. Plus, with all of this, you will still be saving 50% to 70% compared to your all-in costs of hiring an equivalent person in your local market.

That is worth repeating:

Considering all of this, you will still be saving 50% to 70% compared to your all-in costs of hiring an equivalent person in your local market.

Price Structure

Since outsourcing is such a diverse industry with many valid approaches, it is impossible to capture or represent all of the different pricing models fairly. Also, since a big component of the cost is someone's salary, which can vary by many multiples, it is not a straightforward exercise to give accurate pricing guides or estimates.

Coming back to the hypothetical question at the beginning of the chapter, "How much does a salesperson cost?", unfortunately, in isolation, the question is still not any easier to directly answer. To get a full picture, I would likely ask some follow-up questions, including:

- Are you hiring one person or a team?
- What specific skill sets are needed—including technical or industry-specific knowledge?
- What seniority and experience level is required?
- What is the industry and product they will be selling?
- Would they be working from office facilities, with hardware provided?
- Do you want to recruit from major city centers or provinces?
- Will you create and manage the process yourself or will your outsourcing partner do this?
- What timezone and hours will they be working?

With these questions answered, it is possible to give a pretty accurate guide on pricing.

While it is hard to give a simple price, there is a formula for thinking about the various components of outsourcing and how they are valued. If you work with this formula and piece together each of the parts yourself, then you will arrive at a pretty decent estimate.

To tie it all together, I will provide a brief overview below.

As discussed, a complete outsourcing service is just the sum of its constitutional parts. There are two core components and two auxiliary. With outsourcing, you can choose to take all services or take just one or none. There is still the option of just contracting someone direct or through Upwork—though the likelihood of repeatable, reliable success is diminished.

Let's recap the four components of outsourcing now:

(1) Office and Facilities

As discussed, the office and facilities are a core value-proposition of many outsourcing firms. While it's not essential to provide an office for your staff, and certainly since COVID many are not, it is advisable to do so—at least when starting out. Typically, they are priced on a 'per seat' basis and charged monthly.

(2) Staffing and Employment

For staffing and employment, there is (a) the salary, (b) the employer costs, taxes, and government contributions, and (c) a service fee to the official 'Employer of Record' (EOR). Again it is not essential that you properly employ your staff, but it is the prudent approach.

With the above two components, you have the foundational requirements in place.

(3) Operations and Oversight

It is possible, and even likely, to get operational assistance from the outsourcing firm. Depending on who you engage, they might even bundle this into a package and work this into an all-in price. It is important to be clear on exactly how much support you will get, how much it costs, and ultimately, who is responsible for the deliverables.

(4) Auxiliary Services

These are ad hoc services, which other than recruitment, may not typically be required.

Price Components

Typically, the office, facilities, and employment services are bundled into one single monthly fee. Usually, this would include the office space, facilities, dedicated desk, hardware, Internet, legal employment, payroll, HR, and account management. Generally, this is referred to as the 'seat fee' or 'service fee.'

For the Philippines, depending on quality and location, this service fee would be within the rather wide range of $350 to $1,000 per person per month. The price will vary based on several factors, including (a) location—city versus province, (b) quality of facilities, (c) brand strength and quality of the outsourcing firm, and (d) the degree to which support and additional services are bundled in.

For the salary, as discussed, prices can vary dramatically. People can earn up to $10,000 per month, but this would be very rare. The base salary of the vast majority of typical roles in the Philippines would land between $500 and $1,500 per month.

You should allow for another 20% on top of the base salary to cover the employer contributions, taxes, healthcare cover, and accrual of 13th month. This is an approximation only, but is a reasonable rule of thumb.

Once you have a clear picture of the above components, it is easier to view the cost-versus-benefit of any additional operational or process management support services. Depending on the services offered and the value they can bring to your team or company, it might be reasonable to pay an extra $100 per month, or even $1,000 per month. Maybe even paying an extra $10,000 per month in assistance is great value if it generates your business many times more value. Certainly, the true cost, and likely value, of such advisory services are harder to nail down than the other components.

This is why it is useful to separate the foundational costs from any advisory costs, then at least, you have clarity over what money is allocated where. Also, with any additional services, it is valuable to be able to stop and start these independently of the core team's activities.

Putting It All Together

A rough example of total costs, for a full-time person doing a mid-level admin activity, might look something like this:

- Base salary: $600 per month
- Employer contributions: $120 per month
- Service fee: $700 per month
- Total: $1,420 per month
- Operational assistance: a variable amount on top

Note: roles, services, location, and prices can vary dramatically, and with inflation over time, all costs will climb.

This example price of $1,420 per month, which works out to about $8.20 per hour, is an all-in price, covering virtually every associated cost of employment. It also includes A-grade office facilities and infrastructure, dedicated desk, and computer equipment. It comes as a turnkey solution and includes a reputable outsourcing firm's expert support and assistance. You will see that this price is considerably higher than the potential freelancer at $3 per hour. However, the results will be significantly more reliable, repeatable, and most likely better with the proposed solution. Plus, it is still much cheaper than the US, UK, or Australian equivalent.

Pricing Summary

To avoid the common frustrations associated with outsourcing, consider the following principles:

- Seek to find the best candidates in the market.
- Employ people that have a stellar education, CV, and career path.

- Pay them well, in line with their market price, but don't overpay.
- Tap into the high-performing, career-driven professionals—not the home-based 'casual-class.'
- Use intermediaries such as a reputable outsourcing firm. Leverage their knowledge of the market and their experience in setting up teams.
- Pay extra for the assistance and guidance of the experts—it will pay off.
- Have your staff work from an office. A-grade facilities imbue certain professionalism and discipline and ensure that the staff can work efficiently.
- Avoid the lower and middle markets. There may be gems in the middle market in the West, but in developing countries, you are more likely to be met with disappointment.
- The Philippine's middle market will likely get you skillsets, conversations, communication, standards, culture, and perspectives that do not translate very well.
- Hire more senior staff at the beginning. Try to avoid working one-on-one with junior and entry-level staff. This will likely be a challenging and frustrating exercise for you both. Instead, work directly with more senior staff, and then as you expand, the senior staff can take on juniors underneath them.

Accept that you might be slightly over-paying at the beginning. Take any assistance that is offered. Do not spend recklessly, but don't try to save every penny. You will still be saving significant money overall—i.e., 50% to 70% compared to the West—and, importantly, mitigating frustrations and chances of failure.

Eventually, as you become conversant and comfortable with an offshore team, you can cut away the extra support. And as the team grows, you can hire more junior staff within your hierarchy.

Over time, you will build a brilliant structured team and save extraordinary money—but the savings should be a by-product of building a world-class offshore team, not the focus.

Can I Pay 'Commission-Only' for Sales?

There is probably some business guide out there telling would-be entrepreneurs how to hustle hard and build a sales team for free. It's a compelling story; after all, why pay for a sales force when you can get one for nothing. The simple idea is that instead of earning a salary, the sales team will get paid a generous commission—when and if they succeed.

On the surface, it sounds like a win-win, and the entrepreneur is willing to pay an impressive amount of money for each sale they make. If they can only make a handful of sales each week, they will earn many times a normal salary. The entrepreneur promises that the sales agents will get rich from the bountiful commission—they just need to make enough sales. They also assure the workers that the product is fantastic, it's an easy sale, and only a fool would say no. Usually, they want just a small team to test this and get it started. For the entrepreneur-cum-hustler, this sales arrangement gets the wheels of the business turning—for no cash down—allowing the company to self-fund its expansion.

However, after the initial inquiry, it turns out that the entrepreneur does not yet have an established sales process, has sold little of the product themselves, and has minimal traction in their business generally.

For some reason, many people approach the Philippines asking for commission-only sales arrangements similar to these…maybe this is because outsourcing attracts thrifty people, or maybe because they feel that people in the developing world should be desperate enough to take any job.

With most readers of this book not looking for a free salesforce, you might be wondering why I am dedicating a section to this topic? Many people do want to build a sales team, so the question of salary and commission structure regularly comes up. But even if you are not building a sales function, a lot of the principles below —as with many things in outsourcing—can equally apply to most other people and roles within an organization, as well as most other countries.

In the vast majority of cases, commission-only arrangements simply do not work. It is not to say that they cannot work. It is possible, but it is not likely. I have offered some considerations below as to why this might be the case.

Salespeople are Not Entrepreneurs

If you look at the best and biggest companies in the world — few, if any of them, have commission-only sales teams. Think of Salesforce, Hubspot, Google, Amazon, Walmart, or Disney. Sure, they do get paid significant commissions, but they also get hefty base salaries plus all the standard healthcare and benefits. Why? Because good salespeople are in demand and so attract good employment packages to match—just like any other employee in a business. In fact, because sales can literally make or break a company—the top salespeople are often compensated better than most other employees in a business. Proper companies realize that sales processes do not just happen. It takes months or years of building, testing, and refining processes before you can scale an effective team and build out a cost-effective sales function.

Risk and Entrepreneurship

A commission-only scheme is, in essence, trying to transfer the role of innovator and risk-taker from the entrepreneur over to the employee. However, it just doesn't work like that. The entrepreneurs are the entrepreneurs for a good reason. They are the self-appointed innovators and problem-solvers of their businesses. They also take on considerable risk to innovate, and they stand to win big, if those risks pay off.

The reality is that an employee is very different from an entrepreneur. An employee is not there to innovate, and they are certainly not interested in taking on the risk of the project. Naive entrepreneurs think that with the right pep talk, they can get employees to think like them and absorb some of the risks. But it doesn't work like that.

How Much Does It Cost to 'Sell'?

If you have a good proven sales process, with supervision and training already in place, then you can get entry-level, lower-cost people to follow the procedure, execute well, and generate good sales. However, you have to consider who has built that sales process. Has anyone built it yet, or are you expecting the first sales person you hire to come in and do it? It is a very different skill to design and engineer a process than it is to follow and execute one.

I know some sales experts who charge $50,000 for an 8-hour training day. They are leaders in their field and can generate enormous value for their clients. In fact, the value created is considered to be worth at least $50,000—otherwise, they wouldn't get paid. This demonstrates that sales processes and techniques aren't inherent—you have to design and build them, and it takes skill, experience, and talent. If you expect highly paid experts to design your sales process and build a winning sales strategy and team for you—for free—it will not happen.

Interdependence

Sales do not happen in isolation. A successful sales process touches every aspect of a company, which inherently means that in order for there to be a successful sale, then every other aspect of the company needs to be in good working order. If someone is working for commission-only—or for free—they are working independently of the company, yet their success heavily depends on all other aspects of the company being perfectly tuned.

Generating sales requires a lot of cooperation and codependence, testing and iteration throughout the company, especially at the early stages of the sales process design. And so it is unlikely to happen if someone isn't getting paid.

Moving the Flywheel

If I could sell $1 billion of your product this year, I would make your company a multibillion-dollar company. How much is that worth to you? And why has no one done it yet? Generally, there is an inverse relationship in selling. It is harder to sell the first $100,000 of a product than to sell the last $1 million of $10 million of sales. If you are already selling $10 million of product, it is very easy to sell the next $100,000. But setting up the process to sell the first $100,000 is a big and complex job. Don't underestimate the difficulty of getting the flywheel spinning its first few turns.

Desperate Candidates

If determined, you will eventually find people that take up the challenge of working for free. If you kiss enough frogs, you will find your prince. If you ask around enough, scouring Upwork and Freelancer, you will find an inexperienced optimist who accepts your offer. They might be wowed by the enthusiastic pitch of your product and excited by the potential commissions—so they sign up. But they are not sales experts, and they will not be able to build the system you are hoping for. Neither are they likely to be the A-players of the industry—those people will have much better, salaried offers from elsewhere. Instead, the role will attract the inexperienced, desperate, and those with nothing to lose.

Overpayment

Most entrepreneurs are willing to overpay the commission amount to save on a salary. They argue that the seller can make much more money if they just sell enough products. This argument is flawed in that it is self-defeating and short-sighted.

If the product were easy to sell, and selling regularly and reliably, then with high-paying commissions, the entrepreneur would quickly realize that they are paying more than they need to do that job. If the sales process was tested and reliable, then it would make sense for the entrepreneur to lock in the staff for a considerably lower but reliable salary. Commissions would still be paid in the form of small bonuses on top, but most of the compensation would come from a salary, meaning that the entrepreneur would keep considerably more upside.

If the entrepreneur was asked about their commission-only scheme, they would likely come up with a story of their generosity and a willingness to share the spoils of success. However, in truth, the entrepreneur is trying to conserve cash, can only afford to pay on the backend, and probably doesn't have enough confidence in the process yet to bankroll it themselves.

If, or once the process is proven, the sales outcomes look reliable, and they see that they are overpaying for the sales, then the entrepreneur would undoubtedly switch over to the lower-cost option of having people on a regular wage.

Selling for Nike

If I were to build a sales team working for free, why would I choose your product to sell? If I work for free, then I am taking on the risk that your product is worthy of my time. So if given a choice, it would not be sensible to take on the risk of selling a new, untested product with low brand recognition. Instead, it would be much easier to sell Nike, Coca-Cola or Apple products, or at least a product that has an established track record of sales and an existing process in place. The bigger brands are already selling billions of dollars of a proven product, to a proven market, through proven channels, and can leverage strong brand cachet. If I was to work for free, why would I choose an unknown small company that doesn't have the cash to pay a basic salary?

10,000 people

If the sales team costs you nothing, then why stop at five people? Why not blitz the market? Go all-in. Why not? If it costs you nothing, why not hire an army of 10,000 people—for free. After all, 10,000 people hitting the phones for free, will outperform five people hitting the phones for free. The reason why you never see big commission-only sales teams like this is simply that the sales process is not successful enough.

Without a successful process in place, the subsequent lack of promised commissions will quickly cause staff to get despondent and leave. You can generally train someone up in two to three months to become good, and most jobs require a period of training and skill development, but this is not feasible within a commission-only role. People will not be able to self-fund their learning curve. If they do not see results within the first week—they will leave. It is difficult to build a team without them quickly churning for these reasons. It's like trying to fill a leaky bucket.

Smallest Sales Company

The same principle also applies to sales companies. Generally, you will find that the businesses that accept commission-only arrangements are small and unsophisticated operations. This is a truism because as soon as a company gets good at selling and has a proven track record themselves, they would start to command more control and ask for a retainer to cover their downside.

The sad reality is that the companies that are willing to work for free are desperately hoping to snare whatever opportunities come their way. They are far from being an expert in their field.

If they were an expert at selling, they could pitch and win more clients for their own business. If selling was no problem for them, then they should have already grown into one of the biggest service companies in the world. Ironically, if they did do this, it's not likely that they would still be offering their services for free. I would expect that they would start to charge more for their services, including upfront retainers and maybe even a $50,000 fee, like the coach above, to share their secrets. For these reasons, high-caliber sales companies just don't accept commission-only arrangements.

◇◇◇◇◇◇◇◇◇◇◇◇◇◇

In short, the issue with a commission-only arrangement is that it transfers the risk away from the entrepreneur and onto the employee. If an employee did want to take on the risk of an entrepreneur, then they would not be an employee—they would probably be setting up their own business.

Most employees are exactly that—employees. They are not entrepreneurs or business owners. And so, for a project to work in a long-term, repeatable and scalable way, the compensation, risk, reward, and process design must align with that of an employee, not an entrepreneur.

About Virtual Assistants

Oompa Loompas

Do you know the Oompa Loompas? They're the mystical workers that ran Willy Wonka's chocolate factory. In the movie, they were short, dressed like elves, had bright orange skin and radiant green hair. According to the story, Wonka imported them from Loompaland, an island in the Hangdoodles.

When people tell me that they work with Virtual Assistants, especially if they have a lot of them, I get an unnerving sense that they think of them a bit like Wonka's Oompa Loompas.

Some people I talk to proudly announce that they now have 20, 30, or 50 VAs, while other entrepreneurs brag that they run their entire company. And I speak to Virtual Assistant companies that employ hundreds of them.

Virtual Assistant is only a term, so maybe I shouldn't get so riled by the semantics. But I really believe that words matter and can influence many other things beyond the title.

Virtual Assistants are known to work on a broad range of activities. Some do secretarial or assistant-type services, but many do marketing, social media management, design, and even coding. Others do bookkeeping and accounting, while others write blog articles and SEO. A group of Virtual Assistants can run almost every part of a business.

My issue is that, if these people were sitting in your own office, in your own hometown, working for your business in a traditional manner, then they would not be called a Virtual Assistant. And there wouldn't be one name for all of them. Instead, there would probably be a content writer working in the content department, a social media manager overseeing the digital marketing, or a bookkeeper in the accounting department. It mystifies me why people clump all Virtual Assistants into one classification when they are covering a diverse range of activities across every part of a company.

It may be slightly pedantic, but my concern is that the all-inclusive moniker severely misrepresents the capabilities of a virtual workforce. It paints them all as being capable of basic administrative tasks—things that are not important enough to warrant their own designation—and nothing more.

It almost creates two classes of workers. The 'real' workers are sitting in your office, and the Virtual Assistants are sitting somewhere else. It unknowingly relegates and confines, Virtual Assistants to exactly that. An assistant. This is extremely limiting for the staff, but more so, for you and your company.

Many people outsource with the unspoken assumption that while offshore staff can maybe help with the basic tasks, and assist with the real work, they could never take on the full roles, the important stuff, or the senior positions.

In truth, Filipino staff can, and should, be involved right up and down—and throughout—the entire hierarchy of a company's org chart. There are highly educated and enormously capable people in the Philippines that can outcompete on a global stage. The country has 110 million people, 750,000 college graduates each year, and already services most of the world's major technology, gaming, banking, and consumer goods companies. You can find highly qualified and brilliant executive and technical talent in the country.

In reality, if you have 50 Virtual Assistants working in your company, then I suggest you have 50 staff working for you that you haven't yet bothered to allocate proper roles and titles. I assume that those staff have some sort of a departmental structure internally— and are probably sorted into a hierarchy of juniors, seniors, and managers. This is called a business. And businesses have staff, not VAs.

Even in sports, there is a conscious organization around the division of labor and specialization, with every player having different positions, roles, and responsibilities.

If someone defines their company and its people to just a group of Virtual Assistants, then they are limiting their company's prospects, as well as everyone within it, and are missing out on the full extent of the global workforce. There are 8 billion people on the planet, and they are all waking up to the opportunity of globalized and remote employment. These 8 billion people offer every skill, role, and profession under the sun.

I would rather build a business filled with the brightest minds, best professionals, and the most keenly educated and career aspiring people. They will be specialized in their chosen roles and passionate about what they do. They will be developers, accountants, marketers, sales professionals, analysts, growth hackers, and HR professionals. They will have particular qualifications and abilities and know exactly how they contribute to the company's success. If you hire top-flight offshore professionals on this basis, then you will build a much stronger business that everyone can be proud of.

Compliance

Another niggling concern I have with Virtual Assistants, but most especially with the Virtual Assistant firms and agencies, is that they are, in most part, unlawful and are not correctly employing their staff.

We are starting to see the informal economy become normalized worldwide—with Uber drivers, food delivery apps, dog walkers, web designers, and VAs all participating in the casual gig economy. It is an open secret that the Virtual Assistant world is largely based on freelance, contract, and gig work arrangements. But I don't think people realize that there is a proper way of doing things, and that there are very viable alternatives.

The Virtual Assistant firms, of which there are now many, are mostly operating illegally—or certainly, they are non-compliant with the Philippines' incorporation, tax, and employment laws, which is clearly not a good thing. To repeat—most VA firms do not properly employ their staff, are not properly incorporated, and do not pay local taxes.

Many of these VA companies are US, UK, or foreign-owned. In fact, many of the owners of these companies have never even stepped into the Philippines. So while they tap into the Philippine talent pool, many of them only really have a very loose association with the country. Certainly, they don't deem it necessary to incorporate, pay taxes, or abide by the labor laws. The problem is also not helped because the major freelancer platforms do nothing to sufficiently encourage or enforce formal employment practices or compliance.

Many VA firms would explain to their clients that they have an 'agreement' with their 'contract staff' and that the staff have agreed to be responsible for paying their taxes and managing their compliance. However, these arrangements are not actually legitimate, and they do not comply with the labor laws in the Philippines.

I want to be clear that there is not actually any direct coercion or abuse of VAs in this regard. The VAs understand the terms of the agreement, and they know that they are not being properly employed. They also know that their taxes will not be paid, and they will forgo proper benefits. They know this, and they are happy to make the deal. For the VAs they would be earning considerably more than what they could elsewhere, and also—they avoid paying the tax themselves. This means that they are already getting a relatively high salary, and they are saving extra because of the tax-free arrangement. Good jobs can be hard to come by in the Philippines, especially in the provinces, so few would pass by such an opportunity—especially when there isn't an alternative.

So it is valid to point out here that the VAs are very much on board with this approach. And they can be earning great money, work from their home, and be very productive and happily engaged in their job or career in this way. So there is not necessarily any direct abuse of power or privilege in this respect.

The VA companies suggest that they agree with the VA that it is up to them to submit their own documents and set up as a contractor and pay taxes—but 99% of the time this does not happen.

The problem is that the VAs are getting a good deal in the short term—which is wonderful. But in the long term, they are doing themselves a disservice. The government systems are pretty cruel in the Philippines. Without any contributions, these people will not have any public health cover, and no pension—even though the support is meager anyway. But in their need to pay for today, they are not ensuring a safe and secure tomorrow.

I don't want to come across as a nanny-state zealot trying to wipe away people's free will and free choice—but I believe that these people need to be properly employed, and the companies need to abide by the country's labor laws in this respect. The system of proper employment has been a long-established facet in almost every society for many hundreds of years now, and while this system isn't perfect, it brings with it some sort of stability and downside protection for the employees.

The VA companies are taking advantage of a wide-open opportunity in that the government simply doesn't have the resources to identify, chase, and enforce the rules across the massive gray market economy. Equally, the government is between a rock and a hard place. Parts of the government are happy that this big thriving online digital economy provides much-needed high-paid work for the provincial population. Some estimates suggest that between 1 million[19] to 4 million[20] people are working online in this way. But alternatively, this entire sector is completely sidestepping the formal employment sector, and tax, pension and healthcare regimes. A system will simply fail if it does not participate in a major—and fast-growing—part of the economy.

I really believe in the free market. And I believe that the private sector, not the government, will bring affluence to a population. I also believe that the digital economy is generating an incredible opportunity for a wide range of the global population that would have otherwise been completely left out in the cold. So there are incredible benefits to this. But I think that each country's employment laws should be abided by.

Part of the issue is that the Philippines is enormously bureaucratic, is filled with red-tape, and is highly complex to navigate. To get it all done, you almost need superhuman persistence and a Ph.D. to set up a company and be compliant with taxes and the multitude of filing requirements. Small-time freelancers mostly don't have the resources, time, or understanding to jump through

---

19   Paypal Newsroom.(2018).Global Freelancer Survey.https://newsroom.apac.paypal-corp.com/paypal-global-freelancer-survey-categoryId-company-news

20   Payoneer.(2019).The global Gig Index.Retrieved from https://explore.payoneer.com/q2_global_freelancing_index/

all of the endless hoops needed to be compliant. And why should they? If everyone they know is working online for direct Paypal payments—why should they be the only ones to go through the rat race of setting it all up properly?

The system creates enormous friction and barriers for people to legitimize themselves. This is both the case for VA companies and their staff. It is very hard for companies to incorporate and stay compliant in the Philippines—and it is almost hostile towards full foreign ownership. These numerous hurdles discourage companies from even attempting to do the right thing.

Equally, for basic administrative staff stuck in the provinces of the Philippines, having to negotiate the enormously complex bureaucratic systems is overwhelming. Most people would not understand the complexities of the tax systems and the innumerable documents that need to be completed monthly, quarterly, and annually.

As a result, and is the case in nature generally, if there is too much complexity, friction, and obstruction, then people will find an alternative route. And this is what's happening right now. The alternative route has created a thriving gray-market digital economy. In many ways, this is a wonderful thing. It is much better to have a thriving digital economy, instead of not having one at all. But there now needs to be work done to give these contractors an easy way to participate in the formal employment system and give them a job and career that they deserve.

The VA companies are taking advantage of the weak enforcement environment. If they were ever assessed or tested, they would likely all be in direct breach of the labor laws of the Philippines. As a result, they stay on the low within the Philippines. But this has little impact on their ability to market their services to overseas clients in the US, UK, and elsewhere. And they are all quickly growing as more businesses discover VAs, and the benefits of working with Filipino staff.

The VA firms are discouraged from going the formal route simply because it costs a lot of time and money. Equally, if these companies legitimize, it will cost them, and ultimately the client, more money to employ their people properly. Formal employment adds about 10% to 20% of various employer contributions on top of the salary and additional administrative work for the VA firm. Additionally, and significantly, it requires them to be compliant and accountable to the Philippine labor laws, which means that they are no longer able to hire and fire at will.

Typically, with a VA, if a client is unhappy or leaves, then the VA will be let go immediately. This is most certainly not possible when they are properly employed. When employed, the staff have the right to notice periods and redundancy pay. These things are all thorns in the side of VA companies and can add up to cost significant money. So if there is no one forcing them to go legitimate, then, of course, no one is going to do it voluntarily.

Again, the VAs know what they are getting themselves in for when signing up to an informal contractor agreement. They know that there is less job security and likely no redundancy or 13th-month pay. However, in most cases, these staff simply don't have an alternative option. There are no other 'proper' jobs, and so they continue to exist within the freelancer economy.

Of course, the vast majority of the outsourcing industry is legitimate. And this is why—for many wide-ranging reasons—I encourage you to use the professional industry and steer clear of the informal counterparts. The formal outsourcing industry, in fact, is the single biggest sector in the Philippines. It contributes to over 12% of the country's GDP, is one of the biggest employers, rents the most office space, and is one of the largest taxpayers in the country.

There is a divide between the professional outsourcing sector and the online, gig worker, and freelancer economy—and it doesn't seem to be going away. This is maybe not helped by the fact that there is a general movement towards gig-economy services right across the world. Everything from Uber drivers and food delivery to handyman services and dog walkers are all now available online with a click of a button. In 2020, the gig model used by Uber and the like was challenged by California state in the US, and narrowly defeated in the now infamous Proposition 22.

It is well beyond me to say whether gig-work and freelancing is the right approach to the future of work, or not. However, from a business point of view, I would suggest that if you're jumping in a cab to get home, then a gig-worker might be a good solution for that. But if you are hiring full-time professional staff, in specialized roles, to run your company on an ongoing basis, then I would suggest you hire them legitimately, on a full-time basis. And while you're at it, you might as well abide by the local employment laws when you do. As a client of a legitimate outsourcing firm, this is not hard. The BPO industry has developed specifically to provide these critical services for your company—so that it is easy, cheap, flexible, and convenient to hire a team properly. As a client, it's not hard to be compliant, and it costs relatively very little. And when you employ people properly, giving them the benefits they deserve, you will attract better people and stand to get better results yourself.

For the VA community, I suggest that they take one step backward to legitimize their businesses and employees. If they do this, they will have the proper foundations in place to take many more steps forward. If they continue to exist within the gray economy, they will never progress further beyond basic back-alley administrative services. I want the VAs, or more accurately, the offshore industry, to be so much more than this.

Limiting Beliefs

People that know about Virtual Assistants tend to think that Virtual Assistants are the entire offshoring industry. But actually, they really just represent a tiny corner of a much bigger picture. They are more like a kiddies league compared to the highly sophisticated outsourcing industry.

It's like watching a bunch of five-year-olds playing basketball and thinking that that is the extent and peak of the sport. And then you suddenly see the NBA, the LA Lakers, and LeBron James working their magic and realize that there is so much more than you have previously known.

The Virtual Assistant movement—led in part by Tim Ferriss and the freelancing platforms like Upwork—has at least shone a bright light on the possibilities of offshore staffing. It has certainly played a part in boosting people's awareness of the online Filipino workforce, which is great. But I know that the broader industry has so much more potential, which is often overlooked.

If you are looking for a great sport and world-class players, then the kiddies league is very limited. The same applies to the Virtual Assistant community. The sector consists of mostly self-taught freelancers from very humble backgrounds who work from their provincial homes, from very basic machines. I don't want that to sound disparaging in any way. These people are all fantastic, and they are doing great work. They are elevating the prospects for themselves and their community and making their way in the global online economy, which is wonderful.

However, I am desperate for the Philippines to be known, not just for administrative assistants but also for its capacity to work in highly technical and professional roles. Instead, many people have only ever heard of VAs, and so they go looking for VAs, and then, surprisingly, all they find are VAs. This circular loop creates a self-fulfilling pattern of people thinking that when you hire offshore, you hire Virtual Assistants, and there is nothing beyond that.

This could not be further from the truth.

People need to realize that they can just as easily hire quantum physicists, data scientists, blockchain developers, animators, and metaverse engineers. And they are working from labs, universities, city centers, and shiny offices. These exciting and dynamic roles are just as prevalent, if not more, than the typecast Virtual Assistant who's managing someone's inbox, working from their bed, in their pajamas.

When speaking to clients, I sometimes ask them to envisage the kinds of people they want on their teams. Sometimes I suggest a little visualization exercise.

First, I ask them to envisage a quintessential Wall Street banker and how that sort of person might contribute to a business. They get up early in the morning, put on a crisp suit, and make their way to an impressive office in the world's central financial district. They're wearing a fancy watch, shiny shoes, and holding an elegant leather satchel. Commensurate with this image, you might assume that they have had a stellar education and an even more impressive CV. You expect that they will be earning good money, but in return, you know they're hard workers, capable of some fantastic stuff, spend long hours in the office, and are dedicated to their company and career.

Next, I ask them to visualize a low-paid casual worker. Instead of Wall Street, you might have bumped into them on the bus or in a local bar. They're not particularly well presented, and they're in no rush to get anywhere. They are just getting by in their career, never really shone at school, and haven't actually ever worked in an office. They do a lot of their client work from their bed, interspersed with some Netflix, and usually hang out in their pajamas. You chat, and they are happy to do a bit of work for you on an informal basis—it isn't full-time, and the pay isn't that great, but that's okay, they'll give it a go.

Both of these types of people are out there in the market. While they are both generalizations, and cliches at that, I know that I would prefer to power my business with the Wall Street bankers, rather than the part-timer working from their bed. The same applies for marketers, developers, designers, and any profession for that matter. When offshoring, I would strongly suggest that you look to work with the brightest people in the industry. Seek out those who have invested a lot into their education and have painstakingly built a career they are proud of and committed to furthering.

These principles are inherently understood and taken for granted when hiring traditional staff in your local setting. But when it comes to hiring offshore, for some reason, people think that the home-based, freelance gig-worker is the best option to go with. This is incongruent at best, and most generally, does not work.

It's great to get your groceries delivered by a DoorDash rider; in this respect, the gig economy is invaluable, but I wouldn't recommend that you have them run your business. When offshoring, seek to employ the top professionals, on a full-time basis, and within a commensurate business environment.

Part 3

Evaluating
Ousourcing

The Bad Boy of Business

Everyone Loves to Hate Outsourcing

Outsourcing is, unfortunately, one of the most controversial topics out there. It has a somewhat unique ability to infuriate people on both sides of the fence, at the same time—and for almost completely different reasons. Meanwhile, for the casual observer, outsourcing is at best an unfamiliar but contentious topic, so they naturally default to a skeptical uncertainty. Consequently, we are faced with two very unhappy parties on either extreme, and an apathetic majority in the middle. It's kinda like if you walk into a bar and there is a fight going on—you don't want to get involved in any part of it, so you just walk out of the bar again, and avoid it completely. That's what you have with outsourcing. You have the hot-minded right and the woke left going at it, which causes anyone in the moderate middle to just play it safe and give the whole subject a wide birth.

There are two main objections that cause both sides of the political spectrum to bristle. These two objections are in some ways diametrically opposed, yet they are almost the same issues, like different sides of the same coin.

One of the key objections to offshoring is that it takes jobs from 'our' people. The other concern is that offshoring is akin to slavery, taking advantage of vulnerable populations and paying them less than a reasonable wage. Generally, those on the right are concerned about the loss of local jobs and opportunities to offshore competitors. Meanwhile, those on the left are more concerned about the unethical treatment of offshore staff and what they consider underpaid labor.

Another throwaway criticism of outsourcing is that it is of bad quality, or just doesn't work. People from all walks of life quickly associate offshore staffing with low standards, bad accents, and poor service.

This ominous tripartite of objections understandably causes significant headwinds against outsourcing. And it's no wonder. They're all quite damning accusations.

In short, outsourcing is an industry that everyone loves to hate.

◇◇◇◇◇◇◇◇◇◇◇◇◇

To me, there is just no argument that outsourcing works. Which I suppose is a good thing, since I am writing the book on it.

In its simplest form, offshore staffing is really just applying the basic concept of employment—on a global scale. It's like traditional employment—on steroids. In this respect, it's so simple and almost impossible to argue against.

As discussed in earlier chapters, offshoring is both the manifestation and embodiment of improving technology, increasing global trade, and human cooperation. There are obvious benefits for both the client-, and supplier-sides—and ultimately, for all stakeholders, including the workers, shareholders, communities, nations, and ultimately humanity itself.

The world's largest and most successful businesses have been offshoring for the last 30 years. If it didn't work, then they would not do it. And if it did not work, the industry would not have consistently grown at double-digit rates every year for that time.

You would think that 30 years of breakneck industry growth, and almost complete penetration of the Western enterprise market, would be proof enough that the concept has clear advantages. However, the West's small and medium-sized businesses are slow to catch on. I find it quite amazing that not only SMEs have missed out on this incredible opportunity up until now, but they also still need convincing of its merits.

Today, with cheaper technology, flexible turnkey solutions, and widespread adoption of remote-work tools and methodologies, offshoring is easy and accessible for everyone. However, amongst the SMEs, there is still a very limited understanding of exactly what it is, and how it is used. And so more often than not it's treated with uncertainty or disdain, popped into the 'too-hard basket,' and ignored.

With education and awareness, these perspectives and habits will change. I know they will, because there's a big wave of globalization and technology rolling in, that will eventually make offshoring a completely normalized practice.

Part of the problem with outsourcing is that not enough people talk about it openly. Instead of being seen as a magnificent feat of global cooperation, it's looked down upon as a kind of national betrayal.

Offshoring does have a lot of happy clients, devotees, and supporters. There are now countless businesses that outsource globally, but since it is generally an unpopular topic, most choose not to fly their flag of support too high. After all, "Buy American Made" is a more compelling slogan than "I offshore all my staff," causing most businesses that outsource to keep it to themselves. And this is a shame for the industry—and the global economy generally. This tendency to not talk about it amongst peers has a dramatic dampening effect on the industry's awareness, acceptance and uptake.

There's also a commercial reason why a lot of happy clients aren't shouting about it from the rooftops. Outsourcing creates a significant competitive advantage over those that don't do it—and so it makes sense not to overly share. After all, there's not a lot of business upside in giving away successful competitive advantages to others.

As a result there isn't a big network effect to outsourcing—it's quite the opposite to 'viral.' So I encourage you to break this cycle. Talk to your colleagues, staff, company leadership, and entrepreneur friends about how outsourcing can be used in your business.

In doing this, you will be identifying the benefits of outsourcing, specific to your business, for yourself. In isolation, outsourcing has little inherent value, it is really just a conduit to global staffing solutions. It is more the integration of offshore staffing into your businesses that will get you the transformative gains.

So when exploring the potential benefits, don't actually ask —"How can we harness outsourcing?" This question means very little to most people because they simply aren't familiar with the concept. Instead, ask something much simpler, more compelling, and core to your specific business.

Ask questions like:

- What could we do if we could hire equally-capable staff at a 70% discount?
- What could we do if we could triple the current workforce for the same amount of money?
- How could we outcompete if we had easy access to the best of 8 billion people?
- How could we grow if the labor shortages, skill shortages, jumping salaries and 'Great Resignation' did not apply to our company?
- How could our company thrive if we participate in the global economy, not just our local market?

These questions should get the creative juices flowing and may kickstart some exciting innovation inside your company. If you can answer these questions for your business, then you are at the same time discovering the benefits of outsourcing.

◇◇◇◇◇◇◇◇◇◇◇◇◇◇

With all the criticism, some might wonder how the industry even exists. Yet, it has been powering on for 30 years, racking up $273 billion in annual revenues, sustaining enviable growth rates, and servicing virtually all of the world's leading companies—bar none. With this impressive performance, there must be something positive to be found in outsourcing. Indeed there is.

So why does outsourcing have such an image problem? Maybe, the bad boy of business is actually a misunderstood genius. I want to attend to the many criticisms and controversies facing the outsourcing industry, as well as some of the more macro benefits, in the following two chapters. I will first confront the swirling storm of contention and then follow up with the advantages.

Criticisms of Outsourcing

Ethical Battleground

In most Western countries, offshoring has become a dirty word synonymous with job loss, plunging salaries, worsening job markets, slave labor—and even a threat to national well-being. These criticisms are largely unfair, and I would go as far as to say that it is entirely unfounded. But it exists nonetheless. Let's explore why this industry is so regularly maligned.

Ironically, the resistance to offshoring is more prevalent in economic powerhouses such as the US, UK, and Australia. These are countries that you think would not be troubled by competitive threats from weak developing nations. It's like an elephant being fearful of mice—there is no threat—quite the contrary. Being from a leading developed country and having access to significantly discounted resources from developing nations can only be a boon.

Employee salaries are a significant component of overall expenses for any business. For most modern companies, especially those in tech, SaaS, and online commerce, their employee salaries can easily represent 40% to 80% of their total costs. If businesses from already affluent countries in the West can access significantly cheaper salaries from developing countries to supply their needs, you would think that this is a clear benefit for the wealthier countries, their companies, employees, and the community. Generally, in any economic model, if you can source key resources for significantly less than your competitors, you have a profound advantage. It doesn't stand to reason then that having access to a cheap pool of labor, as well as cheap computers, materials, and products, actually undermines a country's prospects. If anything— and the evidence supports this—this asymmetrical access to cheaper Human Resources, inputs, and tools should make the richer countries richer.

And indeed, we are seeing the rich countries getting richer. We also see that the unemployment rates in most Western countries are at all-time lows. In fact, unemployment levels are now so consistently low that many developed countries are suffering severe labor shortages and a significant hike in salaries due to the spike in demand.

I am no economist, so I can't dive too deep into the analysis, but if you zoom out, the big picture seems obvious—and conclusive. The world has seen 30 years of rampant offshoring—both in manufacturing and employee services. The world has also seen enormous advancement and penetration of software, automation, robotics, and machinery in that time. The combination of all of these factors has collectively destroyed many tens of millions of jobs across every industry, touching every facet of life. Quite frankly, the technological and offshoring shifts of the last 30 years have had a significant impact on virtually every job in the world—in fact, there would be few jobs, if any, that remain untouched.

However, three decades on, instead of seeing widespread unemployment and downfallen economies, the world is seeing sustained levels of employment, rising salaries, and strengthening economies. In fact, unemployment rates in most developed countries are at all-time record lows—and this is despite having just gone through a near economically catastrophic black swan event of the global pandemic. Meanwhile, salaries have not only stayed strong, but they have significantly risen. And generally, the quality of life and prosperity for the vast majority of society has markedly improved. So there is just no evidence that the much-feared specter of offshoring will, or ever has, 'taken all of the jobs.'

Of course, not everyone in society has prospered in the last 30 years. Inevitably there will be some winners and some losers. And also, unfortunately, some members of the population will have completely slipped through the gaps and have had a really rough time due to the evolving market. For these unfortunate individuals, the impact of change is universally devastating, and they would probably do anything to wind back time. But overall, society, employment, quality of life, and salaries for the great majority have vastly improved.

When analyzing the impacts of technology and globalization, to form a complete picture, you would also have to examine various changes to regulation, trade agreements, national strategies, security, international relations, and political posturing. It's a complicated situation.

For example, many successful American businesses were immediately and summarily ruined when US President Donald Trump in January 2018 began his trade war with China. To hurt China, Trump, with little warning, imposed a raft of pernicious tariffs and other trade barriers between the two countries. While the impact for China is undetermined, there was certainly significant collateral damage. Trump's trade embargo harmed, and ultimately destroyed, a huge number of well-meaning US businesses that either relied on Chinese raw materials as inputs or sold their finished product back to the Chinese market.

As the global population continues to work, trade, socialize, holiday, and live more closely together, inevitably arguments will arise. Like any cooperation among large groups of people, there will be instances of disagreement and even outright unrest. But I firmly believe that directionally, the world will continue to move closer together, and increasingly towards some sort of concentrated unification. It is certainly harder to imagine the reverse happening. There are about 195 countries globally and five major economic trading zones. It is hard to imagine a future where the world becomes increasingly fractured, with countries splitting into many hundreds of sovereign states, and opting for less cooperation and more segregation as different regions of the planet choose not to connect or work together.

I don't want to appear overly naive or pollyanna about the complexities of international political relations—in this respect, we are all pawns in an infinitely complex chessboard of life, and I do not claim to have the answers. Political stability needs to be managed, and I'm glad that there are highly qualified specialists in the area dedicated to the careful navigation of this particular gauntlet. For example, maybe there are political risks in having all of the world's semiconductors produced in Taiwan. Or maybe if China becomes too powerful, it could enact nefarious plans for the world. Or maybe, Britain should have remained within the European Union. All of these things are very complex issues and they do need monitoring, managing, and attending to. However, the world has never been in a perfect state. It is always a work in progress, and there will always be issues that need addressing. But I would argue that the world is directionally heading the right way. It is, on the whole, becoming a better place, cooperating more than ever, becoming more prosperous, and its people are living better than ever.

With outsourcing, there is an oversimplified knee-jerk fear that all jobs will be shipped offshore one day, and 300 million Americans will have nothing to do. This is simply not the case. It will not, and could not ever, happen. What is more likely to happen, as discussed, is that the world will increasingly become one globalized marketplace for products, consumers, and employees alike. Companies will be able to source the best staff for a role, regardless of where that person is sitting. This offers an enormous opportunity for a business to find the best possible employee, producing the best possible output, at the best possible price. Equally, it gives all citizens of the world an incredible opportunity to participate in the global economy, support their families, progress in their life, and chase their dreams.

There will be bumps in the road along this journey, and there will be some losers amongst the many winners, but overall, it will be a significant net positive for the world's population—both rich and poor alike.

Xenophobia?

Could it be that a subtle form of racism underpins some of the offshoring complaints? Previously, the Dhaka Tribune, from Bangladesh, posted an article raising this question: "Why do some people oppose globalization?"[21] The article's author noted the hostility toward globalization and suggested that it's not simply job loss that fuels this hostility. It may also be the "transmission and blending of ideas, lifestyles, [and] cultures" that angers many politicians and voters of the West. The trend toward nationalism and the negative views of immigrants and refugees who have recently poured into Europe and the US may inadvertently further dampen outsourcing's image.

In-group bias is a human trait identified by social psychologists that explains why people give preferential treatment to others who belong to the same group that they do. We all like to think

---

21   Dhaka Tribune. People oppose globalization. (2018). Retrieved from https://archive.dhakatribune. com/business/2018/02/05/people-oppose-globalization

that we are fair, reasonable people, and that we select our social preferences based on sound logic and reason. However, numerous studies conducted in the field of social psychology have clearly demonstrated the almost arbitrary application and impact of in-group bias. Experts have observed that an in-group bias appears almost immediately after people have been divided into groups. Even if the group was created just for the purposes of an experiment, and even if the group members were knowingly randomly selected —an in-group bias quickly appeared and persisted.

We all have a solid affinity for in-group preference—we just don't know it. The preference might be between you and the person that you love. Or it might be you and your family. Or it could be you and your town, you and your state, or you and your country. And equally, it could be you and your sports team, your workplace, or your friends at the gym. It might also be your culture, race or gender. What—or who—that in-group is can vary. But we do all have preferences for some people over others, and these are referred to as in-group preferences.

The dangerous corollary of this is that we also naturally possess an out-group skepticism, and maybe fear, and maybe even distrust. Awful as this may sound, it is almost a universal trait among humans—and even all animal-kind—that we prefer people who are part of our group. And conversely, we are inclined to treat those outside of our group with hesitation, caution, or worse.

Taken to an extreme, in-group bias can easily be distorted into something quite akin to xenophobia or racism. We even see it play out, very obviously, among most animal species. Dogs and cats are highly territorial—this is a given—and as Jane Goodall, the famous English primatologist and anthropologist discovered, it affects our closest genetic relatives equally.

In the 1970s, Goodall found that chimpanzees actively sought out neighboring territories and went on merciless raiding forays. She noted that if they outnumbered the foreign chimps they came across, they would tear them to pieces. The anthropologists reticently reported that the human tendency for war was so innate that our closest animal relatives even shared it. So the idea that in-group preference is something that human beings struggle with is, to some degree, an inbuilt truth. These deep psychological traits are thankfully dulled in modern society, buried under layers of social conditioning, and mitigated by conscious civility and general security from modern-day safety. We now no longer have to go to war with our neighbors to ensure the survival of our offspring; however, the shadows of our deep territorial traits still persist.

The positive aspect of in-group bias is that people hold other people in higher regard if they are from the same group. However, the flipside of that same coin is that it can account for a big component of prejudice and discrimination, leading people to extend extra privileges to people in their own in-group while denying that same courtesy to others.

In-group bias can harm relationships with people who don't belong to the same group that we do. Our tendency to favor in-group members can make us mistreat others and cause us to perceive the same behaviors among other people very differently depending on their group. We might even feel justified in committing immoral or dishonest actions so long as they benefit our group.

I really believe that the in-group bias contributes to the generalized opposition to outsourcing. It makes sense. The threat of job losses is magnified by the jobs and opportunities being taken from 'our group' and given to 'that group.' In contrast, some software might be installed or a computer delivered to the office, which wipes out dozens of jobs—and this is okay. Despite both the outsourcing and technology equally impacting job security, offshoring inevitably invokes more outrage. In fact, it's more likely that the new software installation is actively celebrated.

I believe that this is because humans are wary of, and easily riled by, the activity of other humans. Yet, they usually ignore the impact of inanimate objects like a computer, ATM, or lawnmower. This is just like a dog getting immediately agitated by the sight of another dog off in the distance. Dogs pay ten times more attention to another dog than they do to almost anything else. Most dogs are blasé about humans and certainly completely disinterested in most inanimate objects and even moving images on the TV. But they immediately come alive, jump to attention, and prepare to either meet, play or fight when they see another dog.

The benefits of globalization for businesses and the world, in general, is immense. Not only can companies leverage the output, skills, and resources of 8 billion people, but they can also now sell their product or service to an ever-expanding audience. There are now 8 billion prospective customers, collaborators, and producers for your products. This is an incredible opportunity and one that the world has never seen before. So while it is natural to have preferences for those we are familiar with, people should actively resist their predisposition to reject outsiders and embrace the opportunity for progressive globalization.

Outsourcing Fails the Middle Class

One of the biggest, most pervasive, misconceptions about outsourcing is that it is stealing jobs from Western workers and causing big problems for home economies.

An article published by the Washington Post tackles this issue head-on. Rather than accepting the fear that globalization and outsourcing models will 'hollow out' entire industries in the West, it states that "rearranging where and how work is done has been going on ever since the first shepherd and farmer decided to trade milk for wheat on a regular basis. Outsourcing is merely an extension of the age-old story of specialization and exchange, whether it is done within a village, or country, or across national borders.[22]" The article points out that "the resentment seems to grow exponentially with geographic distance—which heightens the 'us' versus 'them' tension—and the gap between the original wages and the new ones."

There is a far bigger offender if the critics really want to find the true source of job disruption. Instead, they should look at threats to workers that come from the inevitable and far more pervasive development of technology, automation, machines, and robots.

How many self-checkout lanes does your favorite grocery store now have? Tech-enabled processes like these mean that fewer workers are needed to deliver a necessary service. Technology has shown to be relentless with its displacement of people, as it sweeps through society, and is responsible for the loss of an almost infinite list of roles, jobs and livelihoods. Before looms, garments were all handmade. Before washing machines and dishwashers, clothes and tableware were hand-washed. Before computers, people manually processed tasks, taking many times longer and requiring many more people. Before heavy machinery, society largely constructed its roads, bridges, and buildings by hand—and possibly by the hand of human slaves. Few of humanity's earliest roles still exist to this day. Technology and evolution have wiped out virtually every job we have historically ever known. However, the same technology and economic progress has also added just as many new ones and many more on top.

In the UK, for example, every week, 51,000 jobs are lost. However, in the same week, about 53,000 new jobs are created. Clearly, outsourcing or offshoring aren't the only reasons for these weekly job losses. According to the Leverhulme Centre for Research on Globalization and Economic Policy, only about 2.3% of these

---

22   Washington Post. (2012). Outsourcing: What's the true impact? Counting jobs is only part of the answer. Retrieved from https://www.washingtonpost.com/business/economy/outsourcings-net-ef-fect-on-us-jobs-still-an-open-ended-question/2012/07/01/gJQAs1szGW_story.html

job losses can be attributed to outsourcing.[23] In addition, their findings show that "offshoring creates jobs and boosts turnover within the UK Economy" and that "offshoring was responsible for an estimated 3.5 percent of job losses in the UK in 2005. But this research shows that job gains by far outweigh the losses." While according to a study by The Reason Foundation titled "Offshoring and Public Fear: Assessing the Real Threat to Jobs," they concluded that "most American jobs are lost to other Americans or absorbed by technology.[24]"

However, despite all of this, after 30 years of rampant technological development and offshoring, there has been little, or no, net impact on employment. In fact, the labor market and salaries are stronger than ever. As the Washington Post puts it: "Global outsourcing has been a net job creator for the United States —that as a result of shifting work overseas, more jobs were created back home than were lost, even though the jobs and the workers may not be the same." These studies are in keeping with the basic tenets of economic theory—that specialization and healthy trade are win-win propositions for all.

So, yes, job loss may occur. For instance, many manufacturing jobs were indeed lost in this sector over the decades. However, the loss was offset by much greater job gains across the service, technology, and professional services sectors. So, certain workers do have a legitimate gripe that their specific line of work may eventually become obsolete as a result of outsourcing and a trend towards specialization, but this is an economic reality and cost that comes with progress. If there is a net gain in total jobs, more higher-skilled and better-paid jobs are produced, and generally, the

---

23 Leverhulme Center.Offshoring and the UK economy. Retrieved from https://www.nottingham. ac.uk/gep/documents/reports/gep-offshoring-report-06-08.pdf

24 The Reason Foundation.(2005).Offshoring and Public Fear: Assessing the Real Threat to Jobs.Retrieved from https://reason.org/wp-content/uploads/files/4275b89640247336408d391422ad2c9a. pdf

society is better off then, unfortunately, the hammer will likely fall in favor of this progression.

There aren't blacksmith stalls in London anymore. But nobody is mourning. At some point in the past century, all blacksmiths, candlestick makers, telephone operators, and ladies' maids had to find a new line of work—as was necessitated by change. The blacksmiths would have felt the pinch at the time, but now, no one is concerned about the lack of blacksmiths. No one would complain that they are out of work as a result of there being no demand for blacksmiths, and the economy as a whole has more than moved on.

Political Dynamics

While a New Yorker whose job is moved to India or Mexico certainly has a legitimate personal gripe to make, much of the case against outsourcing and globalization, in general, comes from certain political corners that play on fears of job loss and diminishing national security dominance.

However, can politicians who passionately rally against offshoring jobs actually provide a viable alternative or sustainable solution? Can these politicians actually bring jobs back to their struggling economies, impact the nature of change, or stop a potentially inevitable change? As with the Luddite attempts to keep handweaving relevant, can they stall progress?

Western politicians have won votes by promising to slay the offshoring monster. They promise to either penalize companies that engage in the practice or offer incentives to companies to keep all their processes within their home country. To a large degree, these politicians have made unfeasible promises, proffered flawed solutions, and spun false hope for an unrealistic future. Certainly, the policies have not worked because we can see that globalization of the world's population and offshoring along with it has increased and is only gaining speed.

Case in point: Take the former Trump administration in the US —and I apologize here for picking such a soft target. The former US president waged a campaign to bring overseas jobs back to America and to "Make America Great Again." It is clear from his rhetoric and trade-busting actions that he was seriously against offshoring—and this solid nationalistic bent viscerally resonated with his audience.

However, savvy onlookers will, no doubt, notice his hypocrisy. As a business leader, Trump had long exported much of his production and jobs to other countries, all of which were far from American shores and, more specifically, American workers. According to The Independent, "For Trump, highlighting US-made products is inconsistent with his practices as a businessman. For years, the Trump Organization has outsourced much of its product manufacturing, relying on a global network of factories in a dozen countries—including Bangladesh, China, and Mexico—to make its clothing, home decor pieces, and other items."[25]

The "Made in America" mantra of the Trump campaign is an example of the liberties that politicians take when attempting to score votes. However, when the rubber meets the road, companies are forced to find the most efficient means of production for their businesses.

The politics surrounding outsourcing is hardly a uniquely American problem. A recent article by HR Director reported how "unsubstantiated claims of loss of employment due to offshoring have played a part to the UK voting for Brexit and the rise of right-wing protectionist governments across the world."[26] Despite

---

25 The Independent. (2017). Donald Trump's 'Made in America' week marred by criticism of company's overseas manufacturing deals. Retrieved by https://www.independent.co.uk/news/world/americas/donald-trump-made-in-america-week-overseas-manufacturing-products-outsourcing-a7844651.html

26 The Director. (2018). Study Finds no Evidence That Offshoring Destroys Jobs. Retrieved from https://www.thehrdirector.com/business-news/globalisation/study-evidence-offshoring-destroys-jobs/

extensive conjecture from every corner of society, much of how Brexit will actually impact the pulling out of certain trade and offshoring agreements is still very much unknown. In another analysis, according to a report by Deutsche Bank, there are genuine fears that Brexit could actually cause a labor market shock and send a big increase in jobs overseas. The bank warned that a tighter labor market would not necessarily result in higher wages for the British.[27]

Regardless of the realities, the fact remains that outsourcing is a dramatically polarizing concept. Even if the research does not back up the claims that outsourcing steals jobs, politicians will inevitably blame globalization if it suits their platform. Businesses must look past this rhetoric and find the real evidence for the real benefits that come with outsourcing for themselves.

Labor Exploitation and Unsatisfactory Conditions

Another important concern that cannot be overlooked is the claim that overseas workers are exploited, forced to work in poor conditions, or treated as veritable slaves who earn next to nothing for the same work that would otherwise earn a Western worker a living wage.

While the gravest concerns here are reserved mainly for the manufacturing sector, the same issues can spill over to the offshore service sector. This complaint certainly has merit, as evidenced by the sweatshops in underdeveloped nations and the poor work conditions that many overseas workers are forced to endure.

I want to be very clear on this point. In no way do I support the

---

27   Business Insider.(2017).DEUTSCHE BANK: Falling immigration after Brexit is set to cause a
      'major' problem for the British economy.Retrieved from https://www.businessinsider.com/unem-
      ployment-uk-deutsche-bank-brexit-2017-9

unfair exploitation of people, the underpayment of people, or the act of exposing people to unsafe or inhumane conditions. These practices are completely intolerable and should under no circumstances be condoned. There are enormous disparities in the world today, with nearly 700 million people existing in abject poverty and surviving on less than $1.90 per day.[28] This is an abomination. And the world needs to do all that it can to correct this situation.

However, it is important to note that neither outsourcing, offshore staffing, nor manufacturing created these conditions. It has not played any part in creating the poverty or circumstances that exist today. In fact, these industries offer salvation, and I would argue they are the best hope these countries have for kickstarting their economies and elevating their people out of the poverty trap.

Outsourcing to another country offers a poorer country a valuable opportunity to participate in economic trade with a wealthier state. And as we have seen in the previous chapters, engaging in a fair trade between two parties ultimately benefits both sides. Each party might not necessarily benefit exactly equally, but both parties do benefit—otherwise, it's not trade. Non-free trade is either slavery or some sort of coercion or corruption—and that is not outsourcing.

Yes, bad actors in outsourcing can take advantage of a bad situation, and we must all work to eradicate these from the industry. But they are exceptions rather than the rule, and there is a general consensus and commitment towards improving conditions. There are always abuses, though, and there will likely always be instances of bad behavior, unfair treatment, and exploitation— just as they are happening every day in downtown New York, London, or Paris. It is happening everywhere, but thankfully, it is a rare exception rather than the rule. If there was no outsourcing

---

28   The World Bank. (2018). Philippines Poverty Headcount. Retrieved from https://data.worldbank. org/indicator/SI.POV.UMIC?locations=PH

and no international trade, then the poverty would persist, and in all likelihood, be significantly worse. However, with trade, its economic fruits, and the right intentions, we all collectively move towards a better, safer, and more equitable future, gradually every day. Things do get better, and as we progress, society will continue to install stronger guard rails to ensure that future generations benefit from the improvements laid before them.

One of the worst tragedies in recent memory for outsourced manufacturing occurred in Dhaka in Bangladesh. According to World Bank, a building known as Rana Plaza crashed down on thousands of workers, killing one thousand people, and injuring twice as many more. The workers were sewing garments for many leading brands including Prada, Gucci, Versace, Mango, Primark, and Walmart. According to World Bank, "a chunk of blame for the collapse and deaths was placed on retailers and brands that outsourced their work to Bangladesh, and particularly Rana Plaza.[29]"

As evidence of these abuses comes to light, it has since become completely unacceptable for Western businesses to profit at the expense of workers in underdeveloped nations. Moreover, it has become imperative for Western companies to carefully vet suppliers to comply with acceptable safety standards and work conditions. Many companies in North America and Europe have signed formal agreements to ensure that they will shut down any operations that do not comply with agreed-upon standards. Certainly, abuses still exist, and change might not be happening quickly enough, but improvements and progress are gradual and certain.

Back in 2010, Apple was infamously exposed for the bad treatment of workers in one of their outsourced iPhone factories.

---

29   Open Knowledge Repository.(2019).The Effects of International Scrutiny on Manufacturing
      Workers: Evidence from the Rana Plaza Collapse in Bangladesh. Retrieved from https://open-
      knowledge.worldbank.org/handle/10986/32674

The conditions of Foxconn's infamous Longhua plant came to light when there was a slew of suicides from workers that fell victim to the seemingly intolerable conditions. There was an outcry from the West, and rightly so, but there is no easy answer.

Certain middle-class armchair observers in the West might get riled over low pay, bad conditions and bad actors across the developing world. And it's great that there are people out there looking out for each other. But who are we to say that the conditions of a Chinese factory worker are not sufficient? What are we comparing it to? If they didn't have that job, the typical Chinese factory worker might otherwise be starving or toiling in the fields or down a coal mine. Life for two billion people on the planet is still unbelievably bad. They have no safety net, and not even clean water to drink. So who are we to say that an entry-level factory job isn't a godsend for them?

When the Foxconn outrage was blazing, one Foxconn worker wrote to the New York Times to balance the swirling storm of arguments.[30] He said that he was grateful for the factory. Both he and his mother worked in the factory, and while conditions were tough and pay wasn't great, the conditions were infinitely better than the alternatives. They had previously lived in perennial poverty, with no access to economic opportunity. His mother was forced into prostitution and would suffer beatings and abuse from her clients. The son went on to say how grateful they were for the opportunity of factories like Foxconn, and for the chance for them to better their lives, and have a future of hope. It is too easy for people to condemn a factory worker's livelihood but have no concept of the alternate reality. Unfortunately, there is no better option for many factory workers, and maybe even no other option.

30   Duhig, C & Barboza, D. (2012). In China, Human Costs Are Built Into an iPad. The New York Times. Retrieved from https://www.nytimes.com/2012/01/26/business/ieconomy-apples-ipad-and-the-human-costs-for-workers-in-china.html

Naturally, over time, conditions improve. With millions of people probably suffering right now, it might sound glib to say, but improvements are most certainly being made, and actually, the rate of improvement is really quite staggering. China has struggled with famine and poverty for many centuries, and as of 1990, it had two-thirds of its enormous population living below the poverty line. In just 20 years, China was able to raise 742 million of its people from poverty.[31] Today, the latest figures show that just 0.6%—or 8.4 million—of their population live below that same threshold.[32] This is incredible progress and should be celebrated. And it is largely the manufacturing, factories, industrialization, and emerging capitalism —all products of trade and cooperation—responsible for this outcome.

China has switched from a poverty trap to a world-leading populace in just a few years. Now, certain pockets within the Chinese economy are wealthier, more productive, and far more technically capable than their Western counterparts. These small pockets will continue to expand and increasingly lift the masses. Progress never happens all at once, in a blanket fashion, to everyone all at the same time—and it never happens overnight. But the benefits of incessant progressive compounding improvements over time are extremely powerful.

◇◇◇◇◇◇◇◇◇◇◇◇◇

For the sake of this book, it's worth noting that service-based outsourcing, compared to outsourced manufacturing, is generally far less susceptible to poor conditions and worker abuse. I would

---

31   BBC News. (2021). Has China lifted 100 million people out of poverty? Retrieved from https://www.bbc.com/news/56213271

32   Statista. (2021). Is China Tackling Poverty? Retrieved from https://www.statista.com/chart/25138/people-under-poverty-line-china/

go as far as to say that the offshore staffing industry generally, if not completely, treats its staff reasonably and fairly.

I would posit that you can possibly mistreat a factory worker who is producing a physical good and still get the same physical good produced. However, when you are dealing with staff that are directly fulfilling professional services, you won't get much output if people are not happy at their job. For example, it is hard to run a productive and happy-sounding call center if the staff are being mistreated behind the scenes.

Also, because of the knowledge-based nature, the offshore staffing industry generally needs a workforce that is better qualified and more middle class. These people are usually better educated, less tolerant of low standards, have more options, and are more informed and vocal about their rights and expectations. Equally, in the Philippines, the government tends to be very protective of its workforce and is generally very pro-labor, especially within the largely foreign-led outsourcing sector.

While it is good to have regulatory protections in place, at some point, it just makes more sense to treat staff well. According to management 101, if you treat staff well, then better results will follow. This is, after all, why Western firms spend a lot of money and work hard to build a happy workforce, because the theory suggests that the company will benefit even more if their staff are happy, productive and engaged. This is consistent with management best practice and the basic tenets of economic trade. If there is a mutual benefit for both parties within a trade, then things work out better for everyone. It's just common sense—and this is no different for offshore staff.

For these reasons, I think the offshore staffing industry is inherently less susceptible to the malevolence of unscrupulous labor practices and bad actors. Certainly, this is what I see in my own experiences and certainly the case within the Philippines.

Regardless, concerns for abuse or exploitation are by no means immaterial. Companies today must assess for themselves the conditions and welfare of the people they work with and ensure that no one is being taken advantage of. Companies themselves have the power to ensure that their offshoring activities offer a safe environment, good income, and a great opportunity for their people. The control is ultimately with the client.

Charitable Causes

While I believe that outsourcing can do a lot of good for many people, I would prefer that the concepts of offshore staffing and charity were kept separate. There is a growing subsection of outsourcing referred to as 'Impact Sourcing,' or 'socially responsible outsourcing.'

The sector intermingles Business Process Outsourcing with Corporate Social Responsibility (CSR) by employing people from the base of the pyramid or socioeconomically disadvantaged communities. These businesses might seek to utilize less-educated workers from poor and vulnerable communities to perform lower and moderate skill requirements such as scanning documents, data entry, and data scraping and filtering.

It is excellent that this sector exists, and it is a further testament to the fact that offshore employment really is a positive force for the people of developing nations. However, I am concerned that having two potentially conflicting agendas regarding your staffing could muddy the waters and ultimately undermine the commercial rationale for the employment.

If, at home, your business is also hiring underprivileged staff and incorporating charitable causes into your operations, then Impact Sourcing is possibly an excellent option for you. But if you are running a traditional commercial operation back home, then I think you should also run the same kind of operation offshore—at least when you start out.

I believe that you should only employ someone because you need work done, and in those circumstances, you will want the work done as efficiently as possible. This relates to the economic imperative that businesses seek the most efficient inputs for producing a certain output. I am concerned that if you add a charitable motivation into the mix, it can become unclear what your key determinants are for the project's success.

For example, if certain work is not being done well, or you no longer have any need for the original work to be done, then in normal circumstances, you would either remove those staff or have them do something else. I am not sure how you would navigate this decision if the bad or unnecessary work conflicts with a charitable agenda.

To keep things simple, it is best to treat offshore staffing as you would your own traditional employees. In fact, I would emphatically suggest that you keep the objectives of operational efficiency and charity completely separate. Let me be clear, I am not against charity. If it is a charity that you want, then I can name a range of wonderful organizations that represent some very pressing causes and can even recommend a number of charities that work tangentially with the outsourcing industry.

As for offshore staffing, I suggest that you undertake the journey with a clear singular objective and employ people based on their merits and ability to get the job done efficiently, to a high quality, and at a good price point. Do not give people work because you are doing them a favor, or for any charitable motivation. Only give them work if you feel that they are able to provide output for you at superior quality, price, and volume compared to any other option you have. Outsourcing does not need charity. It simply needs happy clients who are getting a great deal and happy staff who are well paid. If this happens, then all other factors will sort themselves out.

Poor Service

Outsourcing is synonymous with bad service. And to be fair, maybe in the early days of the industry, a lot of mistakes were made. We all know the stories. Everyone has a collection of frustrating tales of phone calls to their bank or airline going wrong. In fact, whenever anyone mentions an offshore call center, people everywhere can immediately resurrect one of these maddening conversations. They usually lament that the person was useless and couldn't even understand them.

First, a note on customer service. I don't want to try and defend the seemingly indefensible—but actually, it's easy for people to underestimate the complexity of doing customer service well—at scale. Customer service is a common function to be outsourced, but there is good reason why it should be one of the last functions of a business to be sent offshore. In most companies, the customer service function plays a critical role and is at the 'coal-face' of a company's interactions with its customer base. Many businesses regard customer service as non-core—and in some ways it is. But what can be more core than your customers? If you think about it, there is no more of a critical interaction point in your business than this. This is especially true since the advent of easy online reviews and social media pages where people can all too easily share their disappointments and publicize them to millions.

In the modern world of omnichannel communications, the customer service function of a business is more important and more complex than ever. Before, customer service might have been a phone conversation; now, it covers phone, email, text, chatbots, webchat, and social media moderation, among others. Customer service extends well beyond reactive problem solving to customer education, retention, assistance, technical support, upselling, onboarding, sales, and even brand development and influencer management. When you combine a complex product with thousands of potential queries juxtaposed against thousands or millions of different clients and client needs, the customer service function is a complex one indeed. When you combine this with the operational side of training up dozens or hundreds of youngish staff, building knowledge bases, systems for solutions management, escalation protocols, and ensuring that enough people are capable and present for a 24/7 unending flow of irate customers—it's a tough job to say the least. For a bank to manage its customers' requirements well, they need to know every possible solution to any possible question that might arise from an enormous, complex system, interacting with millions of people and trillions of transactions at any point in time. And it never gets easier. While customer service tools, training, and processes are continually improving, the products and systems themselves are also getting ever more complex and far-reaching. So there is a never-ending chase to catch up and improve.

However, the industry is improving. I would hope that many of the call center criticisms are a hangover from the earlier days, and that the systems are indeed getting better. Thirty years ago, when offshore call centers began, it most certainly would not have been performing at its peak. Things have vastly improved since then.

Just compare, for example, computers and mobile phones that were around 30 years ago. Even the best computers back then were slow, clunky, and broke down a lot. Cars from 30 years ago now seem primitive, and printers and televisions seem laughably prehistoric. These things, today in comparison, are infinitely more polished, sophisticated, faster, and enhanced. This is simply because the products have been iterated and improved over time. While the latest iPhone you have right now seems pretty impressive—and indeed, it represents the pinnacle of today's global technological innovation—it will no doubt look embarrassingly shoddy in just 10 years' time.

This is the same with offshore staffing and call center operations. Even though people don't fundamentally change much, the systems around them and the tools they use are continually improving. Also, the people within the systems do improve. Filipino and Indian call center workers are now better educated, have more experience, draw on strong role models that have passed before them, are better paid, speak better English, and are infinitely more culturally aligned.

Bad service can happen, though. And there are undoubtedly poor performers within every sector. For example, every householder has had a bad experience with a plumber, electrician, or hairdresser. Every business has had disappointing results from a lawyer, accountant, or web designer. And every business owner has at some point had encounters with poor performing consultants, scandalous partners, or ungrateful staff. Unfortunately, this seems to be an unavoidable complexity of doing business—anywhere, and I doubt this will ever completely disappear. Having a bad interaction with an electrician or lawyer can be painful, but it does not mean that the entire industry is broken or of equal incompetence. You should certainly seek to avoid bad outcomes and people in outsourcing, just as you would any other poor performing business in your own community, and rest assured that the vast majority of people have positive experiences.

A lot of the criticism of outsourcing—whether founded or not —circulates around the call center functions. However, outsourcing is so much broader than just this narrow sector sitting within the overall industry, and for SMEs—call centers are not really suitable for their requirements. As discussed in this book, staff leasing or staff augmentation is more suitable and does not present the same issues in terms of quality control and system complexities. When an SME engages an offshore team, they will be working with a smaller, more generalist team of independent professionals and collaborating with a professional outsourcing firm. With these fundamentals in place, the quality, reliability, and friction are not really different from what would be encountered in a traditional employment scenario.

Confidentiality Issues

Some companies have been bothered by the notion that outsourcing hampers confidentiality. The SANS Institute published a paper dealing with this topic.[33] As sensitive information that includes financial records and social security numbers is transferred to countries like China, Indonesia, and India, the risk for confidentiality breaches is heightened. The paper cited an example of a disgruntled Pakistani medical records transcriber who threatened to post sensitive information about the University of California patients if she was not presented with payment. This one incident alone had many companies worried and taking steps to prevent such breaches from occurring.

According to the institute, "As a result, some American politicians have introduced new pieces of stringent legislation that provide clear guidelines, strict accountability, and penalties in order to keep such incidents from occurring." As America and Europe enacted these tough standards, many outsourcing nations quickly followed suit, updating their own regulations. For example, in response to European General Data Protection Regulation (GDPR), the Philippines launched their own Data Privacy Act (DPA) soon after. The DPA is closely patterned after Europe's GDPR, with experts suggesting that any Philippine company that is fully compliant with the DPA and related issuances is already

---

33   The Sans Institute.(2004).Offshore Outsourcing and Information Confidentiality.Retrieved from https://www.sans.org/white-papers/1438/

90% compliant with the GDPR.[34]

Some client companies are choosing not to export elements of the company that deal with sensitive information to overseas contractors. Some may be waiting for even stricter legislation or simply want to witness the effects of the legislation over time. However, companies should note that confidentiality breaches can be homegrown too. Data security and confidentiality of sensitive information must be well protected, whether at home or abroad.

Most companies generally have very lax data and cyber security provisions. But when they start to offshore, they expect the offshore team to have a Fort Knox level of security. This incongruence can cause unnecessary costs and operational friction and won't necessarily offer broad-spectrum security.

The Philippines outsourcing industry is incredibly sophisticated regarding security standards and protocols. A department can be built to any level of security specification imaginable. However, security is not something physical that is turned on or off. A lot of the security measures involve training of staff and the fortification of processes. It involves a lot of active participation by every user, and regular reporting, logs, and audits. A lot of the process design has to come from the client company itself, because all of the processes belong to and interweave with other aspects of the company. So while it is all possible, high-security setups require a big commitment from all parties and can significantly increase costs and friction.

Security and data privacy is something that should be taken very seriously. And there are many experts out there that can assist with this issue. From my perspective, I try to emphasize to clients that when using an offshore team, the best approach is to treat

---

34   European Innovation, Technology and Science Center Foundation. (2018). Mapping the Philippine Data Privacy Act and GDPR: A White Paper from the EITSC. Retrieved from https://eitsc.com/wp-content/uploads/2018/05/Mapping-the-DPA-and-GDPR.pdf

them the same as you would your onshore team. This applies to cyber and data security, as well as most other operational principles.

Outsourcing Benefits

Most Powerful Business Tool

The most commonly associated benefit of outsourcing is its ability to cut costs. These savings are real, but it is not, and should not, be the only consideration. However, since it is seen as the main draw-card for the industry, it is a good place to start.

As a rule of thumb, you can generally save 50% to 70% of your staff costs when offshoring to a place like the Philippines. The exact amount can vary dramatically—depending on requirements, especially if you are in a lower-cost nation yourself. However, for companies from most developed nations looking to hire most standard roles, the savings are huge. Saving even 30% on something as significant as your employee costs can absolutely transform the prospects of a business.

On this basis alone, I am slightly amazed that not every company is already taking advantage of the profound opportunities of the global workforce. The chance to cut costs certainly is significant and very real.

It is hard to say too much more on this topic since it is what it is.

But before I move on, I want to try to emphasize quite how profound this is.

For many service-based businesses, their staff costs are their single highest expense. This is especially the case for professional service firms like accountants, lawyers, and architects, as well as most of today's tech startups. These companies might spend 50% to 70% of their total costs on their staff. Even most traditional businesses would still spend a vast amount of money on their staff each month. In fact, there are few businesses in the world where staff costs aren't significant.

So the opportunity to save 70% on these costs can be a game-changer. Saving this amount of money can either go straight to the bottom line or be invested back into the business to further its growth and development.

Some financial market traders on Wall Street go to extreme lengths to generate arbitrage margins of just 10 basis points. That's 0.1%. Meanwhile, offshore staffing can save a business 70% on one of its biggest costs, yet most business owners remain unaware of this opportunity or are otherwise unconvinced or apathetic.

There are millions, if not billions of people in the global market that would bite your hand off for a chance to earn a salary of just $6,000 per year. And these people are college graduates, highly capable, communicate well, have a good CV, and are committed to their career.

Prospective employers have access to almost any role, skill, or job in the world. Contrary to popular belief, offshore staffing is not just limited to low-level competencies or basic roles. You can find any kind of developer, physicist, big data scientist, Ph.D., or rocket scientist you need. These people will be sitting in an office, just like you. And they will work in the same manner, just like a traditional employee, and will work alongside you and your team, just like everyone else.

The only difference is that they are sitting in a different location.

That's it.

I cannot emphasize this enough. You can find brilliant staff, for a fraction of the cost of your traditional staff. Typically 70% cheaper compared to the major markets. This dramatic cost reduction can have a transformative impact on your business.

You do not have to outsource. It is entirely up to you. But I do implore you to look into it. After reading this book, of course, spend a few hours to reach out to a few outsourcing firms and see if it is right for you. The benefits of offshore staffing are profound and real. You can save 70% on costs. And you can get started today.

Cost Versus Friction Matrix

If money was not an issue for a company, and there were no resource limitations, then I would argue that there would be no need to offshore. If money was not a factor, then I would think that the ideal solution in any scenario is to have all of your staff sitting in one head-office location, working face-to-face, synchronously, and collaborating alongside each other. But money does matter. Even the world's wealthiest companies like Google, Apple, and Facebook all have to be careful with their resources and how they spend their money.

However, while cost-saving is paramount for any company, it cannot come at the cost of diminished quality, output, or operational efficiency. So the cost-saving benefits of outsourcing should not be assessed on that merit alone and cannot be viewed in isolation.

I am a huge proponent of offshoring, but I am the first to say that the benefits of the cost savings cannot come at the cost of the quality of output or the ease of doing business. When I advise people that they can save 70% on staff costs, I say this with the assumed position that the quality and output of the deliverable, as well as the harmony of culture, will at least be maintained. Equally, the 'ease of doing business' should also be factored in, and should not see an unreasonable jump. I expect this for those that I advise, and equally, for anyone involved in outsourcing.

It will always be easier to have work done in the traditional manner. Offshoring can introduce several unintended complexities and differences that you wouldn't normally encounter in the traditional employment model. Things like time zone differences, remote-work annoyances, cultural and communication difficulties, and the fact that you will rarely, if ever, meet in person. I refer to all of these issues as points of 'friction.' The more friction you have, the less easy or even enjoyable it is to do business and get the job done. There is some point at which too much friction would just simply render the job impossible, or at least intolerable, to do. At some point, it becomes 'just not worth it.' I refer to this broader concept as the 'cost versus friction matrix.'

Before we move on, I want to emphasize that friction is a real factor in any company and is an inescapable part of doing business. There is always a certain amount of friction in getting any work done, anywhere within a traditional setting. You will never have a situation of zero friction. Workplaces always face hiring, retention, training, motivation, growth, culture, funding, quality, and output challenges. This is a normal part of doing business.

So understanding the friction incurred by outsourcing is about assessing the current levels of traditional operational friction and objectively comparing that with the levels encountered when offshoring. The hassles of running a team will never completely be removed—but you do not want it to significantly spike due to your choice to go offshore.

Also, offshoring is new and different. It will require you to learn new skills and approaches and make adaptions to your culture. These necessary changes may or may not be perceived as friction. In some respects, learning to offshore effectively, is a bit like learning to play a new instrument. You can either regard the process of learning as a constructive, enjoyable, and character-building endeavor, or you could see it as an annoying pain. While I don't want anyone to tolerate unnecessary friction from outsourcing, there is a requirement to learn new skills and adapt before getting good. This could be considered a form of friction, but I would suggest that learning these new skills in adapting to the new offshore paradigm is a valuable means to an end.

I raise this issue of friction because, in reality, it is probably the most common complaint of offshoring. It is also the main thing that prevents people from starting and the primary cause of failure. Indeed, many people have tried outsourcing—though maybe incorrectly—and have walked away disappointed. The cost savings were there, but they weren't able to get the results they needed to justify the hassle it took to get the job done. And this is a fair complaint.

It is important to be aware of the friction involved in a process and to see it as a cost of doing business. A low level of friction should be expected and tolerated, but anything above this should not. No one wants a daily battle to get work done. If the friction and complexities of getting something completed are too high, then it doesn't matter if you are saving 10% or even 99% of the cost of the job. At some point, it is just not worth the hassle.

So I am telling you that you can save fantastic amounts of money. But I am also telling you that you should not have to tolerate bad quality work, unreliable service, or endless hassles in return. It is certainly reasonable to expect a slight increase in the level of friction when offshoring for the reasons mentioned above. However, I would suggest that the benefit of saving 60% to 70% on costs for a 10% increase in friction is well worth it. But if you save only 30% in costs and the friction is 40% higher than normal, it simply isn't worth it. Ultimately, everyone is different, and each should find their own sweet spot. Maybe some people are willing to accept a 30% or even 40% increase in the friction they encounter to save 70% on costs. But I would suggest that you aim to tolerate at most a 10% to 15% hike in overall friction to access the 70% savings.

One of the biggest mistakes I see people make in outsourcing is their propensity to try to save too much. Outsourcing is an industry that has built its reputation on cost savings, so I understand why it attracts a lot of thrifty people all looking to save big. But there is most definitely a point at which it becomes self-defeating. Too many people scratch around to save 80% or even 90% of costs without considering the full picture, and most especially the inevitable hit of friction that they take as a consequence. Sure, they might get a great price at an 85% discount, but the friction of getting that work done has rocketed up to 60%. At this level of friction, the work will likely be of low quality and dependability if it even materializes, and the process to get it done is a hassle at best.

We are not yet at the part of the book where I should be prescriptive, but there is a simple solution for this common calamity. Based on the simple cost versus friction matrix, if you want to reduce friction, then, as mentioned in an earlier chapter, spend more money.

One sure-fire way of dropping friction is to follow this simple strategy:

1. pay a little more,
2. use a proper BPO intermediary, and
3. get your staff to work from an office

If you do these three simple things, then the quality of your outsourcing output and experience will dramatically improve. Outsourcing firms are seasoned experts in building offshore teams for businesses like yours. You will be paying for facilities for the staff and will certainly be paying more, but these services will help ensure that you can build and run a highly effective team without encountering too much friction along the way.

But before you slam this book shut in blown-budget outrage, remember that with all this expert support and additional bells and whistles, you will still be saving 70% on costs compared to your home market.

Too many people are scratching around the Philippines trying to find a valuable employee working from home for $2 per hour. Instead, they should be looking for great staff, properly employed, and working from a proper office for an all-in price of $8 per hour and up. If they do this, they will be building a capable, scalable, and reliable team to take their company to the next level and will still save an inordinate amount of money. Think about it.

Anyone and Everyone

People typically think that offshoring is limited to call centers, administrative assistants, and customer service reps. This could not be further from the truth. The reality is that the world's developing countries are home to many billions of people. Many of these people are highly qualified and extremely capable professionals. The Philippines, for example, has a population of 110 million people, many of whom speak fantastic English, have graduated from college, and are focused on developing a good professional career.

Not only can offshoring offer so much more than basic customer service and admin, but it can give you access to literally every single skill, role, and profession that the world has to offer. The Philippines does have a lot of poorer, less educated people. But it also has plenty of highly educated, world-class talent on offer. If you need to employ a Ph.D., or an MBA, or architect, rocket scientist, or engineer—they are all available. The country generates about 750,000 college graduates each year—so there is no shortage.

The Philippines even has its fair share of Harvard, Stanford, and Oxbridge graduates, and it also has its equivalent Ivy League colleges of its own. Equally, the country is home to many world-class multi-billion-dollar conglomerates, innovative startups, a handful of unicorns, and everything in between. Also, most of the world's leading companies have significant operations in the Philippines. Facebook, Google, and Zoom from technology; Citi Group, Deutsche Bank, and Morgan Stanley from banking; and P&G, CocaCola, and Unilever from traditional industry all work from Manila.

So you can rest assured that whatever role you need for your business, it can be found in the Philippines.

So while you can save considerable money by hiring call center agents, you can actually save significantly more if you hire highly paid professionals. And there is no shortage of these to choose from.

Complexities of Employment

The traditional employment of people is an enormously expensive and complex undertaking. Not only are the salaries high, but there are endless other considerations and costs on top.

Hiring another human is a task that cannot be taken lightly. When you employ people, you are not only concerned with their daily activities, training, and career progression; you are also charged with their welfare, safety, compliance, and a whole raft of other mission-critical factors. To ensure that you are fulfilling your obligations, there are a wide range of employment laws and regulations in place to guide and enforce compliance—all of which vary depending on where they are sitting and what work they are doing.

As a result, outsourcing the responsibilities of employing another person is actually a no-brainer. Being compliant with employment is a hornet's nest. Having a third-party specialist to handle these things allows your company to focus on core activities instead—and not so much on the HR, payroll, compliance, and the ever-changing regulations and laws.

Not only does offshore staffing remove all of these issues, but it also enables you to be more flexible with your hiring needs and practices. Outsourcing can allow you to quickly and easily scale a workforce up and then down again. The process of recruitment, onboarding, retention, and offboarding are all complex tasks that need to be done correctly. You can have these things done for you by someone that specializes in doing this. This will enable your company to hire and fire more effectively, allowing you to better respond to your market dynamics.

Outsourcing can also mostly absolve you of any legal liability for your team. As an employer, there is always the potential risk that an employee will hurt themselves, sue you, or file a complaint. There is a myriad of possible points of exposure in this regard. While you might be the best employer in the world, with the purest of intentions, these risks still exist. And even if nothing untoward actually happens to your business, the presence of these risks are already factored into the cost and complexities of your employment —like the regulations that govern your workplace, hiring practices, and more. And the costs of the risks are already factored into your insurance premiums, taxes, and employer contributions.

Working with an offshoring partner does not in any way absolve you of the imperative to treat your team well. It's vital to ensure that all staff are, under all circumstances, paid well, are happy and safe, and their rights as an employee are at all times respected. All of the fundamental principles of properly engaging and motivating employees apply in equal parts and should be closely translated across from your traditional team.

However, offshoring does mostly relieve you from the direct legal liability of employment and most of the administrative work of compliance, payroll, HR, and the general complexities of employment. This allows you, the client, to focus more on operations, growth, and scaling your business.

Capex to Opex

Employing people usually requires a lot of upfront capital. Typically, in order to build a team, you need a fitted office, infrastructure, functional workspaces, and a range of hardware. At least, this was the case before COVID. These hard costs require big upfront investments that only pay off after many years—if ever. And once the commitments have been made, a business is locked into a certain trajectory for many years to come—irrespective of the actual trajectory. Heavy upfront costs and rigid long-term commitments of this nature are the antitheses of running an agile capital-efficient business. However, despite significantly restricting a company's options, agility and flexibility, if you're going to hire staff and build a team, they are most usually a necessary evil.

Offshoring removes any such need for capital expenditure, allows a business to hold onto its cash, and remain light and agile. Instead, the outsourcing firm makes all of the upfront infrastructure investment and grants the client access to this for a relatively low cost with flexibility and minimal commitment. This enables a company to scale up or scale down—with speed and efficiency, without concern for capital investment, space, or infrastructure—according to its operational needs.

Outsourcing converts fixed costs into variable costs, releases capital for investment elsewhere in your business, and allows you to avoid large expenditures in the early and growth stages. All this makes your firm more capital efficient, asset-light, and since you're able to pump more capital directly into revenue-producing activities, ultimately more attractive to owners and investors.

Scalability and Flexibility

Offshore staffing specializes in the efficient scaling of people and teams. The entire industry has evolved to offer a flexible and cost-effective means of setting up and running operational structures. This is what it specializes in, and collectively, does this for many tens of millions of people.

This means that as a client, you can quickly build a team and then scale—as and when you need. You can do that quicker and easier than you would be able to yourself—simply because this is not your specialty, but it is the specialty of the outsourcing firms.

The value proposition of an outsourcing firm is that they can not only do all of this for you, but they can offer fast response times, almost infinite capacity, and flexible terms. Plus, of course, there is the added cherry on top that you save 70% on costs. So if you need to scale up for Christmas and then scale back down again after the rush, then this is possible. If you're a fast-growing startup or just raised capital and quickly need to ramp your teams, then this is also possible. Or if the business has taken a turn for the worse and quickly needs to cut staff, this is also managed for you.

As mentioned above, you can do this quicker than you would be able to if you did it yourself. You have someone else that is looking after all the employment-related operations, the compliance and relieving you of any associated liability or exposure. Plus, unlike traditional employment and infrastructure, you have no capital expenditure, leases, or asset write-offs to worry about. All of this allows you to concentrate on your core functions and ultimately better drive your company forward.

Specialization

Outsourcing is simply better at providing employee solutions — particularly on a global scale. This is purely because managing people and processes is their specialization. Employing people is complicated. And employing people in a developing nation is even more complex. And so hiring people and having them work efficiently, cohesively, and productively is something that outsourcing suppliers specialize in—and have had 30 years to master.

They not only focus on the hiring and basic HR components of employment, they also specialize in process efficiency and optimization. Outsourcing firms simply focus on how to get people to work well together and how they can build and fulfill those processes more efficiently than anyone else. Process design, analysis, and iteration are what these companies do. It's their bread and butter.

By offshoring to an outsourcing hotspot like the Philippines, it not only means that you can hire people significantly cheaper and more flexibly than you could onshore—it also means that you have a highly sophisticated partner working alongside you to build out and optimize the functions of your business. This is an incredibly powerful opportunity.

Your business might be one, 10, or 50 years old. However, the process or department you are building could either be the same age, but more likely a lot younger, or even brand new, or about to launch. In contrast, the outsourcing firm you choose to work with could be 10 or 30 years old and has been specializing in building processes from scratch for clients like you for that entire time.

Therefore, you are leveraging their ability to hire better and quicker than you can, and also their knowledge of building processes can add enormous value to your business. This is the power of specialization and collaboration.

Access Abundant Talent

The world is awash with incredible, highly qualified, and dedicated talent. At the time of writing, businesses in the West are facing a severe labor shortage, spiking salaries and employment costs, and record low unemployment levels. This means that most companies are severely limiting their growth opportunities. If you cannot find the staff you need at a reasonable price, then your business will suffer—if not falter.

I am still somewhat amazed that businesses still limit their talent search to their own geographical location. There are 8 billion people in the world, and most of them can now participate in the global workforce. And most of them are happy to work for a fraction of the price.

We have a client who runs a successful business in a small town of just 15,000 people in the Midwest of the US. He employs 175 people across a wide range of roles, skills, and business units. He was growing fast, but his ambitions were severely curtailed by his ability to find and recruit the people that he needed. Instead of hiring digital specialists, he was forced to hire just anyone that he could find and then train them to do certain tasks. This is not ideal—for anyone—and generated less than optimal outcomes. He lamented that he was recruiting from a talent puddle and not a talent pool.

After introducing him to offshoring, he quickly hired four staff—from Manila. He could find great talent quickly and was generally saving 70% on costs. The staff were specifically qualified in the functions that he required, so they could hit the ground running and quickly contribute to the company's success. Instead of limiting his search to a small town of just 15,000 people, he was now able to tap into the talent pool of Manila's burgeoning metropolis of 20 million. It's a no-brainer. Once these staff had settled in, he hired another 17 people—and now the company is doing better than ever. Thanks to a global workforce, he was no longer limited to his talent puddle.

Outcompete Your Competitors

Saving money is great. Saving a lot of money is even better. But saving money has a finite capacity. You can only save so much. And at some point, you are quickly met with diminishing returns.

It is much better not to see outsourcing as a cost-saving exercise but instead think of it as a tool that can allow you to triple your workforce and outcompete your market. If you switch your thinking and strategy to this paradigm, then a whole new world of opportunity can open up before you.

It's an exciting thought exercise to consider how you could improve your business if you could triple the number of employees you had. Think about what new functions you could do. How could you better perfect your existing product or build more new ones with three times more staff? Would you be able to ramp up your marketing and sales activities to knock out the competition? If you were able to triple your customer service and client success teams, how would you better be able to service the needs of your customers, retain them for longer, stop the churn, and 'wow' them? Or what research and development activities could you do to ensure that your company leads your market?

All of this is possible when you have access to the most cost-effective resources. You can effectively triple your workforce overnight for no extra cost. When you look at offshoring from the lens of abundance and opportunity instead of the lens of cost-saving and conservation, it can quickly become enormously exciting.

To help you envisage how these opportunities could be applied to your business, try asking these simple questions from the chapter above:

- What could we do if we could hire equally-capable staff at a 70% discount?
- What could we do if we could triple the current workforce for the same amount of money?
- How could we outcompete if we had easy access to the best of 8 billion people?
- How could we grow if the labor shortages, skill shortages, jumping salaries and 'Great Resignation' did not apply to our company?
- How could our company thrive if we participate in the global economy, not just our local market?

Supporting Developing Countries Such as the Philippines

There can be some political tension between the outsourcing country and the place receiving the outsourcing work. As explained above, it seems that you have people worried that outsourcing is taking 'their jobs' and undermining their country on one side of the coin. For these people, there is generally little concern for the welfare of the receiving country. And if the country doing the outsourcing is actually benefiting from the transaction, then it is like rubbing salt in a wound. So describing the benefits of outsourcing for the receiving country can be a sensitive topic.

Conversely, on the other side of the coin, those worried about the ethics of outsourcing seem to assume that the people offering the outsourcing work are oppressors, and the countries doing the work are underpaid, mistreated, and should be pitied.

I have seen, from first-hand experience, the incredible opportunity that outsourcing creates for both sides of that fence. It is most certainly of benefit to the client company, and also its staff, owners and ultimately its stakeholders and community.

It is also highly beneficial to the developing nation that provides these services, for example, the Philippines. The success that the Philippines is enjoying, because of its outsourcing industry, is literally transforming the nation's economy. Headline after headline flaunts the country's improvements and its evolution from a nation of migrant workers who travel abroad to perform menial work to a nation of skilled professionals who are competitive in areas that require a high degree of expertise.

The sustained growth of the Philippines' outsourcing sector is directly impacting the country's ever-strengthening and maturing economy. In addition, forecasts all suggest that this success is likely to continue as increasing numbers of businesses from the West—including countries as disparate as New Zealand and Australia, US, UK, and even Scandinavia—choose to partner with outsourcing firms in the Philippines.

With continued patronage, the Philippines is, in turn, able to further invest in this sector with programs designed to support its growth. Far from feeling exploited, the employees themselves have been thrilled with the job opportunities that await them in the outsourcing industry. In many cases, standard rank-and-file outsourcing employees make more than general doctors. Jobs and opportunities are plentiful, as evidenced by reports from the country's Department of Labor and Employment (DOLE), which show that the BPO sector continues to offer the most jobs, and the highest rate of job growth, in the country. As the concept of outsourcing expands beyond basic call center functions to generalized professional services, more and more professionals of all walks of life are entering the outsourcing industry and contributing to the global workforce.

You only need to witness the optimism of the nation's millennials to see that outsourcing is a net positive for this once economically-floundering nation. There are generations of Filipinos that grew up without one or both of their parents because of the lack of work in their local community. Filipinos in many cases, were forced to work overseas in order to earn enough income to support their families. There are about 2.2 million Filipinos[35] that work overseas in this manner even today. They are collectively referred to as Overseas Filipino Workers (OFWs), and make up about 10% of the country's GDP.[36] The cost of the OFW's' living their working life away from their family and community has enormous social consequences—and two and a half million families are dealing with that reality right now. Not least, the flight of the best and most capable people to overseas employment causes a significant brain drain on the country, which can further exacerbate the situation.

With the advent of outsourcing and online work, things have started to rapidly change. Now, millions of highly capable Filipinos are joining the global workforce, but they can do it from their own hometown, in their own home country. They no longer need to leave their families in order to feed them. Today, rather than pinning their hopes for a better life from working as an engineer on an oil rig in the North Sea, they have a real option to remain in their homeland earning wages that are good by their own standards.

35 Philippine Statistics Authority. (2020). Total Number of OFWs Estimated at 2.2 Million. Retrieved from https://psa.gov.ph/sites/default/files/attachments/hsd/pressrelease/Press%20Release%202019%20SOF%20signed.pdf

36 Statista. (2020). Personal remittances received as share of the gross domestic product (GDP) in the Philippines from 2011 to 2020. Retrieved from https://www.statista.com/statistics/1241883/remittance-share-of-gdp-philippines/

Eliminate Repetitive Business Processes

People often ask me what roles can, and can't, be offshored in their business. In short, almost anything can be offshored— certainly, any job that is done from in front of a computer.

However, there are easier or more complex processes and also more appropriate, or less appropriate things to tackle. Also, what you decide to offshore can be dependent on the size and stage of your business, its growth trajectory and ambitions, and its niche and sector. Offshoring, like anything, is a skill to develop and build —just like a muscle. So if you are starting out, it is advisable to focus on the easier and more standard tasks first.

Historically, the outsourcing industry focused on fulfilling lower value, high repetition functions, with the traditional call centers still synonymous for these roles today. These tasks are still an easy target for offshoring and can generate great results. But the bigger opportunity for offshoring goes well beyond this.

The main principles being leveraged here are specialization and business process optimization. These are generic business concepts that exist completely independent of outsourcing. If you can identify and delineate a specific process, and then build a specialized team that can focus on getting the process done efficiently, then it is a winning formula.

There can be a negative connotation associated with heavy process-driven businesses—with McDonald's being an example of one of these. Their argument for strong systems is that virtually anyone can walk in off the street and within a few hours of training, easily follow a process without fault, and produce a reliably standard burger at the end of it. Most small businesses rightly resist this rigidity and argue that it is better to have fewer processes and instead hire stronger staff that can work autonomously. I agree with both perspectives.

It is important to see process optimization as a broad spectrum of organizational design and not as a binary yes or no. However, in reality, a business with zero processes is not really a business. It is likely a small startup that is temporarily able to harness organized chaos. Over the long run, businesses need at least some level of process design and organization, and it is more a question of how much, how precise, and how controlled.

Even within a single business, it is likely that different departments will demand different levels of process control. The accounting department might have very rigid processes, whereas the design department might work more from instinct.

In short, though, there needs to be some amount of process design and management within a business—and where this is the case, if you are able to improve those processes, then it is nothing but upside. If you are able to delineate each process, and gradually improve its efficiency, then this is a winning formula. The cherry on top is the offshore component of this. Creating an efficient workflow is fantastic, but if you can get that workflow fulfilled by people that are paid 70% less than your traditional staff, then this is very powerful.

The outsourcing industry is able to add extra value to the task you are trying to get done because they specialize in optimizing processes. They have been doing it for three decades now, and they have a lot of tools, experience, and executive talent in this domain that can help. The industry has effectively made an efficient process out of building efficient processes. This is very valuable for you as a client if you can tap into this experience for the benefit of your business—while at the same time, saving 70% on your staffing costs.

Of course, rigid processes don't always work. There are strong arguments for a generalized and holistic approach to workflows also. Generalization is the antithesis of specialization, and both approaches have their merits. If you have a very new or small company, or your business processes are continually evolving, then hardline specialization is probably not the best choice, and may not even be possible. Outsourcing firms can generally adapt to whatever organizational design that your business works to, and there is usually no pressure to conform to one way of doing work. But it is good to know that you have specialist resources available to you, at a great price, if you ever need them.

Improved Efficiency

Many companies outsourcing to the Philippines naively expect to be met with a third-world level of talent, sophistication, and ingenuity. They are quite shocked when they realize that they are stepping into a highly sophisticated world, and many then realize that it is their company that is looking a little unstructured and ill-prepared.

Philippines offshore industry—for better or worse—is very process-driven. This means that Standard Operating Procedures (SOPs), process maps, org charts, metrics, KPIs, and analytics are all standard fare. Businesses in the West in comparison, tend to be more liberal with their processes, encourage their staff to 'think for themselves,' and often have onshore staff that tend to dislike being strapped down into a process.

There are pros and cons to each approach. But the net outcome is that many Western companies often under-invest in their processes and the documentation of those functions. However, as a company grows, it inevitably has to mature. When it does, it goes through an exercise of consolidating, recording, and solidifying its information and processes. This is a natural by-product of scale and is in some ways inevitable.

When a company starts to offshore, they are usually forced to accelerate this mapping and formalization of processes. This can cause some transitionary growing pains, but the client company is, without doubt, better for it once they have reached a point of improved documentation and enhanced processes as a result.

Expand Business

Employing people is expensive. The decision to hire people cannot be taken lightly. But if a business wants to expand, launch new products, or test new business ideas, then it has to add more staff.

Offshoring is an incredible way to give businesses the extra resources they need to test new opportunities, products, and markets. If, in order to test a new market, you have to hire a $100,000 employee, with heavy recruitment costs, and onerous employment obligations thrown in, then you will think twice about doing so.

However, if the new person was only $30,000 per year all-in and includes recruitment, hardware, and facilities, and they can be relatively easily let go if it does not work out, then the prospect is suddenly a lot more attractive. With offshoring, the cost, risk, hassle, and exposure of adding new team members are all reduced, which means that you can scale faster and take a few more risks.

Hire More Employees

Offshoring enables you to hire more people. There is no surprise there. But it isn't just about hiring more offshore staff. If you can get the non-core functions done more efficiently and for cheaper, it frees up your core staff to focus on higher value and more-core activities. Also, with lower costs, your company should be sending more money to the bottom line, which means that you can reinvest more of that money into either building your core and non-core staffing functions or expanding your business generally.

Once you get a feel for offshoring, you will generally have the confidence to hire more staff, both offshore and at home. As your offshore team grows, you can begin to hire more high-level specialists within that team. These are the sorts of people that drive your company forward and really start to move the needle on your business.

Many companies use their cost savings to hire more specialized employees or use it to invest in, upskill and better serve their core workforce by providing better roles, higher pay, and more benefits. Businesses can use their resources to better develop their internal staff so that they can be trained for new, and more advanced endeavors within the company. When employees are allowed to specialize, they can help the company prosper just as their individual careers can prosper. Naturally, as employees obtain new skills, they can demand increased salaries. And the virtuous cycle continues. Enabling Western companies to upskill their workforce through increased specialization and professional sophistication provides for a future-proof stronger company and home economy.

Improved Business Focus

Businesses that are able to shuffle non-core business processes to outsourcing firms can better focus on their core services.

It is a valuable thought exercise in itself to explore what exactly are your core activities and what aren't. Generally, employees in companies are so under-resourced that many of the key staff end up doing a range of unimportant and urgent tasks and unimportant and non-urgent tasks, instead of the important ones. They do this because the tasks are typically all intermingled with each other, and it takes too much time to properly separate them out and identify what really matters.

Spending time identifying what is truly core to your business and what is truly important—and then taking steps to ensure that the important ones are worked on can be invaluable for a company.

The core focus of a business can be fluid and evolve, so it is valuable for a company to monitor and update its foci accordingly. For example, it's now an accepted norm for companies to outsource their electricity and computer servers—but this wasn't always the case. When electricity was first invented, its use within a product became one of the core propositions of that business. But since it was not yet commercially available, it was up to the individual factories to make their own electricity to power their machines. As a result, the 'magical new energy' would have been a part of a company's 'secret sauce.' However, now with electricity everywhere, it is standardized everywhere and has lost any focal attention.

Not so long ago, a big part of running a tech company was the management of their servers and IT equipment. Fast-growth companies would collapse because they were unable to physically build enough server capacity in time. Now, all of this is pretty much outsourced, and there are very few tech founders who even consider their server needs when starting a business. They can simply subscribe to an online service, and after a few clicks, get started.

In business services, the same principle can commonly apply to the more standardized and stable backend functions of a company. Common examples are accounting work, legal, HR, recruitment, and payroll. These things are often done externally. However, the full extent of what can be done in collaboration with external partners is only limited to your own imagination.

For example, you may choose to work with partners for your customer service, lead generation, appointment setting, sales, marketing, web development, SEO, branding, fundraising, and the list goes on. I do not necessarily suggest that you get external parties to do this. It is possible, and maybe even preferential that you still keep this in-house. However, there is value in identifying these functions, splitting them out, and getting a separate team to specialize and focus on these activities. Doing this will help you to identify what are your core and important activities—and which ones are less so. Having people specialize in certain activities, whether core or otherwise, will help them get that process done more efficiently.

As you split your functions into teams, you can then allocate the most appropriate resources to that function—maybe they are in-house onshore. Maybe they are in-house but offshore. Or maybe they are done by external partners and agencies. Having clarity will aid your focus and efficiency.

Access the Best Offshore Firms Globally

When you are open to the concept of offshoring, you suddenly have access to a sophisticated industry that employs tens of millions of people. Collectively, it consists of about 3,500 firms and generates about $273 billion in revenues—depending on how broadly you define it. Regardless, it is a big, established, and sophisticated industry.

In countries like the Philippines, there are highly capable firms that offer world-class solutions across the full range of business services.

With offshoring, you can not only access highly qualified staff at a 70% discount, you can also tap into the sophistication, support, and guidance of an equally developed professional services sector covering a wide range of agencies, consultancies, and advisories. Partnering with the right outsourcing firm, can propel your company forward as they improve your processes, build your teams, extend your support systems, and enhance your output.

Shared Risks

People are often apprehensive when starting offshoring. They are nervous about selecting and signing up to a BPO as they consider all of the things that could go wrong and the risks they are exposed to as a result.

However, I look at it a different way. It is very much a cliche to say that "a problem shared is a problem halved," but in the case of offshoring, it really is.

An outsourcing firm is eager to win your business. And they are very aware that in order to keep your business, they will need to perform and meet your company objectives. Once you start offshoring with a professional firm, the relationship is likely to last many years, involve hiring many staff—maybe even dozens or hundreds of people—and potentially involve many millions of dollars. The firm knows this, and so they are very committed to making this work.

The outsourcing firm, may or may not get involved in the day-to-day operations of your staff, but they at least are the official employers of those staff, and they all congregate in their offices every day. Those staff inevitably feel attached to both the client company and the BPO's facility. In this respect, it is very much a long-term partnership. And it is a partnership that can become fundamental to your own business. As mentioned, they can help you, by contributing valuable insights and offering process efficiencies for your business. This input can be of great value to your company, and your interests are very much mutually aligned —both parties really want this to succeed.

This kind of partnership can either be seen as an opportunity or a vulnerability—depending on how it is structured and the results that are garnered. If you do it well, then it can definitely be a mutual win.

Business Recovery

Business Continuity Planning (BCP) was thrown into public consciousness after the September 11 tragedy. The prestigious World Trade Center housed the offices of many of the world's leading firms. As the towers collapsed, other than the obvious deplorable human tragedy, many companies were left with the realization that they had very little backup and recovery plans in place. This was further heightened by the fact that back in 2001, there was more paper-based documentation and less cloud-based systems.

Offshore staffing provides a turnkey solution for easy operational backup and redundancy. Having a secondary office, and a team that can be quickly augmented is a great way of limiting risk and exposure to operational interruptions. Such interruptions can be caused by anything from a simple server time-out to power cuts or storms, all the way up to more ominous typhoons, earthquakes, natural calamities, and terrorist attacks.

Offshore staffing can, by default, provide fantastic backup, redundancy, and capacity management solutions. Just by the fact that you have a second office in a geographically distant location can provide significant assurances in this regard. If you actually want to double down on your BCPs, then you can set up third and fourth offices, spread across different regions, and enable your staff to have laptops and work-from-home protocols.

Most of these things would be cost-prohibitive when considering it in your home market, but they are are all highly achievable and accessible solutions when offshoring, many of which come as default.

Global Distribution

There is a significant advantage to having a globally distributed workforce. It is easier to access other markets from both a supply and also a demand point of view when you have staff sitting in different regions. Having trusted staff in different regions makes it easier to form new relationships and carve out new markets.

The Philippines is based in South East Asia, one of the fastest-growing regions in the world. Equally, most other outsourcing destinations are by definition based in high-growth developing regions and can offer a lot of compelling opportunities. Once you have a beachhead of skilled trusted staff within different key locations, it is much easier to explore and take advantage of the full extent of the global marketplace.

Part 4

Ousourcing In Practice

Laying Out the Framework

How to Run a Business

Suggesting that there is only one way to run a business is naive. Companies are filled with endlessly different types of people, personalities, and ways of working. A business responds to, and reflects the rich and diverse tapestry of a broad array of cultures, communication styles, and societal expectations and norms of its owners, employees, customers, and community.

For example, a scientist-led business might lean on numeracy and logic for its company-building framework, while an artist might instead wholly defer to creativity and instinct. In contrast, a quiet but confident introvert would have a very different approach to running their team compared to a lively extrovert. Despite centuries of practice and decades of academic research, there is no clear evidence anywhere that can conclusively identify that one approach to running a business is better than another. This is, in part, because there are an infinite number of factors that can contribute to the success or failure of a business, and so the act of running it and navigating the factors is more of an art than a science.

Not only is there no one clear way to set up, design, or run a business—there isn't even clear empirical guidance on how to run a relatively simpler single department, project, or function. Facebook's culture used to famously embrace "working fast and breaking things," which is an exciting proposition for a dynamic young tech company, but that methodology would not work for a cardiac surgeon, hospital, or law firm. So understand that how you run a business and choose to organize yourself in that business is entirely personal. The choices you make in the early days will become embedded and eventually form the foundations from where your company's culture emerges. Culture is never set in stone, but it will have a lasting influence on whether your company is scientific, artsy, fast, considered, decentralized, or autocratic.

My point of all of this is to say that there is no one right way to run a business. And if some productivity guru or organizational expert tells you otherwise, then run the other way. I highlight this because certain parts of the outsourcing industry is unfortunately overly and all too commonly associated with productivity hackers. Often, everything from Virtual Assistants, to call centers and a myriad of other staffing solutions are sold in combination with a productivity, optimization, or enhancement solution. I'm not suggesting that this is necessarily a bad thing, but I would prefer that the two components—of staffing and process—are presented separately so that they can be assessed on their own merits instead of jamming them together as a single product.

This is maybe analogous to the many varied fitness fads out there. It's easy to attract attention and customers with the latest hyped fitness program and its promised quick wins and fast results. However, the fads rarely last, and the promises eventually fade away. This is a shame because the underlying truth that fitness is good for you, and that fitness really works gets obscured by focusing on the superficial fad. Fitness can mean a game of tennis, going for a walk, running a marathon, pumping weights, or competing in the Olympics. There is no one way to do it. Instead, there are many—endless—ways to get fit and be fit.

For outsourcing, I suggest it is valuable to learn the industry's fundamentals and initially look past the done-for-you applications. It is easy for the more comprehensive outsourcing solutions to appear more attractive, but there is greater value in learning to work with the underlying toolset, and treat the productivity additions, as just that.

It's good to lay plans for your business, and if you're about to scale your teams, then you will need something clear—a playbook of sorts—for your new team to play along with. But understand that even best-laid plans can sometimes be wrong or redundant as soon as they have been settled. As Dwight D. Eisenhower once said: "Plans are useless, but planning is indispensable."

It's very valuable to have certainty and clarity in business, but it is also equally as important to have agility and flexibility. Peter Thiel, the famous VC, in allowing for this dichotomy, suggests having "strong opinions loosely held." In a world where change is the only constant, Mike Tyson probably got it right when he said, "Everybody has a plan until they get punched in the mouth."

As your organization grows, it can become increasingly important to align its direction, mission, and activities. These things add to a company's strength, identity, and fortification. However, paradoxically, as these things become more prominent and embedded, the company becomes less agile and more entrenched. So in some ways, this can be a strength, but it is a weakness in others.

Just as a small boat can outperform a bigger boat as it zips through the water and turns on a dime, it is perfectly formed for nimble agility. In contrast, a large cruise ship can take many hours or even days to stop or turn around. If you're looking for agility, then the small boat wins hands down. But if there was a storm and rough seas, I know for sure that I would want to be onboard the safe and steady cruise ship.

People build plans, maps and processes to reduce uncertainty in business. While a solid plan might increase the certainty of certain things, ironically, it might not help much with the multitudinous remaining uncertainties, unknowns, and risks that businesses face daily. As Carl Richards, author of The Behaviour Gap said: "Risk is what's left over when you think you've thought of everything."

Having said all of that, it's still important to have a consolidated plan of some sort. A plan that exists in your head only is nothing but a dream. For a plan to really exist, it needs to be something that lives outside of your head. Your plan needs to be written down, and become tangible so that others can see it, understand it, join you on your journey, adopt it as their own, and then begin to evolve that journey along with you.

Some people put off outsourcing because they don't yet have all of their planning, maps and processes complete before they set out. While it is good to have something on paper, it is not necessary to have the 'perfect' documentation before you begin. In this case, 'done' is certainly better than perfect, and let's face it, the plans will always be changing anyway. Your plans will forever be an ongoing live process—a living organism even—and will evolve with you, your team, and your business. No matter where your business is on the maturity curve, whatever plan you produce, consider that it will be just one small early-stage snapshot of many continuous iterations to come.

Start by getting an initial plan on paper, and then get your team involved in fleshing it out and formalizing it. If you do get your team on board, not only does it take a lot of weight off your shoulders, but they will feel a greater sense of connection and ownership of the process and outcome and will treat it more as their own. So don't worry too much about having everything in place, before you get going. Having a rough and ready plan in place is much better than having the 'perfect plan' forever in development and putting everything on hold until it has been delivered.

People and Process

If you zoom out, the fundamental concept of outsourcing is simple. It's basically the same as traditional 'employment,' except that the people are sitting in a different location. Equally, employment itself—if you zoom out—is also very simple in concept. It's about paying someone to get something done. Simple.

However, as you get closer to the subject, employing effective people and building a successful team is an incredibly complex process. And as with most things of complexity, the more you learn about it, the more you realize that there is so much more that you don't know. Within the broader topic of employment are dozens of sub-topics, such as management, culture, communication, recruitment, training, retention, legal and compliance, process improvement, change management, goal setting, and HR. Each of these sub-topics alone has thousands of books written about them and millions of disciples who dedicate their careers to mastering their chosen fields.

So I want to reassure people that outsourcing is primarily fundamentally simple in concept. However, there are many nuances and essential skills involved in building a successful offshore team. Mastering these skills might require you to spend many years or decades in analyzing, re-adjusting, and perfecting your practices.

This next section provides a brief overview of some commonly used tools and concepts within the outsourcing industry. Offshore staffing is centered around building, operating and iterating efficient processes and teams, and is highly adept at a range of skills and management tools to monitor and facilitate this. Things like org charts, SOPs, process maps, metrics, and KPIs are all common fodder for the outsourcing industry. For this reason, it is valuable to be aware of them yourself and conversant with their application.

Because the industry is so focused on process optimization, you can see why it gets associated with productivity hacks and gurus. As mentioned, I'm not a fan of the 'productivity' self-help genre, and so I'm most certainly not going to preach here how to optimize your workday to squeeze out an extra 5% from your eight hours. We can leave that to the info-product gurus.

However, if you are looking to build a team or scale a business, having a toolkit of relevant frameworks on hand can certainly help. At least having a familiarity with the common tools of process management can help you and your team on your journey. You might even have them already in place, or maybe you might want to implement some of them if they resonate with you.

Part 4.1

Ousourcing Framework

Building A Framework

Why Look at Your Processes?

It's worth taking a moment here to remind you of the origins of the outsourcing industry. Outsourcing is also commonly referred to as "BPO," the abbreviation for Business Process Outsourcing. The entire industry is built to take a business process and make it more efficient.

This kind of outsourcing began some 30 years ago by taking entire, delineated processes from big multinationals in the West and executing those processes in a lower-cost destination such as the Philippines. The original concept of Business Process Outsourcing is more of a natural fit with big business, simply because it is usually easier to split out a specific process from a bigger company than a smaller one, because they naturally have more people doing more specialized roles. This means it's easier to draw a 'line' around very specific processes that have little crossover into other functions of the business.

An example might be a big company such as General Electric, which may have 200 people sitting in a room just doing a particular part of their accounts receivable function. That's all they do. They would not handle any other part of the accounting pipeline. Compare this with a small company like Acme SME, which may have someone in accounting doing all the bookkeeping as well as both the accounts receivable and payables, plus maybe a little marketing, and also answering the customer-support hotline when their colleague is on lunch. Bigger businesses naturally have more process specialization as they do everything on a bigger scale. This is basically why outsourcing first happened to big businesses—because of the scale of jobs—1,000 seats instead of one—and the more clinical nature of identifying and working on very specific processes.

When a process is split from a business and handed over to a BPO service provider, it places that process—but more specifically the output objectives of that process—in the care of that outsourcing firm. These BPOs are typically highly experienced in designing and running these processes efficiently and remain focused on optimizing them, which further enhances the outcomes. The ultimate objective is that the outsourced process is done to a better quality, more efficiently, at a cheaper cost for the big-company client.

On the other hand, outsourcing has evolved to become a slightly different product and value proposition for small and medium enterprises. Most smaller businesses need more all-rounders and generalists on their team rather than specialists. A typical startup with big plans and little budget might need one broadly capable and adaptive person to cover three departments and 12 ever-changing roles. Whereas a small company needs one person to do five roles, a medium-sized company might need one person to do just two roles. Meanwhile, the large multinational has 200 people doing just one role. When building teams and processes, the difference in the operational needs of small-to-large businesses is dramatic.

However, BPOs have evolved significantly over the last 30 years, and many now focus specifically on the offshore needs of the SME market. In response to the demands of smaller businesses and the enablement of advancing technology, prices have been getting cheaper and the service terms have been getting more flexible. Also, the Philippine labor pool has been upskilling over the last couple of decades, meaning that more broad-skilled and agile generalists are available, which are more suited to SME use. The confluence of all these trends has created an incredible human resource solution for small and medium businesses that is turnkey, agile, scalable, and hyper-affordable. It is a big opportunity for small businesses to easily tap into the sophistication of the offshore industry and access the global workforce.

Before you begin, though, you must have a relatively clear idea of what you want to do. This can be embodied in a vision, mission, roadmap, or process—or all of the above. Using some of these methods for consolidating your ideas is a great way to focus your thoughts and formalize your plans. Let's explore some of the more common tools for this.

What Do You Want to Achieve?

Knowing what you want to achieve with your business is one thing, but knowing what you really want for your offshore team is another thing. Outsourcing can be used to save money. It can also be used to add rocket fuel to growth. It can also be used to replicate and replace an existing function, and it can be used to explore new opportunities and experiment with new activities. All of these objectives are very achievable with offshoring. However, they are all quite different applications of the same tool—and some applications may conflict with others. For example, a cost-saving exercise doesn't jive so well with a high growth objective. Building a team to replicate a well-proven process is different from building an experimental team to explore a new function. So, before you put your outsourcing tool to work, it's good—and in fact, really important—to clarify exactly what you want from the tool.

Eventually, it is possible to run many different, separate, and even contrasting functions consecutively. However, when you are starting out, it's advisable to begin with a narrow focus on just one activity with a clear objective. Once you have become comfortable with your offshore team and have seen some success, you can certainly start many other teams across various functions. But in the beginning, start simple, small, and narrow. This will ensure quicker and greater success.

◇◇◇◇◇◇◇◇◇◇◇◇◇

So that you can build the best possible team, it is good to be clear on the type of team you need. There are many different objectives in business and you need the right group of people doing the right kind of things, according to those objectives. Building a winning football team is very different to building a winning table tennis team, and it's similar in business. Below are just a few of the business objectives and possible team structures that you might encounter when setting up your offshore team:

1. Individual Hire

This is typically associated with an admin assistant role, but can also be role-specific like getting an accountant or a writer. This is the most straightforward process in terms of outsourcing, as you only need to identify and recruit one individual for the role.

Even if you have a clear plan to hire a team of 10 people performing one role, it can be wise to start with the initial one to three recruits. Starting slower and then ramping up more quickly later has a lot of benefits and limits the downsides.

2. Support Team

A support team is characterized by a team of people that directly work with and support other people of an existing team or department. The support team doesn't really have their own objectives; instead, they just piggyback and contribute to the objectives of the headquartered team that they're supporting.

Eventually, as the team becomes proficient and conversant with the department's functions, then their own roles and processes will be more clearly defined and formalized.

3. Break-out Team

The break-out team might be responsible for a new, or as yet unestablished activity for the client's company. For example, they might be working on a new line of business or trying to break into a new market. Break-out teams by definition, are building processes that are as yet undeveloped, untested, and unproven. As a result, their success is less assured and managing a team like this is more complex and requires more attention.

In the beginning, the break-out team's processes and outcomes will only be conjecture. It is really just a guessing game. For example, if you are building a sales team for a new widget, and you have never sold anything this way before, and your widget is as yet unproven, then this will be a very challenging team to build. If you contrast this with the 'replication' of an existing sales team that you might have in the US that's selling an established product, and giving them the same sales scripts and proven processes—then these are two very, very different propositions.

Clients might commonly use outsourcing to explore new projects like the example above. And unfortunately, if the project fails, they might blame the outsourcing firm for its failure to succeed with its mission. This is a shame. In reality, there are many possible, and likely, points of failure to a new project like this. For example, the value proposition might be bad, the widget might be broken, the scripts might be flawed, or the price might be wrong. Who knows?

Running both an outsourcing experiment and a new process experiment at the same time is folly. When you are starting out, try to limit the possible failure points. Business is hard and building a new successful process on the fly, from across the globe, is no simple task. So keep it simple.

4. Independent Department

You might consider outsourcing an entire department such as HR, customer service, accounts, or lead generation. This team has a clear function within the company and easily defined deliverables. These departments would typically have their own hierarchy within the offshore team. For example, a mid-size customer service team might have a blend of junior and senior agents, plus a supervisor or quality analyst (QA), and maybe an ops manager. The ops manager would communicate directly with the home-based management and agree and maintain deliverables.

5. Leadership and Strategic Functions

It is commonly, but incorrectly assumed, that offshore teams can only follow and not lead. In fact, it is very possible to hire high-caliber senior executives, strategists, and expert technicians offshore with the remit of building teams under them and taking your company to the next level. Setting out with this objective is fine and is to be encouraged. But it is important to separate out the different aspects of this objective to identify the complexity and possible pitfalls.

The two key aspects here are: (1) the recruitment of great senior staff, and (2) those staff taking your business to the 'next level.' Finding great staff is relatively easy, but taking a business 'to the next level' is fundamentally difficult. The two objectives are quite separate and should not be blended into one. It is not enough to just hire good staff and then expect them to turn your fledgling business into the next unicorn. It is possible, but not likely. Because of the low likelihood, it is advisable not to attempt these sorts of strategic hires for your first foray into offshoring.

Far too many people hire their initial offshore staff as basic support role employees. However, very quickly, they expect the new employee to grow and contribute to the higher-level project strategy and architecture. This is most certainly not easy to achieve. It is too easy to expect too much from your basic employees. Not everyone can perform like a dynamic entrepreneur and build the next Uber-of-X.

6. **Specialized versus Generalized Functions**
   If you need a strong team of specialists, they will not be very good generalists—and vice versa. Too many expectant employers want their people to be experts in a certain task and also highly capable at most other things. This usually never happens in business—and not even in life. Generally, build your team and the people within it to have skills that are either a mile wide and an inch deep, or an inch wide and a mile deep. But not both. This rule holds true in most countries, but I would say that it applies, even more, when offshoring.

   If you want to ensure greater success with your team, the safest route is to work with specialists and focus them on a narrow set of tasks. You can also get good results with a team of generalists for general functions, but they have more opportunities for disappointment and failure.

Be Clear on Your Objectives

When you know the sort of team that you are building, try to be clear on the core objective of that team. If a single team has both expectations of high growth and significant cost savings, you could end up disappointed. So try to focus your attention on one primary outcome. Below are some reasons why people might outsource—it can be valuable to establish which of these resonate most with your business.

1. **Savings**
    Are you simply aiming to save on labor cost? If so, then have this as your primary objective. To focus on cost savings, you want to ensure that the team will be doing simple, clear processes that are already proven.

2. **Double-down**
    Have you found something that works really well in your business and so you want to double down on this, and is now just a case of scaling that process?

3. **New or Existing**
    Are you building a team to perform a function that already exists within your business? Or is it a new function that hasn't yet been designed, tested, or proven?

4. **Expansion**
    You have a process that's working and is proven and stable. You are now ready to expand and just need additional staffing to support that function.

5. **Personal Assistance**
    You are busy and just need someone to support you and the

activities that you are busy doing.

6. **Handover**

   Maybe you need to clear your plate and you are keen to hand over certain tasks completely to focus on other things. If the roles are technical, this might require someone of different capabilities than an assistant.

7. **External Expertise**

   There are roles you need doing that are beyond your own or your company's knowledge or capabilities. And so you can source external expertise that isn't currently available within your company.

8. **Labor Shortage**

   You are facing a labor shortage in your local market—which is a big problem at the time of writing. You simply can't find the staff in your local market and so you just need to find good offshore staff that can replicate what your existing team is doing.

9. **Simplified Employment**

   Employing people in your local market is complex and expensive. Maybe you are overwhelmed by all of the legal obligations, liabilities and complexities of employment, and so want to employ your team using a third-party outsourcing partner.

10. **Young Startup**

    Fast-growing startups need to access affordable, scalable, and flexible staffing solutions. They are typically still defining the rules of the game, establishing product-market fit and haven't yet built stable processes. Even if they have, everything is changing all the time anyway. If you are bringing staff into this kind of environment, you need to ensure that they are capable of this specific challenge.

11. Stable Company

Maybe you are a mature and stable company where all processes are in place, clearly defined, and routine. This is a great opportunity to just replicate these processes somewhere else for cheaper.

12. High-growth

Are you a high-growth company adding dozens of staff a month and need assistance with hiring fast and scaling systems quickly and reliably?

13. Experienced Builder

Maybe you are an experienced business owner familiar with all aspects of building a team, employing people, and running a business—and so you just need a turnkey third-party employer with minimal intervention and assistance.

14. New to the Scene

Maybe you are a fresh entrepreneur and have to hire people and build processes, systems, and departments for the first time. You not only need assistance with recruitment, employment, and facilities, but you also want help in building the processes and monitoring the metrics and outcomes.

15. Hands-on or Hands-off

Maybe you are personally willing to dedicate a lot of time to building the team and the processes they follow. You're happy doing it all yourself. Alternatively, maybe you are determined to focus on your core activities and you want someone else to build all of the other auxiliary activities for you.

You can build a highly capable team suited for any of the above circumstances. But if you are trying to build one team to cover a variety of the above circumstances, all at the same time, then it could be challenging to succeed— especially at the beginning. When starting your outsourcing journey, it is better to set yourself and your team up for success by narrowly defining the objectives and activities of the team. Doing this will increase your chances of a more favorable outcome for your new offshore staff and reduce the possibility of disappointment, time-wasting, or failure.

Building a Clear Plan and Process

Knowing your objectives for outsourcing is a great start. However, to build a high-performing team you need to get all your ideas and plans for the business out of your head and onto paper. The better that you can consolidate your ideas into a coherent strategy and plan, the more chances you have of it turning out positively.

As you bring on a new team of people, that are as yet completely unfamiliar with you, your business, and mission, it is important that you have some documentation in place to help transfer your ideas, plans, and processes to them.

While you don't want to spend too much time on the documentation, getting things written down and formalized can be invaluable— both for you and your staff.

I find two documentation tools useful for both business generally and outsourcing alike. The first tool is the one-page strategic plan—which provides an easy orientation to your business. The second tool is some kind of process mapping—which provides deeper insights into the processes that drive your company forward. Let's review both of these now.

Consolidating your Strategy—One Page Strategic Plan

A one-page strategic plan is exactly what its name suggests—a strategic plan that fits on one page. It is the brainchild of Verne Harnish and his team at the Growth Institute, and has grown to become a very popular and valuable planning tool for business. It is maybe one of the best ways to help identify and communicate a company's strategic direction and core activities. It is best thought of as a 30,000-foot view of your business, outlining what it's trying to achieve, and how. It is designed to be visually succinct so that you can put it in your notebook, use it as a screen saver, or stick it up on your wall, so that you and your team remain aligned to the company's mission at all times.

It might not be the most comprehensive document, but it is succinct and conveniently contained on one single page. In planning, there is sometimes power in simplicity.

The one-page plan structure is designed to be brief to provide an easy visual reference. The small sections allow only a very limited explanation of each field, which forces you to distill everything into a concentrated, simple summary.

The One-Page Plan includes these core elements:

1. **The Foundation**

   The foundation contains the standard but important mission, vision and values:
   - **Mission** – Why you exist and what drives you
   - **Vision** – Where you are going
   - **Values** – The guidelines for how you behave on your mission

2. **Your Competitive Advantages**
   This section gets you to provide a clear analysis of why and how you are going to win. Where you will focus your energies and who you will specifically serve.

3. **Defining Your Strategy**
   This section has you outlining the higher-level objectives and the actions that will get you there:
   - **Broad objectives** – What is your three to five year long-term focus?
   - **Annual goals** – What is your specific focus for the next 12 months to align you with your broad objectives?
   - **Actions** – What are the short-term 90-day actions that align you with your annual goals?

   The actions are to be updated quarterly, the annual goal each year, and the broad objectives ideally remain stable for three to five years.

4. **Key Performance Indicators (KPIs)**
   The KPIs form the stepping stones and the pathway that allow you to both measure and move towards your defined point of success. The KPIs help you identify how you measure success, and what metrics you need to use.

5. **Implementation Model**
   The implementation model asks you to detail how you will carry out the actions needed to get you to your goals. Including, how is responsibility allocated among your team, and what is your method for implementing the plan?

Once it's all down on one page, it allows everyone in your organization to be more aligned to your ambitions and accountable for their actions.

I'd like to invite you now to create a one-page strategic plan for your business. This will help you determine your company's current state and direction, and can help point towards what you can best outsource first. Both 'doing' the strategic plan, and 'having' a strategic plan enhances your ability to think strategically about your business, and have a solid foundation for its planning and execution.

While you can certainly do a strategic plan on your own, it is recommended that you involve your staff and team members for a more collaborative effort. Involving your team will allow you to see things from their perspective that you might otherwise miss. It will also inspire them to work with you in executing the plan they helped create. Getting their suggestions and commitment can lead to a more effective use of your company's collective time and energy.

Reviewing your plan after a certain period will allow you to reflect on your progress and gauge if the plan is working or not. Your team can then make the necessary course corrections that will steer your company in the right direction.

While it may not be perfect, it's always better to be guided by some sort of plan. Done is better than perfect.

Strategy: One-Page Strategic Plan (OPSP) — Organization Name:

People (Reputation Drivers)

Employees	Customers	Shareholders
1.	1.	1.
2.	2.	2.
3.	3.	3.

CORE VALUES/BELIEFS (Should/Shouldn't)	PURPOSE (Why)	TARGETS (3–5 YRS.) (Where)	GOALS (1 YR.) (What)
		Future Date	Yr Ending
		Revenues	Revenues
		Profit	Profit
		Mkt. Cap/Cash	Mkt. Cap
		Sandbox	Gross Margin
			Cash
			A/R Days
			Inv. Days
			Rev./Emp.

	Actions To Live Values, Purposes, BHAG	*Key Thrusts/Capabilities* 3-5 Year Priorities	*Key Initiatives* 1 Year Priorities
	1	1	1
	2	2	2
	3	3	3
	4	4	4
	5	5	5

	Profit per X	Brand Promise KPIs	Critical #: People or B/S
			▪
			▪
			▫ Between green & red
			▪
	BHAG®	Brand Promises	Critical #: Process or P/L
			▪
			▪
			▫ Between green & red
			▪

Strengths/Core Competencies:	Weaknesses:
1.	1.
2.	2.
3.	3.

BHAG is a Registered Trademark of Jim Collins and Jerry Porras.

Source: One Page Strategic Plan, Growth Institute[37]

---

37 Growth Institute. (n.d.). The Ultimate Guide To Complete A One-Page Strategic Plan—Your Fast-Track To Alignment. Retrieved from https://blog.growthinstitute.com/scale-up-blue-print/the-ultimate-guide-to-complete-a-one-page-strategic-plan

Your Name:	Date:	**Gazelles**
		GROWING LEADERS · GROWING COMPANIES

Process (Productivity Drivers)

Make/Buy	Sell	Recordkeeping
1. _____	1. _____	1. _____
2. _____	2. _____	2. _____
3. _____	3. _____	3. _____

ACTIONS (QTR) (How)	THEME (QTR/ANNUAL)	YOUR ACCOUNTABILITY (Who/When)

		Your KPIs	Goal
Qtr #		1	
Revenues			
Profit		2	
Mkt. Cap			
Gross Margin			
Cash		3	
A/R Days			
Inv. Days			
Rev./Emp.			

Deadline:

Measurable Target/Critical #

THEME

Rocks

	Quarterly Priorities	Who
1		
2		
3		
4		
5		

Scoreboard Design
Describe and/or sketch your design in this space

	Your Quarterly Priorities	Due
1		
2		
3		
4		
5		

Critical #: People or B/S	Celebration	Critical #: People or B/S
▢		▢
▢		▢
▢ Between green & red		▢ Between green & red
▢		▢

Critical #: Process or P/L	Reward	Critical #: Process or P/L
▢		▢
▢		▢
▢ Between green & red		▢ Between green & red
▢		▢

Trends
1. _____   4. _____
2. _____   5. _____
3. _____   6. _____

BHAG is a Registered Trademark of Jim Collins and Jerry Porras.

Creating Structure

Business Process Mapping

Once you are clear of the company's broader ambitions, it is time to get more granular and focus on individual roles, functions, and processes. For this, process mapping is a valuable exercise. It helps clarify the procedures of a business for both the management team, and the people who are carrying out the work.

Depending on the size and age of your business, you might or might not have an 'organization chart,' or commonly referred to as 'org chart.' An org chart visually maps your company in terms of its people and the roles they cover. An org chart can also be function-based, where the specific activities of a business are mapped out, and then people are assigned to one or maybe more of those activities. Depending on the size of your company and complexity of the functions, a single person might be assigned to multiple activities, or alternatively, multiple people might be assigned to just one single activity.

A process map is similar to an org chart, but it zooms in on the specifics of each process within your business, such as production, sales, marketing, business administration, and accounting—to name a few. Its focus is more on the processes than an org chart, which focuses more on the people doing the processes. Process maps can stay as just simple representations of a department's functions, or they can be built out to be highly detailed representations that document every step within every function of every role in every department.

As with anything, it is better to start with something simple. There is value in having your key processes mapped, it gives a clear roadmap for your team to follow, and will allow them to get up to speed much faster. But don't let the process of building process maps distract you from the real business of operating your business.

Doing this exercise helps to clarify each business process and helps identify whether each of the processes is core or auxiliary to your operation. It also helps you identify who should be doing these processes and which have the best chance of moving your business forward.

For example, if you, as the business owner, are spending excessive time in the deeper layers of auxiliary processes such as scanning receipts for your bookkeeping, or posting content on social media, then you probably aren't spending enough time on developing your company. Conversely, if you have already delegated much of the low-value work and are spending most of your time in the upper layers of the core processes, then you're probably getting a lot of high-value strategic work done, which will likely propel your business forward. Completing the process map will help you to see exactly where you are spending your time.

Below is a simple guide to building an effective process map.

Start by listing down the broad process categories of your business. As mentioned above, they might be production, sales, marketing, business administration, and accounting.

Once you've identified the top layer of your company's 'primary processes,' zoom in a little more, drop down a layer, and outline each major process within each of the primary functions. For example, under sales and marketing, other major processes may include social media marketing, prospecting, lead generation, appointment setting, distribution, channel management, and so on.

Once you've done this, you can drop down another layer to identify the key processes of those processes, and then even drop another layer, and repeat. Eventually, you can get so granular that you describe every individual function of everyone's jobs.

Try and write down every business process you have in your company. Some may be big and some small, others separate and isolated, while some are intertwined into the fabric of the business.

As you go through this exercise, you'll discover that some processes are clearly key tasks for the business while some are auxiliary ones. Some functions will have 4th, 5th, and maybe 6th and 7th level processes, while some are more straightforward and end at the secondary level. The final 6th, 7th, or 8th layer might start to look more like a simplistic task-based to-do list if you take this mapping to an extreme.

The next step is to identify which of these activities are core to your business, and which are non-core auxiliary activities. Your core activities are the things that make your company different from every other company. They are the unique skills you possess, and the aspects closest to your value proposition.

In contrast, auxiliary activities are generally generic functions common to most companies. Examples of these are your bookkeeping, accounts, business administration, back-office and secretarial services, among others. There might also be some crossover roles such as content generation, marketing, sales, or customer service. Depending on your business sector and specific business modus operandi, these might either be core or auxiliary activities. Auxiliary activities might still be very important to your business, but they are still supplemental to the core functions that define your company.

Let me give you an example: The online retailer, Zappos, is a shoe company selling footwear online. However, Zappos is not only known for its shoes, but it is world-renowned for its exceptional customer service. Its stated purpose is: "To live and deliver wow." Its actual core product—shoes—comes almost secondary to its main differentiator—customer service. They say that Zappos.com wants to be a world-leading customer service company that just happens to sell shoes.

So, in this case, customer service is actually a core process for Zappos. But for many other companies, customer service is commonly seen as an auxiliary function—and one that is a good candidate for outsourcing. There is no right or wrong approach to any of this, but it is valuable to at least consider your company's functions and identify those that are most critical to your mission.

As Peter Drucker, the founding father of many modern business principles put it: "Do what you do the best, and outsource the rest."

Once you have completed your business process map, it's time to think strategically about which types and levels of processes you might want to retain or outsource. After careful consideration, you might decide to retain 90% of your top-level processes and start with outsourcing the lower level accounting functions—process levels 3, 4, and 5—and social media and marketing functions—levels 3 and 4—while keeping the CFO and marketing strategy functions—process level 2—in-house.

Alternatively, you might eventually choose to keep all upper-level processes at home—i.e., process levels 1 to 4—for all core and auxiliary functions; but get a back office to carry out all of the lower processes—i.e., levels 5 and 6—across the board.

It is safest and a common default to apply offshore staffing to the lower level and non-core activities of a business, especially at first. However, outsourcing can be used equally as effectively in the top-level strategic functions, as well as eventually, the core company activities. It is prudent though to start with offshoring the less critical roles, and then once you're more familiar with the process and the team is showing signs of success, you can begin to outsource more broadly and deeply.

The exercise of process mapping can be valuable because it identifies exactly what you are doing, what you should be doing, and maybe what you could be doing more of. It will also help identify the resources and skills required to fulfill each of the processes.

Figure 1.0 is a sample business process map that can guide you as you make your own.

Identifying Your Processes

To identify the best roles you should outsource first, start by brainstorming a big list of activities. Pull the activities from the process chart you completed above, or failing that, list down anything and everything you have ever wanted to get done in your business.

The best tasks are probably those that come to mind most easily at first. There might be an obvious list of items that you have on your daily agenda every day. You would love for someone else to do them, and you know that someone else could, but you always put it off because you thought it would have been too expensive, or too complicated to off-board to someone else.

Maybe you have had a long list of activities that you've always wanted someone else to do. Everyone has a list of those simple, repetitive things that you find yourself, or your team, kept busy with every day but seemingly don't contribute much to anything. They are mostly mundane items, rarely change, and are of low individual

Figure 1.0

Business Process Mapping

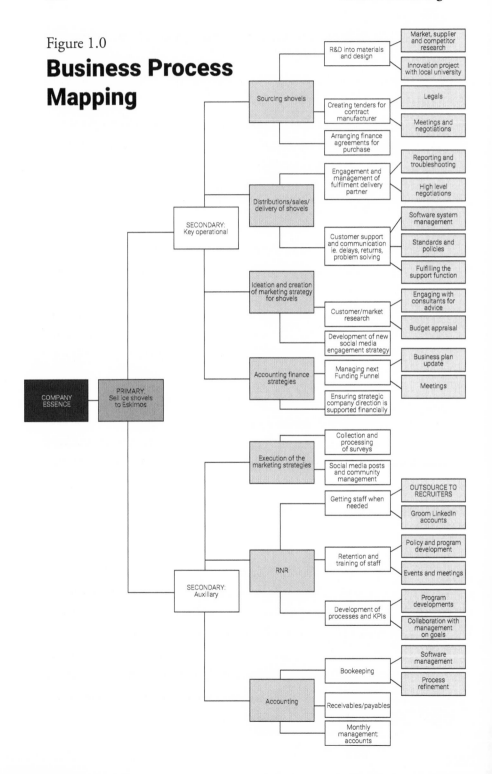

value—but they need to get done. These are ideal activities to get off your plate, as soon as possible.

So get brainstorming. You might be surprised. You might find that 80% of your day is filled with repetitive work that doesn't really impact big outcomes. Maybe, there's just 20% of your day spent working on those important high value tasks that really have the potential to move the needle for your business. Maybe, you find that when you finally get around to those mission-critical tasks, you're already exhausted from dealing with all of the earlier dross. This is common for most businesses, and is a common culprit for preventing a team from really pushing the business along.

If your agenda is looking pretty optimized already, then look at the agenda of your company's high-value staff, rainmakers, and core teams. Are those people spending too much of their time doing unimportant and non-critical jobs? How much more could they contribute to the business if they could focus more on higher-value tasks and avoid the low-value chores?

All too commonly, a company's urgent and unimportant activities get prioritized over the un-urgent but hyper-important activities. Taking a step back to be conscientious about building your operations, and getting the right people to do the right tasks, can add rocket fuel to your business and its development cycles.

◇◇◇◇◇◇◇◇◇◇◇◇◇

Once you have built a big list of current and future activities, try working through the following questions to help you analyze their suitability for easy offshoring. With this process, you can begin to narrow down the ideal tasks to be outsourced.

You can objectively rate the activities by attributing a simple score to each. Allocate a 1 to 5 rating depending on the criticality of various factors: where 1 = low difficulty and an easy transition, and 5 = high difficulty and complexity.

Add a score to each activity, based on the following criteria:

A. Process complexity (1 to 5).

B. Back-office or front-line processes (1 to 5).

C. Process criticality (1 to 5).

D. Non-core or core process (1 to 5).

E. Low to high seniority, autonomy, expertise (1 to 5).

F. Is this already an existing process or needs to be built (1 to 5).

G. Is the skill generic in nature (i.e., accounting or coding), or highly nuanced or culturally unique (1 to 5).

H. Is the process an ongoing permanent function or a finite project? (1 to 5).

Once you have scored each activity, there should be a range of scores from a low of 8 to a maximum of 40 allocated to each. The activities with the lower scores are easier, safer, and possibly better candidates to be outsourced. The activities with higher scores are more complex and should be outsourced with caution—at first.

It is certainly possible to outsource high complexity activities, and in fact, you are leaving a lot of money on the table if you think that outsourcing is only suited to basic tasks. Outsourcing higher skilled and complex activities can yield far greater cost savings and have a much bigger impact on your business than any of the basic activities. However, be warned that outsourcing, like anything, takes experience and practice to master. And so it's advisable not to attempt the more complex activities first. Crawl before you can walk, get an initial taste of success with outsourcing, and then a little bit later on, you can take on the more complex opportunities.

Having scored your activities, it should become apparent which are the best to start with. Here are some other things worth considering:

1. Keep It Simple

Look for the processes that are simplistic and repetitive in nature, can be easily taught, and can most easily be handed over to someone else. As much as possible, they should not rely on an intimate esoteric understanding of you, your business, your clientele, or geography.

2. **Start Small**

   Depending on the scale of your existing organization, you will want to identify just one or two easily 'replicable' roles at this stage. Don't attempt too many disparate or divergent roles at the beginning. If you are a bigger company, then identify one clearly delineated, simple and stable function or department to focus on first.

3. **Non-Critical Roles**

   Prioritize the activities that are auxiliary and non-core to your business at first.

4. **Narrow Focus**

   Unless you are looking for a virtual assistant (VA) to cover some general tasks, try and avoid as much as possible the concept of finding someone great that will do a wide range of... everything. If your initial success depends on you finding that incredible generalist employee, then you're possibly heading for disappointment. To play it safe, first try to find someone great at doing a very specific function.

5. **Established Roles**

   Ideally, try to start with an already established and proven role within your current operation. It is much safer and its success is more assured. You can certainly start by creating a new, untested process, role, or team function that you don't currently have in your organization, but it is more likely to be a bumpy ride.

Some things simply should not be outsourced. At least, not in the beginning. There are no hard and fast rules to this, as realistically, 99% of jobs can be outsourced; however, some things are more complex than others. You will want to try and minimize this complexity when you start. To ensure early and easy success, seek out the low-hanging-fruits at the beginning of your journey. Once you have more confidence in outsourcing and your team, then you can quickly scale to take on more and more complex activities.

In the beginning, to play it safe, try to avoid offshoring roles with the following attributes:

1. Jobs Requiring a Physical Presence

This may sound obvious, but it's hard to offshore an electrician's work. However, nowadays, there are relatively few of these jobs left. For simplicity, things such as plumbing, electrical, and HVAC engineers should be— somewhat obviously—excluded from your outsourcing list.

However, a wise business owner would spend time unpacking these roles, and make sure that everything these high-cost people are doing—is essential. For example, a plumber should not be wasting their time answering phone calls, managing their receipts and bookkeeping, arranging their next job, or writing proposals for clients. If your business requires someone that is physically present—ensure that they are just doing those high-value tasks that utilize the fact that they are physically present. Everything else they do that is lower value and doesn't require that physical presence could potentially be offshored.

2. Passion Jobs

Jobs that you, the boss, or the internal team have a particular skill or passion. Keep this in-house—for now.

3. **Core Competencies**

   Core competencies of the company should be kept in-house, initially. We have mentioned this now many times. It is possible to eventually offshore key competencies but keep them close to your chest—for now.

4. **Regulated Functions**

   Compliance with regulatory and legal frameworks can get complicated when offshoring. Some roles or industries might be regulated. Examples include the finance, banking, healthcare, and roles that come in contact with personal data, health information or payment details. These guidelines should be taken very seriously and abided by. There are many highly regulated roles that are done offshore, but they can be more expensive and complex to set up. It is very possible to do all of these activities offshore, but avoid these areas when you're just starting out to keep things simple.

5. **Localized Knowledge**

   Roles that heavily rely on localized contextual understanding can take a long time to develop. We all take the subtleties of localized knowledge and contextual understanding for granted, but if someone doesn't have it, it is very difficult to quickly or comprehensively pick up.

   For example, people that live in Alaska could hardly imagine what it would be like to live on a beach on a tropical island. Conversely, people from the tropics simply can't comprehend what it is like to live in the freezing Alaskan climate. And it can be really hard to learn, and even harder to try to fake these things. So if your company or product deals with highly specific subject matter, that is critical to the outcome, then try and avoid outsourcing these items. For example, if you are a

New York tour guide selling tours, then it would be hard to get someone in the Philippines to speak with knowledge and authority on your product. Whereas someone from New York, with no training at all, would have inherent capabilities in this domain and pick things up much quicker.

Once you have worked through these various considerations, you should have a clear idea of the roles you want to get started with first.

4.1.3

Outsourcing Requirements

Defining Your Outsourcing Requirement and Roles

Based on your one-page strategic plan and business process map, you should be able to confidently identify the initial roles or processes that you want to offshore and the number of staff for your team.

After determining the roles, the next step is to create a job profile for that person or team.

Your goal when hiring is to find the best, brightest, most passionate, versatile, dependable, and multi-faceted employees available to you. You need to do all this within the budget you can afford and within a reasonable timeframe of searching.

A detailed job description, despite sometimes being a little bit of a creative straitjacket, really does help your recruiting process. When you're doing things remotely, it further increases the requirement to have things better structured and properly written down—and this is an example of that.

Your outsourcing needs will vary tremendously depending on your company's type, size, and maturity. If you have decided to start with a 100-person accounts team, your needs will differ from someone starting with a part-time virtual assistant. However, here are some key considerations when looking to produce a description for your new person or team:

1. **Don't Expect Too Much**

   I have seen all too often, mainly from inexperienced entrepreneurs, an expectation of recruiting a magical all-star generalist who can do virtually everything—perfectly! I've had people who want a single hire to be an A-grade personal assistant, while at the same time proficient in IT, digital marketing, content writing, bookkeeping, and also comfortable making some sales. Plus, they want 10 years of relevant experience, but only want to pay them $400 per month... This simply will not happen. It's unlikely that you would find such a capable generalist in your hometown, and it is just as unlikely, if not more unlikely, to happen in the Philippines.

2. **Don't Start Too Big, Too Fast**

   If you want to expand to a team of 10 people in 10 days, you're going to struggle to attract the good candidates that you need in such a short time. Start with a small team, train them well, to the standards you want, and then they can help grow the team themselves. Be wary of outsourcing firms that have a pool of staff on a bench that are ready to start the next day. No company can have a lot of good staff on the payroll just waiting around for the next paying client, and even if they did, it would mean that you are getting whoever is there at the time. Instead, it is much better to recruit handpicked staff according to your specific requirements—although it will take a bit longer.

3. **Start with Pioneers**

   'Pioneers' are strong, typically more mature, mid-career employees. You will want to spend extra time and attention training these people, making sure that they become proficient and strong ambassadors for your mission. Once you groom a good pioneer, then they are worth their weight in gold. As they get up to speed, you can empower them to scale and train the team and its processes alongside you.

Creating a Job Description

It's generally best practice to write a clear job description for the role you want to outsource. The process of creating a job description will actually establish clarity for you, your company, and all other stakeholders. It helps to bring everything and everyone onto the same page.

An effective job description creates a base agreement, which helps an employee to be efficient and have an early and comprehensive understanding of their performance objectives and expected contribution to your organization.

Some other benefits of creating a job description are:

- It forms the basis of the agreement of the responsibilities and scope of the position.
- It helps the recruiters know the educational background, knowledge, skills, experience, and capabilities you require and will help them generate an effective and targeted recruiting plan.
- It informs candidates about the tasks and responsibilities of the position they are applying for.

- It informs other employees who are helping with the interview process to come up with the right questions to ask the prospective candidates.
- It safeguards you legally to explain why the candidate selected for a position was the most qualified and culturally-suited applicant.

Job Description Considerations

1. **About You and Your Vision**

   Finding the perfect employee is a two-way street. To attract the best, you have to not only pay well, but you have to offer a vision for your company—and their role in it—that people can relate to and get motivated by.

2. **Mission and Values**

   Share and explain your mission and values. Leave out the templated mission statement though and just try to succinctly describe what your company is about, why you are doing what you do, and where you're going in the future.

   If your company is mundane, hasn't really been anywhere, and isn't really going anywhere in the future, then it's not going to inspire many candidates to join that journey.

3. **Describe the Role**

   Spend time to describe the role that you are looking to fill. Briefly explain what they will be doing on a day-to-day basis, as well as the broader purpose of the role and how it contributes to the company's overall mission. Tell them who they will be working with, who will provide support and training, and who they are accountable to.

Be realistic and open about the highlights, as well as the lowlights of the job.

4. **Hard Skills and Qualifications**

   List all hard skills required for the job, including degrees, qualifications, professional association licenses, or registrations. Also, spend time identifying any specific skillsets such as coding, relevant experience, or proficiency in using certain tools or software.

5. **Soft Skills and Attributes**

   List any soft skills or attributes that come to mind. If they are going to be doing customer service, then you might want them to be happy and bubbly, and if they are an accountant, you might have specific concern for their diligence and less concern about their extroversion.

6. **Experience**

   List any relevant experience you would like or expect. Sometimes direct experience in a specific task from a similar company is ideal, and sometimes it can hinder.

7. **Opportunities**

   As well as knowing the company, its mission and the role, prospective candidates will want to know how they could progress their career when working for you. Does the role have any growth opportunities or is it a dead end? Does the company have an active training system in place so that the employee can apply for promotion? Outlining the opportunities and pathway to progress can be a valuable incentive for people to join your company as well as a strong motivator for them once they have joined.

8. **Specifics**

   Be sure to outline any specific terms of the job, such as salary range, hours worked, timezone to be worked in, and which days and holidays they'll be getting off.

9. **Logistics**

   Check with a candidate to see if the job logistics are consistent with their own circumstances. For example, if the jobs is 100% office-based, then make sure that they know this. Also, find out where they live so that you can be sure that coming into the office each day for them is viable. It is not unheard of for people in the Philippines to commute two to four hours each way for a job—but it is not sustainable in the long term.

10. **Technical Requirements**

    When specifying each role, be sure to consider any special tools they might need to get their job done properly. Typically, the outsourcing firm would provide these things, so it isn't a direct concern for the candidate, but it's good to list any standard tools to avoid surprises later. For example, an animator might need a high-powered computer, some analysts might need two to three monitors, call center agents might need a VOIP auto-dialer, and an architect might need a CAD software license.

The above items might sound like a lot, but the job description doesn't have to become a novel. These 10 considerations can easily be contained within one or two pages. Make it short and concise. Critically, your job description needs to identify the person you're looking for and communicate why they want to be a part of your mission.

Setting a Budget

Once you get started, you will probably be amazed at the relative cheapness of highly skilled and motivated candidates in the Philippines. Moving from a situation in your own home market where hiring is prohibitively expensive to one where people seem ridiculously cheap can feel almost exhilarating. It can get you excited to start 'shopping' for the team you need right away.

However, try to contain your early enthusiasm, and more importantly, try to resist overspending. Make sure that you're aware of the going rates for salaries and avoid paying over the market price. Your outsourcing partner should help you with this process.

I've seen the situation many times before where outsourcing newbies see how cheap the salaries are and suddenly feel empowered to offer vastly more money and perks. For once, their budget seems to go such a long way and so they feel emboldened and a little unstoppable with their spending. It is not uncommon for foreigners to glibly offer a 20%, 50%, or even a 100% salary hike if they really like the candidate. After all, the all-in price is still considerably cheaper than what they would find in their own hometown. Try and resist these urges.

Keep in mind that one of the primary purposes of outsourcing is its opportunity to create cost-effective business growth. Individual salary hikes might seem like small change in the short term, but they can add up over the long term, and can cause all kinds of trouble once you build a team and need to implement some sort of salary standardization. It is always easy to boost a salary up, but it is virtually impossible to adjust a salary back down.

Also, remember that money is only one motivator for an

employee, and it's actually quite a blunt tool when used improperly. So get to know the market rates for the staff you are employing, and be guided by your outsourcing partner when negotiating a salary. Instead of splurging, save your money, and build your team with thoughtful consideration.

Don't Be Cheap

Some people overpay and others struggle to find fair value in anything. Sure, outsourcing is synonymous with saving money. But I would caution prospective outsourcers not to 'pinch every penny'—especially at the beginning.

You can and will save a huge amount when outsourcing, but it can be self-defeating if you try to go for the cheapest partner and seek to pay the cheapest salaries. Millions of people are out of work, illiterate, and uneducated in the Philippines and across the world. If you really wanted, you could easily hire an army of people at less than $100 a month for each. And they would be grateful for the work. But it's not really about the number of people; it's about their output, the quality of that output, and your company's growth as a result of those outputs.

To quote the wise Warren Buffett again: "The price is what you pay. Value is what you get."

Don't focus too much on the face price of the salary and service fee, instead focus more on the quality of the person and the value of their contribution to your business. Following this principle does not necessarily mean that you will overpay. Compared to your local labor market, it is still possible to save as much as 70% on the salary and all-in costs. Be happy with this incredible opportunity, and don't push too hard to save incrementally more.

It is possible to save even more money, but be reminded that you are engaging with a developing nation—where many standards are not the same. If you try and save every penny and cut every corner, then you will no doubt encounter disproportional friction and frustration on your journey, which might cost you far more money, frustration, time, and results in the long run.

Outsourcing should not become your company's main focus. Sure, you could spend more time building a slightly cheaper team in the Philippines if you put the extra time into it. But why focus on this? You already have a big complicated business of your own to run and should focus on the opportunities of that business rather than trying to squeeze out an extra 5% of savings from the offshore team.

In the context of Philippines salaries, allow yourself to pay well or very well for your team, and give yourself permission to pay middle of the road, or even top of the budget for your outsourcing service provider. Doing this will still save you a huge amount of money over the long run—and you will encounter considerably less friction and frustration as a result.

Finding the Perfect Employee

Try to have realistic expectations of the capabilities of your future employees. If you build processes where only a genius can succeed, you are building too many possible failure points into your systems. It has become a default assumption and aspiration to hire brilliant employees. But what if you don't? What if an employee turns out to be…. gulp… average? What then happens to your business?

In reality, your employees will probably be average. It's better to face that fact and build systems to accommodate this, rather than live in a fantasy world and get disappointed each time that someone average in your company does something average. Everyone subscribes to hiring the best possible employees, but if everyone is hiring the best, then there just simply won't be enough best people to go around. The reality is that most people are average —and that's okay.

Employers are also prone to overestimating the impact of their job offer in the market and overvalue the impressiveness of the company that they own or run. While most business owners treat their company as if it's their first-born child, the painful truth is that most businesses are also just average. If you are a Google, then you should rightly shoot to hire the top-of-the-top employees, but otherwise, it would be sensible to temper your employment expectations.

The truly perfect employee is in high demand globally. They are by definition a smart cookie, and so they are very aware of their market value and will only entertain the best possible employers. The top-of-the-top employees will be working for a Google or Facebook, a JP Morgan or SpaceX, or be starting their own business and raising millions in capital.

Despite being one of the most famous and most cashed-up billionaires in the world, even Warren Buffett is realistic about his expectations. When investing hundreds-of-millions or billions of dollars into new businesses, he says: "I try to invest in businesses that are so wonderful that an idiot can run them. Because sooner or later, one will." There's a lot to unpack in this simple statement, but he is suggesting that a good business should have robust systems in place so that it can survive and even thrive, if, or when, an idiot is employed to run it.

If your company's success depends on your finding a genius to run it, then you are placing too much of your company's success on someone else's capabilities. Instead, take responsibility for your own outcomes, and build fantastic systems that a broader range of people are capable of running. Then, if someone fails in their job, your systems and business won't break. If a business comes tumbling down because an employee was complacent, then it is maybe more the business's fault than the complacency of the individual. Having strong processes and robust systems in place means that you will find good staff easier and cheaper because the systems are easier to run. If your systems require hiring the one-in-a-million unicorn employee to run them successfully—then you might be in trouble.

A Note on IT Project Outsourcing

It is common for people to outsource their web development, coding, and engineering tasks. There is a sensible argument for this, as it's unlikely you would have all of these skillsets in-house, especially if you are an early-stage, small, or non-technical company. Outsourcing such technical roles can be a great idea because you can save significant money with Philippine salaries, for example, and access a big pool of highly-qualified people. However, I want to caution that outsourcing technical projects can be enormously complex.

In fact, delivering a complex technical project on time and on budget is generally a very advanced process—regardless of whether you're offshoring, outsourcing, using an agency, or doing it in-house. So, while it's more than viable to do this in the Philippines and highly likely to save you a lot of money if you do so, it's not necessarily easy. If it is a highly technical and complex project, make sure that you have experience, intensively plan for it, use appropriate project management methodology, and be prepared to work closely with the team.

A Note on Delegation

For some people, the problem is not about what or how to outsource. For some, their issue is their ability to delegate effectively. Many people hide behind the hoarding of work, solopreneurship, and the culture of workaholism as a bit of a humblebrag. They may rightly feel that only they can do the job as good as themselves, so they are locked into battling through the journey themselves.

The reality is that you need to add staff for a business to grow. And to add staff, you need to add processes that support those staff. You will lose some degree of efficiency by adding more people and processes. But if you want to grow, you don't really have an option. A company really is just a collection of people, all pushing towards an agreed goal. And so if you don't have a collection of people, then you don't really have a company—you just have a job.

Delegation is a skill—and like all aspects of business—it needs to be practiced. Some managers and owners struggle to delegate—even at the best of times. So, make sure that you don't allow your personal bias of controlling tasks to prevent you from properly identifying roles that can be scaled and offshored. Try and be completely objective about identifying what you should outsource.

To help you get started, begin by identifying the roles you hate doing. Even the die-hard control freaks have a few things that bore them to tears or other tasks they keep deferring and never get done. Start easy and simply. Once you get a few successes under your belt, you will see the advantages of delegation and begin to build new systems that enable you to scale.

How Far Can It All Go?

I see a common journey with many outsourcing clients—which is one of exceptional growth and unmitigated success. Ironically, most people are so fearful of starting outsourcing—because of all of the perceived risks—that they ignore the enormous opportunities that can occur if their offshoring is actually a success.

In my experience from observing and working with many outsourcing clients, it only takes a few weeks for them to see results and start to build some confidence around their team and the concept.

Very quickly, once teams are in place, and deliverables are met, clients finally start to realize outsourcing's power and see how it can transform their business. They then start exploring what other roles they could offshore and start pondering the question: "How far can this go?", closely followed by: "Why not outsource everything?", and: "Is it possible for the entire company to be run from another country?"

When a business realizes that outsourcing really works and they start asking these sorts of questions, they have reached the point where the true opportunities of offshoring get really exciting.

Consider for a minute, a more extreme example of an outsourcing opportunity. A big, complex accounting firm with $50 million in revenues and 180 employees is headed by three executives working from their New York home office. At the same time, everyone else is sourced and working from Manila, in the Philippines. This is certainly possible, and those companies are already out there.

Or maybe, instead of doing everything in-house, you could have just one single person running a multimillion-dollar company with zero employees. Instead of employing a workforce, the entrepreneur relies upon a few select, highly-skilled offshore contract partners to fulfill the requirements of this business. This is also happening right now.

The possibilities are endless.

These are indeed extreme examples, but it is valuable to just stop for a moment to think about the alternative possibilities. It's an interesting thought experiment to consider the first principles of what actually constitutes a company, and why the traditional 'company-and-onshore-employees' model remains the default. Before the modern era, with its remote work, Internet, global workforce and online tools, the traditional company structure was the only real option. But now the world is much different, and there are many more options.

There are strong academic arguments both for and against in-housing or outsourcing a company's core skills and functions. Equally, there are raging debates around the benefits of specialization versus generalized roles. No one is certain where, or what, the optimal blend is.

Regardless of practicalities and preferences, as an academic exercise, it's interesting to consider what a company actually is if it doesn't have any employees or retain a core in-house competency. If taken to an extreme, there's a hypothetical scenario where all roles within a company are outsourced to a range of different specialized BPOs and contract partners—all of which are experts in their field. Even expert consultants could handle even the leadership, strategy, and capital allocation functions. It is an exciting concept, and is certainly a possibility.

We may still be some way from such extreme scenarios, but it's fairly common to have both manufacturing and delivery processes outsourced nowadays. It is also common to have marketing, distribution, and customer support outsourced. Who knows, maybe eventually the core product development—and even outsourcing itself—can be outsourced? There is simply no right or wrong way of doing things, and there is no limit.

Just imagine if all your operational functions are executed by domain experts, in a cheaper environment, for just 30% of the cost compared to your competitors. Ask yourself, what opportunities would open up for you and your business then? The possibilities are endless.

Okay, enough with the fantasizing for a minute, let's get this back to reality. You would probably want to keep the management, strategic decisions, and innovative ideas in-house for most companies. Generally, the leadership and key decisions should come from and be confirmed by 'the top.' For now, at least, the leadership, brains, and core essence of a company must be kept and operated in-house. But the rest, can potentially be offshored—at a fraction of the cost. This is an exciting proposition.

Get Started

Depending on the size of your company, company functions, and the specific needs of your business, you will have very different outsourcing requirements compared to any other prospective outsourcing client. Companies are highly individualized, and so are all of the functions and departments within them. So the way that outsourcing could and should be implemented will also be very different in each case.

Some companies might find it best to start with a virtual assistant just to get them familiar with remote and offshore-staffing concepts. Alternatively, another company might start outsourcing with a team of 10 to launch an entirely new line of business in an as yet untested market. Another company might set up their first offshore department alongside, and in competition with, an existing in-house department. They will run them side by side for a while, and then compare the results.

All approaches are valid and viable, and each approach is very individualized.

However, to manage expectations, you should remember that doing business is by nature complex. It could be the case that outsourcing your first VA is a runaway success, but when it comes to outsourcing your sales function, it gets snagged with quality and training issues, and takes longer to find its stride and prove its worth. Success will not always be easy, nor linear, and is not always guaranteed. Success with outsourcing means that you have built and mastered a set of complex business processes, and done this in a new environment with a team of new people from a different culture. If you manage to do all this without too many complications, then that is something to be celebrated.

Outsourcing is, by its nature, a highly human-based function—and people are intrinsically complicated. As a result, you will have to accommodate the variability of the human resource that you are working with. The reality is—some employees will be fabulous, and some will not. So if your first offshore employee turns out to be a bit of a flop, don't take it too personal. Try not to lose faith in the potential for the project, or in outsourcing as a concept, or in the Philippines as a destination. It was simply one person that didn't work out. And that could happen anywhere. As with any human-resource-based activity, you sometimes have to kiss a few frogs before you find your prince.

Every business is different, working in different spaces, and doing different things, and all with very different needs. There is no 'one' ideal approach to starting outsourcing. However, from my experience, I found that the best strategy generally for SMEs is to consider the following:

Start soon, start small, start with the least critical roles, and start as if you were just hiring someone in your own hometown—and build up from there.

One of the key messages there is to 'just get started.' Don't overthink it too much; don't over-prepare and just get started. You will never look back.

Part 4.2

Engaging
the Right Provider

4.2.1

Ways To Outsource

Broad Concept

There are almost as many different ways to outsource, as there are roles and functions within a company. This is great news, since you'll most certainly be able to find an outsourcing model to perfectly suit you and your company's needs—whatever those needs are. However, this oversupply of options might be a little daunting, given the abundant choice and seeming lack of service conformity across the sector, especially at first. Luckily though, there are some strong commonalities within the various market offerings. Despite similar service offerings being called different things, there are now many standardized categories within the fractured market.

The broad concept of 'outsourcing' encompasses a whole raft of different employment and structuring options. As with the concept of traditional 'employment' itself, like in your own home market, there are many different options. For example, with traditional employment you have the standard default of a full-time employee, which is the dominant solution across most of the market. However, you also have the option of part-time employees, interns, contractors, consultants, temporary workers, apprenticeships, and even consultants, advisors, and agencies. All of these different arrangements fall within the broader concept of employment—and this is similar to the broad umbrella term of outsourcing. In many ways, to simplify the concept, outsourcing should really just be seen the same as employment—except that the people are sitting—usually—in a different country.

The default structural option for outsourcing is similar to traditional employment—full-time dedicated employees. It is generally the best way to structure things, in most situations for most people. However, you don't have to be all or nothing. A standard business in the US for example, would usually have full-time employees as its core team, but it might also utilize some consultants, agencies, interns, and part-timers as needed. The same also applies with offshore staffing—all options are available to you—and you can blend them to suit. However, at first, it is generally better to get a stable core of dedicated full-timers. Once you have a beachhead of a reliable and trustworthy offshore team in place, you can easily blend things up from there.

There are common outsourcing offerings in the industry, and it's good to be aware of them and understand how they work, so I will cover these below. They are structures that specifically apply to outsourcing. For the sake of focus, I won't cover the broader range of employment services available offshore—such as agencies, consultants, and interns. In short summary, these services basically work the same as they do in your own home market—so you're able to approach and engage them, in very much the same way— although the cherry on top is that they would generally cost 50% to 70% less than in your own home market.

A Note on Projects and Agencies

If you are looking for help with a short-term project, you would commonly be looking for a freelancer or contractor, or a company that provides project-based, agency-type services—a.k.a. an agency, dev shop, or consultancy.

It is easy to find and engage with agencies; they are everywhere. But be warned that you have to do your homework, as there can be many poor performers in this area. This equally applies to any contract-based project work, whether outsourcing in the Philippines or working with an agency in your hometown.

If you are looking for a project initially, and then you are hoping to turn it into a long-term, or ongoing process or function, then starting with a freelancer or agency might not be the best approach for this. This is where you have to be clear from the start about what your short, medium, and longer-term ambitions are.

It is also worth noting that the most difficult part of any working relationship is the initial onboarding stage. The first stages of a project where you are searching for and selecting an ideal person to work with, outlining the scope of work, getting used to each other, critiquing work, and learning each other's nuances are by far the most complex of any journey.

As a result, it is the early stage of any project, engagement, or employment that is most commonly fraught with frustration, disappointment, or failure. Regardless of who, what, or where you are employing someone, this initial search, selection, and learning phase is by far the most time-consuming and error-prone.

So, if you start multiple new projects with numerous new people all the time, then you are exposing yourself to a high proportion of the 'early stage' of an endeavor. If the early stage is the toughest, and you spend the most time in the early stages, you're creating a lot of work for yourself, and it's work that can commonly be met with disappointment.

Therefore, if you want to give offshoring a good try and want it to succeed, it is best to take the easy route first. That means hiring someone full-time for a clearly defined role, using a reputable outsourcing firm, preparing to spend a reasonable amount of time with them at the beginning for a comprehensive onboarding, and taking things slowly. The chances of this route failing are far lower, and overall it will demand much less of your time to set up and operate.

Then, once you are familiar with your first person or team and have a good working relationship, you can easily increase the scope of the work they perform. You can then also easily add team members, roles, and increase the complexity of roles. If your foundational team or person is strong, then they can spend their time training the newer staff. It will be your staff spending time in the early time-consuming stages and not you. And so already, you will be seeing good leverage and the benefit of having a stable team, and having spent the initial time to train them up properly.

This is a far safer approach, as you only have to onboard the initial person or team once. The 'stakes' are kept relatively low, and if you treat them well, they will likely stick with you for many years to come. All of this means that you minimize the exposure to the early stages of a project or employment relationship.

If you are looking for help with a one-off project, such as building a website or an app, this is by nature a short-term project. And so hiring someone full-time for this function is probably not the best option. So using an agency or freelancer for this is most certainly the best approach. Typically, a standard BPO wouldn't be interested in these short-term service offerings, and even if they are keen to accommodate it, they most probably wouldn't be the best at getting it done.

There are some BPOs out there that will offer a full range of services—from short-term projects, creative and dev teams, to long-term seat leasing and full-service solution management—but like anything, you might get better results if you select a company that specializes in a certain vertical. This might certainly be the safer bet if you are just starting out. It is hard to find a company that is good at everything.

Outsourcing Service Models

Four Main Models

The outsourcing sector has undergone continuous evolution in its relatively short 30-year life. The benefit of this progress is that there are now many varied providers offering a huge range of flexible services. One of the biggest benefits is that outsourcing has now become available to smaller businesses. In the beginning, it was only accessible to the large multinationals. This industry development, helped along by extensive technological innovation, has made outsourcing more affordable and accessible than ever to micro-, small-, and medium-sized companies.

Most BPOs work hard to differentiate their services. They do this by describing them in different ways, emphasizing different aspects, calling them different things, and introducing small variations. After all, it's within a BPO's interests to maximally differentiate their offering from the rest of the market—it's marketing 101. Doing so allows them to highlight their uniqueness, focus on their value-add, and avoid being compared on a like-for-like basis with their competitors. So it is your job then, as the prospective client, to understand and align the different offerings available so that you can better compare apples with apples.

The seemingly endless variety of outsourcing firms, services, and price structures makes the market appear complex and disparate. This is not quite the case, and in reality, beneath all of the marketing fluff, there are really only two or three fundamental business and pricing models. It's good to be familiar with the models in thesis and application so that you can better find the best match for your needs.

I will review four common models typically offered by the BPO industry below, namely:

1. Comprehensive or full-service outsourcing.
2. Staff leasing.
3. Seat leasing.
4. Build-Operate-Transfer (B-O-T).

Some BPOs offer only one of the above; others offer a choice; and many offer all in some form.

1. Comprehensive Business Process Outsourcing

Dubbed as 'traditional outsourcing,' a common example of the comprehensive model is for a company to have an external outsourcing firm manage its entire customer service operation. In this case, the BPO would take care of the entire scope of the engagement based on the client's requirements. Notably, the basis of the agreement between the two parties is typically not centered around the actual staffing requirement but is instead based on agreed outcomes and deliverables.

For example, to cover your customer service needs, you might specify to the BPO that: (1) All customer inquiries are answered within one hour if via email or three rings if through phone; that (2) only severe complaints are escalated to company management; and (3) the success for this program is determined by a customer satisfaction level of 8 out of 10 and above.

Notice here that there is no mention of staffing numbers or discussion about 'people' to hire, or 'seats' required in this scenario. Within a full service BPO arrangement, it is common to set agreements based on the output or outcome, and not on how many people are working, or the internal activities required, to get to the outcome. Once you have agreed on the set terms with the BPO provider, it is then up to the provider to meet these targets. Internally, the BPO will leverage their experience in managing similar processes and build a team to meet the desired outcomes. Once awarded a contract, and the deliverables are agreed upon, then it is within the interests of the outsourcing firm to build this team and process as efficiently as possible, and will continually be looking at ways to optimize and refine it.

The billing or cost of this service might possibly link back to the number of people employed, but more commonly it will be linked to the volume, output, or results achieved. For example, you might pay them based on the number of calls answered, along with some sort of performance bonus or clawback, depending on an agreed customer satisfaction rating, and not necessarily the number of people or person-hours required to get that job done.

The huge benefit here for the client is that you can get a wide range of complex and critical functions of your business managed by experts, without any direct involvement in the process or the people running the task. In these cases, the BPO will carry out all internal operational tasks such as recruitment and operations management, IT support, and payroll services. The provider will build the process and drive results with dedicated staff working on the client's behalf, using the provider's facilities, infrastructure, management, and experience.

Comprehensive process outsourcing is most applicable to any part of a business that a company wants to, or is able to, outsource completely—hence, the emphasis on the word 'process.' Again, this is why the industry is traditionally called 'business process outsourcing.' Commonly outsourced functions could be call center or voice services, non-voice services, accounting, sales, customer service, administrative or professional services, and any tasks that fall under these major categories.

It is essential though, that there is little or no crossover between roles when you use comprehensive outsourcing. For example, if you contract a BPO to provide customer service, then unlike traditional employees, these BPO agents won't pitch in to help you with any additional admin work or social media management in their spare time. Nor will they help with a client invoicing issue, or any proactive sales when on a call, if it isn't within their clearly defined remit. Their function will be very clear, focused, and delineated from other activities of the business.

Because of this black and white role segregation, the comprehensive BPO model is usually reserved for bigger, more mature, and more structured companies. There is a close analogy to this kind of structured service provision and mass-scale outsourced manufacturing.

For example, in manufacturing, a car-production facility can build one million cars relatively cheaply. They can set up a manufacturing line and build a set process that builds cars with extreme efficiency. But it is only viable to do this if you are manufacturing in large quantities. If you are producing just one motor car, then the cost of setting up the manufacturing line would far outweigh the cost of the individual car. These big systems are very efficient, but they are big and typically very narrow in scope. Equally, they offer little in the way of flexibility and agility. If you suddenly want to change the process or design, or want one slightly different version, then it can become very expensive and slow, if not impossible, to change.

The clear and certain role delineation and definition of a full BPO service offering certainly has many pros, but just as many cons. It is very effective at a large scale, but it is much less applicable at a small scale. It is for this reason you don't see SMEs engaging in this full-service BPO offering so much.

2. Staff Leasing

Staff Leasing is now one of the most common BPO service models available, especially within the SME space.

To complicate things slightly, the term, 'staff leasing' can be interchangeably used with offshore staffing, staff augmentation, virtual staffing, and even seat leasing.

In short summary, staff leasing allows you to basically 'hire' someone full-time for your business, and you manage the daily activities of those people just as you would your own staff, except that the BPO firm manages all of the backend infrastructure and complicated issues of employment, payroll, and facilities. The client's contract is with the BPO and the BPO employs the staff. The BPO provides not only the employee, but also the desk, workspace, IT infrastructure, as well as the HR, payroll, and recruitment support functions. Let's dive a little deeper to understand this model better.

When staff leasing, the outsourced resource remains the legal employee of the outsourcing firm, who then 'leases' the employee to your company on a full-time basis. As the client, you basically work alongside and treat the outsourced resource as your own employee. Like any standard employment arrangement, you would set the operational objectives of each employee, get them on board with your company's mission, manage their workload, and check their deliverables.

The outsourcing firm takes care of the hiring process, benefits, taxes, employee welfare, compliance, workstations, computers, and technology—while you, the client, simply focus on your team's operational aspects and deliverables.

Generally, with staff leasing, part of the setup process is to recruit the people that you need on your team. You can generally have as much input into hiring each resource as you desire. However, many clients leave most of the recruitment process to the staff-leasing provider, at least up to the short-listing stage of last-round candidates. The final interviews and testing can be conducted by the client, who then makes the final decision on which candidates are hired. Alternatively, clients can also leave the whole process up to the provider, but it is generally better to be involved in at least some part of the final hiring stages.

Ultimately, you have the choice and flexibility, which is the beauty of this model. It is basically the role of the outsourcing firm to make the job of finding and employing people much easier.

Once the person is hired, the BPO will provide staffing oversight regarding their HR, payroll, compliance, and basic supervision. They would also usually provide health insurance and most commonly cover the required 13th-month pay and other standard salary and pension contributions. Certainly, this is what should be happening. It's important to check who will be providing these and be clear of any of your obligations in this respect.

It is also prevalent for BPOs to provide a stimulating work environment and community vibe for the staff to make them feel as much 'at home' as possible. This might include regular social activities, and major social events such as Christmas parties, summer retreats, and karaoke nights. This has a dual benefit in that it keeps the staff happy and keen to work longer with the client, and it also means that the staff member will stay longer within the BPO, meaning the BPO will spend less resources on recruiting new people.

Many BPOs will monitor for shift punctuality and absenteeism, and some might even aid with training, skill development, and IT and hardware support among others. Some might also have established turnkey service templates such as customer service, Virtual Assistant, or bookkeeping procedures, which the client and employees can work from. However, the BPO is typically not 'involved' in the business function or output of the staff member. So, it is generally the client's job to train, oversee, and mentor their staff. It is also up to the client to set the tasks, assess the output, and teach them what they need to know.

However, if the staff member does not perform, then the client might speak with the BPO and ask for a replacement. At this point, the BPO would need to get increasingly involved to ensure that the client's concerns are accurate and attended to; however, they would also need to see that the staff member has been treated fairly and that due process is followed for replacement—if needed.

So as you can see, there is a considerable crossover of 'involvement' from both parties. Because of this codependence, it means that there is considerable 'blurring' of responsibilities—which can either be of great benefit or a big problem—depending on the results. This approach is very much a hybrid approach to hiring.

The BPO officially hires the employee, but they are basically, for all intents and purposes, an employee of your company. So you must treat and train them as you would any of your employees. If you are getting bad results, then you can't really blame the BPO, as they are effectively just providing a 'seat' and employment structure from which 'your' employee works. This do-it-yourself approach is in stark contrast to the comprehensive BPO model described above, where the people in the process are almost invisible, and it is the results and output on which the BPO is assessed and paid.

A Tight Partnership

With staff leasing, the BPO will become very involved in the staff member's legal, employment, payroll compliance, and basic welfare. But they generally do not get involved in the operational activities that the employee performs for you, the client.

This point here is worth emphasizing—and repeating. There is a division of responsibility for the outcomes, and this division can sometimes cause confusion, misunderstandings, or worse, between the BPO, the client and the employee.

To clarify, the BPO will look after the employment and welfare of the outsourced staff, but it is up to the client to manage the activities and deliverables of each resource. I refer to this division of responsibilities as a kind of 'co-parenting.' And this is where things can get a little complex. As with any co-parenting, it is almost impossible to draw a clear line of separation between inputs and responsibilities. There will inevitably be a lot of crossover of involvement and roles, causing a lot of gray areas.

For example, if an employee isn't performing well, is this the fault of the employee, the BPO provider, or the client? To add more context, let's use a scenario where a client wants to hire someone to sell 1,000 widgets. Someone is hired for the job, but they cannot sell the widgets, so the project fails. But what is the reason for the failure?

BPO Failure:

Possibly the BPO hired the wrong person, or the company's facilities or setup, for some reason, didn't allow the person to perform the necessary tasks well.

Employee Failure:

Alternatively, maybe the BPO was great, but the employee just didn't have the right skills, and they misrepresented themselves in the job interview.

Client Failure:

It could also be the case that the BPO did a fantastic job, and the hired employee was the best in the industry. But the client had never actually been able to sell any widgets previously and had no established process or training in place.

Product Failure:

Maybe the client was well organized, but the widgets they were expected to sell were defective and overpriced.

This example is overly simplified, but it hopefully illustrates the complexity of establishing any root cause of failure. In reality, business is a highly complex affair with millions of overlapping factors. Being successful at anything is by its nature very difficult and never guaranteed. So there can be many factors that contribute or lead to a failure. And so, it can be difficult to unpick the core reason for failure, and so it can get complicated when a client is unhappy with their results.

As a result, the co-management of employees can become complex, and it can sometimes be hard to define who is responsible for what. But don't let this concern put you off staff leasing. In general, the relationship is harmonious and works well. The beauty of the co-management concept is that the client can wholly focus on building their business with the staff they need. At the same time, someone else manages all of the complicated and time-consuming backend aspects of employment and facilities.

Staff Leasing Pricing Models

There are two distinct pricing models associated with the staff-leasing sector, which I will outline below. These different cost structures generally also impact, or at least should correlate with, the level of service and support that you receive from the BPO.

Transparent Pricing

The transparent pricing model is becoming far more common nowadays within outsourcing, which I believe is a good thing for the client. Most SMEs typically favor this model, not least because the name infers a lot more clarity and trust in the pricing structure. Generally, along with the transparency comes keener pricing and the lowest margins for the BPO intermediary.

The transparent pricing model means that you pay a certain set monthly fee to the BPO for the desk space, hardware, facilities, support, and services. And then a separate transparent amount for each employee's salary and overhead costs. Generally, the employees' salary—and any additional government-mandated employer contributions—are fully disclosed to the client and are passed along at cost, with no mark-up or margin.

So the BPO makes no margin on the employees' salary, and only makes money from their service fee component. This outsourcing service component is usually referred to as a 'service,' 'desk,' or 'seat' fee. At the time of writing, the seat fees for the Philippines market can range between $350 to $1,000 per month per person, depending on the BPO, where its located, and the range of support that they offer.

At first glance, these fees can sometimes seem steep, but it is easy to overlook exactly how much infrastructure and support they provide. Below is a list of services that you would commonly get within your service fee—as you can see, there is so much more than just a desk.

BPO Seat Fee Provisions:
- Dedicated work areas, including all standard office equipment, furniture, hardware, software, high-speed Internet connectivity, infrastructure redundancies, and resources.
- Facilities management, redundancy provision, and IT, hardware, and network support.
- The staff are legally employed by the BPO, including all associated liabilities and exposures, and they manage all of the payroll and compliance associated with employment.
- Staff welfare is managed by the BPO, including social functions, community building, and team bonding.
- Operations and quality management oversight and support.
- Employee search, selection, recruitment, and HR oversight— and performance management if employees need to be let go.
- Management support, training, and quality assurance of day-to-day operations.

Some BPOs might also offer operational oversight within their service fee, including:
- Operations and quality management.
- Service Level Agreements (SLAs) and Key Performance Indicators (KPIs).
- Shared support services.

People might also be surprised at the hard costs of setting up and running an A-grade office facility in the Philippines. The assumption that everything must be cheap in the Philippines is not necessarily the case, and in fact some things can be relatively expensive.

Metro Manila, the bustling capital city of the Philippines, is home to over 20 million people. The city generally has expensive land and property prices, and there is a shortage of available high-grade office space. Additionally, due to booming outsourcing growth and demand, the high-quality office space is relatively expensive.

Additionally, all utilities are generally costly in the Philippines, specifically the electricity and high-grade Internet connection. It is not uncommon for Internet and power interruptions, so BPOs have to invest considerable money into generators and redundancies that prevent any downtime. This all means that the electricity and internet bills for BPOs are generally enormous.

The Philippines might be a 'cheap country,' but fitting out an office to Western standards is almost the same price as in the West. The imported materials for a modern office fit-out are at least as expensive, if not more. Also, the cabling, networking, computers, and hardware are considerably more expensive due to tariffs and taxes.

When you consider all of these hard costs, the BPO service fees are good value, and are a great way to get you set up and started with an offshore team quickly and easily. It is easy to see the desk fee in an invoice and think that it is a lot of money to pay. But generally, it is easy to overlook the real and hard costs associated with setting up and maintaining facilities and connectivity and managing employment compliance.

In the West, typically the costs of employing someone can add another 45% on top of their salary, and this does not include the office space. Including the office space, the full auxiliary costs of employing someone can easily match the salary of that person— which is many thousands of dollars per month. It is generally easier to overlook each of these costs as they aren't shown in one itemized invoice each month, but the costs are real, and they are massive.

And Then There's the Salary

On top of the desk fee, you then pay your 'employee's' salary. And this is why it is referred to as 'transparent.'

The splitting of costs between the BPO services and the employee's salary means knowing exactly who is getting paid what. It also makes good business sense to split out the various costs.

For example, if you want to hire a cheap assistant or intern, then you know that their salary costs will be minimal. If you hire a senior professional, then you know that their salary will be high. However, regardless of the role and salary, the desk fee will remain the same for all roles. Having a transparent relationship with the employee's salary also enables you to manage your people's remuneration more easily. If you want to give someone a rise or pay them a bonus, you can, without it getting complicated.

Typically, attached to the salary are additional 'pass-through costs,' which cover a range of government-mandated contributions such as the employee's pension, healthcare, insurance, and 13th-month payments.

The labor laws and salary allowances are complex in the Philippines, so it pays not to get too involved in these things. However, it is important to know that these statutory benefits are being paid and that the employment is compliant with all labor law and government requirements.

Be aware of the '13th-month' pay, which is mandated by the government. This is an additional month's income, which employees are paid just prior to Christmas. This is a compulsory payment mandated by law, and is a minimal expectation by all employees in the country. The concept of the 13th-month pay understandably shocks most new clients, but it is very much standard. In fact, it's not unheard of for certain executive roles to negotiate for a 14th, 15th, and even 16th month as an additional incentive. Though, thankfully they are not too common.

It is common for there to be many additional benefits on top of someone's base salary. The labor laws are strict in the Philippines and are mostly in place to protect the poor and vulnerable workers across the broader population. This is a good thing, of course, but they aren't all that relevant to the relatively highly paid employees of the outsourcing industry as the allowances generally only add up to an extra few dollars each month.

The result is that there are many little allowances to account for and manage, which makes payroll a highly complex undertaking for the BPOs. On the upside, all of the benefits combined add up to very little when compared to a relatively 'good' Philippine salary. However, they do create considerable paperwork if you ever have to get involved in payroll yourself.

Seat Leasing Bundled Pricing

The bundled pricing model is typically similar to the transparent pricing model in terms of service provisions; however, the BPO charges the client one single flat monthly fee per employee. There is no transparency with the pricing and the client does not get to see how much goes to the BPO, and how much goes to the employee.

It is probably no surprise then that the BPOs that charge this way are usually making more margin than they would in a transparent model. They say where there is mystery, there is margin. This is not always a bad thing, though. If the BPO believes that their service can add value beyond the basic placement of an employee, then it is a fair argument, and they should feel free to charge accordingly for this value.

However, as with the transparent model, the employee would still be considered your employee in relation to their activities. The operational oversight from the BPO would typically be limited to the basic account management, payroll, and HR functions.

Generally, the BPOs that charge on a bundled price tend to offer, or at least claim to offer, a higher support and service level than a straight seat-leasing model. In this case, they might work closer with the client and employees to build out the operations and make sure that the team achieves their goals more effectively. In this respect, you should have an enhanced partner working alongside you to assist in operating your team, and this can sometimes be an invaluable partnership to have. However, the net value of this isn't always certain.

As mentioned, there are lots of variables that can influence the outcome of any offshore team, including: (1) The expertise of the BPO provider; (2) the quality of the staff that are recruited; and (3) the functions or roles that they're dealing with.

Generally, good BPOs can offer a supreme amount of experience and expertise in respect to building processes and getting the best out of remote teams. So a bundled service, ensuring a closely aligned partnership with aligned goals, can be an extremely valuable proposition—as long as you get the right partner at the right price.

If someone is charging a bundled price, you should expect to receive more operational support and possibly even get their proactive involvement in running your team's processes. For this reason, you might generally see more bundled pricing structures within more specialized BPO verticals such as those offering customer service, web development, accounting, animation, or game development services.

You would also commonly get a bundled price from telesales BPOs offering inbound or outbound sales solutions. Telesales is generally a very specialized area, and to be frank, you would be best to avoid managing yourself—unless it was a core function of your company. Telesales taps into a lot of industry knowledge and skill, advanced operations, and infrastructure. It is also a sector that's plagued with super high employee churn rates and low morale. If you want to test the efficacy of telesales in your business, but don't want to get sucked into its complexities, then a bundled rate with a trusted telesales BPO is probably a good option and could work out to be a fantastic partnership.

If you are looking to start outsourcing and find a great provider, then a bundled option is worth considering. But you might find it frustrating that your employees' salaries are not revealed to you, and it could cause issues as you scale.

Towards Commoditization

It is slightly sad but true, that as an industry starts stripping out the costs of a service, like in the transparent pricing model, it is in response to the sector maturing and becoming more commoditized. This process of service commoditization generally strips out all non-essential costs, and provides any additional service options as optional upsells. You can then add or remove services and employees as you see fit.

Common commercial examples of this are the low-cost airlines. Over the decades, much of the airline industry has moved from a luxury experience to a commoditized utility. The low-cost airlines emerged and have gradually reduced their service-offering and price to bare bones. You can, of course, add back extra services as you see fit, but they are typically set at a prohibitively high cost.

This is in some ways good, but it means that as the outsourcing industry matures and becomes more commoditized, we will see more and more 'no frills' service offerings. While this might present as a lower 'up-front' cost, it might equally result in poorer output and outcomes, which can ultimately cost you far more—money, time, and stress—over the long run.

3. Seat Leasing

Seat leasing is similar to staff leasing, but it is an even more hands-off approach. Typically, the seat-lease supplier provides the desk and associated infrastructure such as hardware, Internet, and the office environment. The client then provides their own staffing, and they manage their staff members in every respect, including payroll.

Seat leasing is often referred to as a turnkey office solution. It is ideal for foreign clients looking for a flexible alternative to renting or buying an office space and the need to buy expensive infrastructure to maintain their business. This setup is both efficient, user-friendly and enables companies to decrease or limit capital expenditures. It also allows them to concentrate on the more vital aspects of their business and have the less relevant backend infrastructure managed for them.

This model might suit an SME who has been outsourcing for a while, but wants a cheaper lower-service option. Since they have already been outsourcing, they have probably already built their team. They already have many processes in place, so can turn their attention to finding cheaper office solutions.

Alternatively, if someone has built a small team of remote freelancers, but now wants to formalize and build the team, they might find a seat-leasing partner who can provide the team's desk, office, and infrastructure.

Seat leasing is generally more expensive than standard office leasing options. However, the model provides done-for-you infrastructure and easy scalability. This means that as a company, you don't have to worry about any of the desks, cabling, Internet, utilities, or any of the massive upfront capital—and time—required to build out those things. It also means that if you need five seats one month, and then 200 seats the next month, you will be able to get this, and you will only be paying for what you need, when you need it.

4. Build-Operate-Transfer

A build-operate-transfer (B-O-T) model isn't necessarily an operational thing—it's more of a structural design that gives greater optionality and flexibility for future operational structures. In this respect, B-O-T provides the opportunity to switch between differently structured models, however, the B-O-T itself doesn't really impact the day-to-day operations. Allow me to explain...

The B-O-T model was born out of the realization that as clients progressed with their outsourcing journey, their needs changed as they grew. Every case is different, but generally, as time passes, clients would increase their team's sizes, and they would eventually require less supervision and support.

Typically, SMEs need a lot of support at the start of their journey as they start with very small or single-person teams. These factors are generally true at the start, but generally never the case a few years down the road. At the beginning, they are happier to pay more margin to the outsourcing firm, in return for extra support, infrastructure and guidance. The client receives enormous value from the outsourcing firm in the early stages as they help to set up the operation and processes, and guide them through the thorny learning curve of setting up an offshore team.

However, as they inevitably grow, they become progressively independent, need less oversight and support, and consequently start to look for a discount on fees. As they grow a bigger operation, build their team size and become increasingly self-sufficient, they start to question the value added by the outsourcing firm. The client can begin to see the outsourcing firm as an expensive intermediary, instead of the invaluable solutions provider they once were.

The client inevitably looks around and sees that they can save lots of money if they cut out the middle man by employing their staff direct and leasing their own office space.

However, the journey is by no means this simple, and the pros and cons of going it alone aren't always this clear-cut. Generally, it is not worth moving out on your own until you have at least 50 to 80 staff. But it is understandable that when a client has 20 staff with a BPO partner, they start to look at the monthly invoice and wonder if they can save significant money by going out on their own.

If a client grows to the level of 30 to 50 staff, they will typically start to seriously consider the alternatives. From there, some might then start the journey of incorporating their own entity in the Philippines and eventually moving out on their own.

As you can imagine, this is not a good outcome for a BPO. The journey means that if a BPO successfully builds a team for its client, then the client by virtue of this success is likely to leave the BPO. So, unfortunately, many BPOs work to resist, deter, or prevent this outcome. Many BPOs use contracts that include expensive tie-ins that make it very difficult for clients to leave.

Generally, when signing a contract, a shrewd client will look for the ability to terminate the contract and the costs of doing so, if things go wrong. However, they very rarely consider—at the beginning at least—the costs of terminating a contract if things go right. This small detail can trip up a lot of successful outsourcing endeavors. And so, it is not uncommon for BPOs to have very restrictive or costly clauses for the release and transfer of staff over to a new arrangement.

In short, BPOs usually try to lock people in and discourage them from leaving. Contractual tie-ins are not overtly malicious, and it is common in most businesses across most sectors to try and secure future income by some sort of tie-in. But it is something that you should be aware of when outsourcing. Ironically, if your outsourcing fails, then these tie-ins are not particularly relevant, and it is generally easy to depart from your outsourcing firm in this case. However, if your outsourcing is highly successful, then the tie-ins can become highly relevant and costly.

For example, you might have been outsourcing for three to four years and in that time have built an incredible multidisciplinary team that runs most of your business. At this point, it can become almost impossible to drop or change those staff as they are core and critical to your business. In fact, those people basically 'are' your business. And so it can become a little concerning when you realize that you don't have full control of those employees—from a legal perspective—and that you aren't able to port them over to a new structure if the need arose.

So while some BPOs still plot to lock in their clients covertly, other more progressive BPOs decided that it was better to help their clients traverse the different stages of their outsourcing journey, and so the B-O-T model was born.

You don't necessarily need to decide if you want to Build-Operate-Transfer from the start. However, if you choose a BPO that does not offer this option, it might be hard—or expensive—for you to transfer out if you eventually decide to follow this path. So you don't need to decide at the beginning of your journey, but it's generally wise to check if your BPO offers such services, or at least supports the notion of an eventual transfer-out.

If you do eventually find yourself venturing out on your own, the more comprehensive BPOs can generally offer and support many of the complex professional services associated with incorporating a company, managing the HR and payroll, and finding, leasing and renovating office space. If you ever find yourself wanting to move out on your own, then their assistance in this matter can be invaluable. It would help if you didn't underestimate the complexity, cost, time taken, and the mind-boggling level of bureaucracy associated with doing these sorts of things in the Philippines.

In short, here's how the B-O-T model works:

Build

During the build stage, the outsourcing company handles all administrative and legal matters, including setting up the infrastructure and office spaces and providing the personnel and other necessary resources.

Operate

During the operation stage, all administrative services including human resources, recruitment, training, finance, and accounting including expenses and payroll, facilities, IT support, and quality assurance are provided and managed by the outsourcing company.

Transfer

During the transfer stage—which may come after a few months, or more usually, a few years later—once the company determines that it can take on the entire operation as well as all the auxiliary activities that support the operation, the outsourcing company will help the client transition across to the new autonomous arrangements and essentially work to remove their own support services from the organization.

The B-O-T model offers ultimate freedom and flexibility, but it is not accurate to assume that transferring out of a BPO and becoming autonomous is the best option for all companies. Many businesses have offshore teams with hundreds or thousands of people, and they stay working with a BPO partner for years, and might even have them manage the operations in their entirety. Whereas an entrepreneur with a small team of five people, after just 12 months of outsourcing, might prefer to move out into their own facilities and manage their own operations. While there is no clear right or wrong approach, I would strongly suggest that people do not consider fully managing their own operation until they have at least 30 to 50 people on their team—and to leave it even later if they are high-growth or quickly evolving. It is very easy to underestimate the complexities and costs of going it alone.

If you're looking to transfer and set up your own company in the Philippines, my advice is not to incorporate too early. It is generally a huge pain to incorporate, set up a company, get a lease, and remain compliant in the country. It's also worth pointing out that you can't—legitimately—start to hire people, run a team, get a lease or internet connection, or buy hardware in the Philippines unless you first incorporate a company. And if you do decide to incorporate, then you will be thrown headlong into the dizzyingly bureaucratic world of Philippine red tape and paperwork.

In many countries, you can incorporate a company online in minutes. This is not the case in the Philippines. It is expensive, complex, and might take you six-to-nine months before you get all the approvals in order. It really is a bureaucratic slog. And the challenge doesn't end once you have incorporated. The obligations of running a company in the Philippines are intense. You have monthly, quarterly, and annual reporting, and submission requirements in order to remain compliant. It all takes a lot of work, and it's easy to get tripped up. For the uninitiated, it is extremely easy to make a few mistakes, which can come back to bite you many months or years later. They might seem minor at the

time, and indeed might be minor, but compounding fees, random
penalties, and the opportunity for corrupt officials to profiteer
could cost your business dearly and could even leave it in ruins.

And that is just the incorporation and basic compliance. When
going it alone, you also have exposure to the country's labor laws
and employment courts, local government permits, commercial
property leases, office fire hydrant scams, a Byzantine taxation
system, and almost unenforceable contract law.

This is why BPOs are so popular and so valuable. Put simply,
they shield you from all this faff. BPOs offer incredible value on
many levels. But if it were just for the fact that they protect you
and your business from the compliance quagmire, then this alone
would almost justify their full cost and render them invaluable.

Ironically though, people don't know what they don't know.
Most clients have no idea of the complexities, hidden costs, and
potential liabilities of incorporating and building a team offshore.
And neither should they; it's not their job. But this blissful
existence from within their stress-free BPO bubble can lead clients
to undervalue the unseen protection they get from the complexities
outside and underestimate the difficulties of going out on their
own.

Luckily, the outsourcing industry now offers a full spectrum of
service offerings. Everything from comprehensive outsourcing to
the lightest-touch leasing arrangements mean that you can tailor an
offshore team infrastructure to your specific preferences. There are
now endless design configurations available meeting any budget,
structural and operational guidelines.

For example, after outsourcing for a few years and having a
fairly stable team, you might want to remove as much of the BPO's
operational involvement as possible. It is possible to have your staff
employed by a third party, but you manage literally everything
else in this scenario. You can also sub-lease an office space, based
on square footage, instead of by the seat. Combining these two

activities leaves you with the most control, and you're paying the least possible margin to any intermediary. Yet, you don't need to worry about the employment complexities and liabilities yourself, and you don't need to incorporate. However, you would have to do your own recruitment, manage your own functional HR, and possibly arrange your own office furniture, computer hardware, and internet connectivity. This scenario is the closest proxy for standard employment and gives you the best price possible without getting into the complexities of doing business in a foreign developing nation.

Thirty years after its inception, there is now enormous flexibility within the industry. There are endless options, and you should, in theory, be able to scale up and down your services, facilities, and support as you need them. The key is to ensure that both your BPO and your agreement with your BPO allow you to tap into this flexibility, as your requirements evolve. In the beginning, try to take advantage of the incredible outsourcing infrastructure that is out there. It is fine to go it alone eventually, but it is much better to partner up with an experienced outsourcing firm as you start. They will likely make your offshore journey more successful and save you from unnecessary heartache and hassle.

Find the Right Partner

Finding the right outsourcing partner can be a consuming process for most. However, there are certain steps you can take to ensure that you find the right one for you. The following section outlines some steps you can take to create a shortlist of possible partners and the types of questions you can ask them as you begin to engage.

The BPO directory on the Outsource Accelerator website

catalogs over 3,500 BPOs globally. That's a lot of BPOs. There are a lot to choose from, and so its understandable that the vast array might get a little overwhelming.

Picking up the phone and having a conversation with a few of them is an invaluable exercise. You can learn an enormous amount about the industry and how outsourcing can help your business with a simple call, it can be really valuable, and I encourage you to try it. However, before you reach out to them, you can first take a look at their business and do a little tire-kicking—from the comfort of your laptop. You can find a lot of information about a BPO remotely through Outsource Accelerator's directory or by doing some quick research on Google. Let's take a look at some helpful indicators to consider.

Check to see if they have:
- A good website with reasonable domain authority and monthly traffic.
- A reasonable digital footprint of their company when you research them online—for this, check LinkedIn, Glassdoor, Facebook, Outsource Accelerator, and any other reputable third-party source that pops up in a Google search.
- Easy-to-understand pricing and menu of services with simple terms.
- A reasonable business size—or number of seats, relative to your requirement.
- A reasonable trading history and have been in business for at least a few years already.

Once you have identified some BPOs that seem to match your needs, you can reach out to a few of them. When you do, be conscious of their speed and quality of response.

When you talk to them, do they demonstrate:

- Good response times and processes when responding to your initial inquiry.
- An understanding of your business needs on a deeper level.
- The ability to answer more complex questions competently.
- Willingness to openly share information about their company—such as their size, years in business, and specialties.

If you get a good feeling from their initial responses, then it's time to pick up the phone and have a few conversations.

What to Ask a Prospective BPO Partner

There is a lot of value in just reaching out to several firms and having a call with their business development teams. Generally, the sales process with an outsourcing firm should feel consultative and not 'salesy.' You should have conversations with people who can understand your requirements and advise you accordingly. Their advice should be valuable and insightful and the pricing model should be clear and concise.

The success of outsourcing is more often less determined by the obvious big things like price and standard inclusions, and more by the many smaller and often overlooked nuances, like what are they like to work with and how competent are their responses. Getting on a call with people will allow you pick up on the unexpected details, go wherever the conversation takes you, and dive deeper into topics that resonate with you at the time. A call is much more powerful than a templated email response, RFP, or PDF proposal, so don't be afraid to get on the phone.

Once you have made several calls, you will have a lot more insight into outsourcing, the range of services available, the different approaches within the industry—and most importantly, some clear ideas on how it can specifically benefit your business. It can be highly educational just to speak to a few BPOs about what they do and how they do it. However, be mindful that these BPOs are ultimately all trying to sell to you, so a certain amount of their insight and advice will be angled to their benefit.

Once you have identified a shortlist of prospective partners, you will want to eventually settle on the right partner for your business. I have listed some of the things you should consider when making your decision.

1. **Business Goals**

   Share your short- and long-term business objectives with the BPO and see how they suggest that they can help. Are they responding to you with a rehearsed spiel and pricing schedule, or do they really understand your needs, and are they able to offer valuable insights and strategic solutions?

   Having close alignment with your outsourcing partner is absolutely critical to your offshore success. Outsourcing can have a profound impact on your business generally—so don't just treat your outsourcing partner like a simple contractor or vendor—they can be, and should be, much more than this. They really should be seen as a true partner. So make sure that the BPO is completely aligned with your mission and vision, and ensure that you are able to have a sophisticated conversation with someone at the firm who can talk to you on your level, understands your needs, and knows what you're going through. This strategic empathy can be invaluable over the long term as both of your businesses evolve over the ensuing years of the partnership.

2. **Size**

   Make sure you're aware of the size of the BPO and whether they have any specializations—although, it is not necessarily better to have a big or small BPO partner. The best size would depend on your own company size and outsourcing requirements. You can find good BPOs with 100 staff, however, I would suggest that this is right on the lower end of acceptable. Conversely, the biggest BPOs have literally hundreds of thousands of staff, spread across dozens of countries. If you are a small company, requiring just a few people, then the big players would most certainly not be a suitable option. In fact, they probably wouldn't work with you unless you start with 200-plus roles.

Conversely, a small BPO with 100 to 1,000 staff can offer a far more personalized experience. You might also get more interaction with the executive team and be able to leverage their experience. However, you have to be careful that they have all the requisite infrastructure and processes to ensure that you get a smooth, trouble-free operation. There are a lot of startup BPOs in the sector—and while they might be enthusiastic, personable, and give a great pitch—their infrastructure might be lacking and might not yet have a full grasp of the many complex fundamentals required to run a solid BPO.

A mid-range BPO might have 5,000 to 30,000 staff. Companies of this size would typically have far better infrastructure and systemization of processes. However, they would generally focus more on the mid-market to enterprise level clients, and they would not give a smaller account so much attention. Much of the success of an account relies on the proficiency of the account manager that is allocated to your case. If the account manager is young and inexperienced, which is more common in these bigger firms, then it could have consequences for your team's success.

If you are looking to build a team of 20 seats in three months, a BPO with 100 seats will bite your arm off for the opportunity, but they would likely struggle to properly fulfill the requirement. Whereas, if you took this offer to one of the giant BPOs, they probably wouldn't be interested, it would be far too small for them. So take time to find the right-sized partner for your needs.

3. Specialization

Spend time to understand what the BPO's key areas of specialization are. Most BPOs are generalist in nature, especially those that offer the staff and seat leasing models. So for many BPOs, it doesn't really matter much if you need to hire an admin assistant, an accountant, or a rocket scientist.

The typical model is that the BPO will recruit staff according to your specifications and get ultimate approval of the candidate from you before they hire. Since the day-to-day work is between you and the employee, then the BPO only needs to have generalized good practices around facilities, recruitment, employee engagement, and HR to do a good job.

However, you will find that most BPOs do have a few areas where they have found good results and have a lot of clients with these similar needs. If your requirement falls into that area, you will probably hear a lot about it on your first introductory call. They will trumpet their experience and knowledge of the sector and provide many examples of current clients. Alternatively, if they don't have a lot of experience in your particular field, they will default back to the spiel that they can hire any staff you need according to your specifications.

It might seem that it is better to have a lot of direct experience, but it doesn't really make much difference in practice. For example, some clients think that if the BPO already has a lot of digital marketing roles then having that experience will be transferable and help their team get up to speed faster and do their work better. In reality though, each client and their team is completely separate from one another, and while the staff may work from within the same facility, they are very much separate to each other in terms of their work.

At first glance, this might seem silly, but it makes perfect sense if you think about it. Each client account is separate. Different clients are running their businesses in different ways, and they might even be handling confidential information, proprietary processes, or developing some market-leading intellectual property. For example, if a BPO has a lot of SEO agencies as clients, then it is important to each of the agencies that their secrets and methods of success are not shared with their competitors. For this reason, there should be operational firewalls between the workers.

If you are looking for a full-service BPO solution that offers comprehensive management of your processes, this is a different story. It is then essential that the BPO has direct experience in your vertical and with the role they will be fulfilling. Not only should they be able to show experience, but they should be able to demonstrate advanced understanding and strategic insights into the process that you're discussing. For example, if you are looking to outsource your customer service function for your real estate firm in the UK, then the BPO should not only be an expert in customer service management, but they would also ideally have experience in the real estate sector and also have a reasonable exposure to UK clients.

4. **Financial Stability**
Make sure that the BPO is financially stable and has been doing business for a few years at least. Outsourcing is now highly competitive and margins are getting squeezed. You don't want to get your operation involved in a BPO that is on the way down. It is unlikely that a BPO would share their financial statements with you directly, so try to get an idea of their financial position through certain proxies like the number

of 'seats' they have and the number of years they have been in business.

5. **Cultural Compatibility**

You and your outsourcing partner will want to share good business- and cultural compatibility. This ensures that the BPO and the employees on your team have a good understanding of, and alignment with, your company function, values, and culture.

It's not uncommon for BPOs to specialize in certain clients from certain regions. For example, many BPOs might have mostly Australian clients; others might have mostly US or UK clients. If you are from Australia, it may benefit you to go to a BPO used to working with Australian companies. It can significantly smoothen your journey, as the employees of the BPO will also no doubt be used to working with Australian customers more, which could improve your own customer's experience.

So be upfront about digging into the core competencies of your BPO suitor. If the BPO typically serves Chinese online casino clients, this will be a less than ideal fit for you if you're an Australian florist.

6. **Communications, Technology, and Infrastructure**

With the development of cloud computing and innovations in outsourcing, it has become easier to build remote teams and work internationally. However, because of the reliance on communications and technology, your BPO must have sufficient internet bandwidth, infrastructure redundancy, and backup systems. Check that the BPO has all of the infrastructure you require, and at least ensure that they have sufficient internet speed and bandwidth for your requirements. Be mindful that the Internet is generally much slower in the

Philippines and considerably more expensive. Generally, BPOs will need to spend a lot of money to secure a dedicated line, more bandwidth, and maintain fail-safe and redundancies—so make sure this is all in place, and even ask to test the services before signing up.

If you require any special software or hardware, make sure that the BPO is aware of this early on and work it into their pricing. For example, if you need specific phone equipment, CAD software, powerful video-editing computers, or huge bandwidth to send video files back and forth, it is essential that you establish these requirements and costs from the start.

7. **Record and Experience**

Ask for references and possibly even talk to existing clients of the BPO.

Generally, most BPOs will bristle up if you ask for references. So don't be too concerned if you get a cold response initially. Outsourcing is a somewhat unusual industry in that clients generally aren't always open about their use of outsourcing services, and the firm might be managing commercially sensitive activities. So there is good reason for strict confidentiality of clients.

Many BPOs, and specifically Filipino companies, will begrudgingly give out any details of other clients. They might say that the clients want to remain anonymous, which is plausible and not completely unreasonable. However, it is mostly never always the case in all cases. So if BPOs don't openly offer references from existing clients, I would suggest pushing them a little, and if they don't relent, you can move on.

Also, if you are still in the tire-kicking phase of your search, then don't expect that a BPO will allow you to go and bother all of their clients. I generally suggest that BPOs share their references with clients as the last final step before signing up.

So this means that the prospective client has to be completely happy with all other aspects of the proposal and be ready to sign up, and it is at that point, some references can be shared and contacted.

8. Cost-Efficient and Flexible

First, assess the BPO to see if they are cost-effective with your initial requirement. Then, try and see if they will adjust their pricing as you scale up with them. If you take 5, 10, or 15 seats, are they willing to discuss discounts? And what would the price be if you took 100 seats? Also, would they support you in case of a Build-Operate-Transfer scenario? It is valuable to establish these things right at the onset, so that you'll have a rough estimate of how much more you can save once the company grows.

9. Transfer and Exit Costs

What, if any, are the exit costs if you want to either terminate your agreement early or if you want to leave the BPO and take your team with you eventually? It is important to check this right at the start, even if you never expect to leave.

10. Reliability

Ask for full details on the company. How long have they been in business? How many employees are there? How many offices? What are their backup measures for natural calamities like flooding or typhoons? What is their history and experience in the business? Who and where are the employees located if they have multiple offices?

11. Terms

Make sure you document the terms of the project, including the payment, project assumptions, timing, and guidelines for any type of agreement. Of course, the majority of this should be captured within the contract and service level agreement (SLA), but make sure any more subjective intangibles are also written down and agreed upon.

12. Risks

What kind of risks are involved when outsourcing this project? Is the BPO insured for client loss and to what extent? What have they implemented to prevent data loss and ensure backups, firewall security, and regulatory compliance?

13. Turnaround Time

The setup and integration period is a critical time for all involved. Expectations and tensions can run high initially, and new clients are generally excited to get started as soon as possible. It's critical to be realistic with your timelines here. If you want a team of five people to be set up in two days, then you're probably going to be disappointed. Also, if a BPO is telling you that they can find you five great staff in two days, I would suggest being skeptical.

Ensure that the BPO sets realistic deadlines and goals, especially when it comes to the recruitment and screening process. Be reasonable, and see to it that their resources aren't operating on a timeline that may affect the project's outcome and quality. If you demand a super-fast ramp-up period, then it might just result in the BPO rushing the recruitment process and hiring the first candidates that come along. This is not a good result for anybody.

14. Other Considerations

Other things you might want to consider, or ask, might include:
• What separates the company apart from other offshore outsourcing companies?

- What are the escalation procedures if things go wrong?
- What are the educational requirements for employees, and what internal training programs and support are available?
- What employee retention, welfare, and community initiatives are in place?
- Can the BPO scale up quickly? How quickly?
- Are the staff recruited specifically for the client requirements, or are they taken from an existing employee pool?
- What is the company's process for recruiting roles, and what are the costs?
- What is the process for removing and replacing an underperforming employee?
- What measures are in place to protect the client's intellectual property concerning information and data?
- What is the policy for Build-Operate-Transfer, or what are the fees or charges if you want to transition your staff away from the BPO?

Make It a Fair Fight

It is important to remember that when you choose to partner with a BPO, you will generally be working very closely with their people for a very long time to come. Your future staff will be sitting in their office space, and they might all have significant oversight of your business and heavy involvement in your day-to-day operations. So it's important that you aren't too aggressive with your initial investigations and negotiate too hard on the prices and terms. Be gracious throughout the process and allow some give and take. Be willing to lose a battle or two in order to win the war.

Negotiating terms with your BPO is very different from the approach you might adopt with a car dealer. When buying your next car, you have full permission to use whatever tactics necessary to screw every last penny out of that salesperson. Other than living with your own moral compass, you probably won't see the salesperson again, and once you have your car, your relationship is over.

This is absolutely not the case with your BPO partner. Once you have negotiated terms, signed the agreement, and got started, then it is from that point that the rubber hits the road and the relationship actually begins. You need to ensure that the agreement is truly a win-win for all parties involved. If you negotiate hard to secure low service fees, and possibly low salaries for the staff, then you might have won in the short term, but this will backfire on you if there simply isn't enough money to run the project properly. It is a 'fools economy' if you get a seemingly low price, but it leaves the BPO or their staff, unhappy, or worse yet, unprofitable.

Also, be realistic about your value to the BPO. Hiring two to three full-time employees is a big occasion for some business owners. However, for many BPOs, that might already employ hundreds, or hundreds of thousands of staff, the additional two to three employees is just another day at the office. It is saddening to see too many Western business owners approaching Philippine BPOs with a puffed-out chest and a big ego demanding ridiculous discounts and extra concessions for one or two full-time employees. For that client, hiring a few employees may be a big step, and an even bigger ego boost, and so they let everyone know about it. This is the wrong approach to outsourcing and it certainly won't benefit your cause.

A successful outsourcing partnership requires firm but fair expectations, mutual respect, and an appreciation for a win-win outcome for you as the client, the BPO, and your future offshore staff.

4.2.3

Contracts and Service Level Agreements

Getting What You Want

Contract law is obviously very broad and complex generally. It becomes even more thorny when you are dealing with a foreign company from an obscure legal jurisdiction, with whom a significant number of your core staff may be employed, for a total lifetime value of many millions of dollars. The beginning of the outsourcing journey can be a daunting prospect for many businesses, and this is certainly most amplified at the contract signing stage. It can get complicated.

Luckily for the author, and maybe even the reader, exploring this issue in full is well beyond the remit of this book. However, I would like to briefly introduce the process and some guiding considerations below. As a caveat, I am definitely not a lawyer or acting in any such capacity. So I ask that you take this section with a pinch of salt, and proceed only after using your own best judgment.

Don't Overcomplicate

If you treat the beginning of outsourcing as a major life-changing decision, it can easily become complex and overwhelming. If you focus too much on the uncertainty and possible downside risks, then you could be making a mountain out of a molehill and things might never get started.

So I strongly recommend that you don't overthink the process and to some degree, just get started. Of course, you'll need to take reasonable precautions and properly assess the situation, but I would, on balance, suggest that you should not overthink nor overanalyze things in this regard.

To limit downsides and mitigate exposure, the easiest and most immediate remedy is to: start small.

Of course, if your company has 1,000 staff, and your initial foray into outsourcing involves 200 seats, then you will need to properly review contracts, service level agreements, and seek expert advice. But even if your company is as big as that, I would suggest that maybe you adjust your plan to reduce the initial scope of launch to just a handful of people, and in return, the risks are mitigated and you can get started sooner. In lieu of extensive due diligence, why not start by offshoring a small team of three to five people? This will quickly and relatively cheaply get you some fantastic first-hand experience and expose you to many aspects of outsourcing, and the outsourcing firm, that you would never have had insight into otherwise.

For a smaller company, it is also best to start small and grow your team organically. Taking this approach allows you to refine your strategies and tweak your rollout as you learn more about what's ahead of you, once you are on the road. Also, starting small mitigates your risks, which minimizes the stress of ensuring that the contracts and SLAs are absolutely spot on and stone-clad. After all, it's hard to negotiate a tough but fair contract when you don't really know what you're getting yourself into. In most cases, you don't know what you don't know and only experience can really fill in those knowledge and comprehension gaps. You might be negotiating hard for things initially, which you might soon want to change once you have a better understanding of the reality of outsourcing.

Laying the Proper Foundations

I don't want to be too cavalier with my approach. While I urge you not to over-analyze and over-negotiate your terms, I do suggest that you pay them due attention.

If I were to suggest looking out for and doggedly pursuing one thing in your agreement, it would be that it provides you with as much flexibility for future development as possible. But what does this flexibility mean in practice? If I were to summarize the key angles of optimal flexibility, I would suggest that you look out for and negotiate based on the considerations below:

1. **Build-Operate-Transfer**
    See if the BPO offers 'Build, Operate, Transfer' (B-O-T) rights and/or support. You don't necessarily need to sign up for it now, but ideally, they will support this process if you eventually decide to go down this route. Failing the above, at least have a clear and stated understanding of the costs or clawbacks, if you ever want to terminate your contract early and/or take the team you have built away from the BPO.

2. **Contract Terms**
    Be aware of minimum contract terms and tie-ins. Again, the obvious choice is to seek as much flexibility as possible.

3. **Recruitment**
    Recruitment can sometimes be slow and sticky. So be aware of their commitment to recruitment. Try and arrange an SLA

clause in respect to this. However, proceed with caution when setting performance expectations in contractual stone. For example, if you negotiate hard for the BPO to provide any new staffing needs within an unrealistic time frame, then the BPO will simply be forced to cut corners and place inadequate staff into your account. Recruiting great staff can be a complex and time-consuming process, and this is especially the case if you're recruiting in-demand roles. So it is valuable to have a reasonable and balanced approach to this function.

4. **Termination of Employees**
Be aware of your ability to terminate non-performing employees. The labor laws are very strict in the Philippines, so the hands of BPOs are somewhat tied in terms of their conduct. It can sometimes be hard to dismiss someone even in cases of gross misconduct. How different BPOs handle this process are extremely varied—some take full responsibility for the performance management and separation of staff. In contrast, others might pass all the labor law obligations onto you, the client. So, in short, check out the BPO's policies and procedures—for your navigation of the labor laws—for the performance management, onboarding, and termination of employees.

5. **Service Level Agreements**
Be very careful when setting service level agreements (SLA) and key performance indicators (KPIs). Don't spend too much time upfront negotiating on tough SLAs and KPIs. For one, the Philippines are veteran experts in the KPI field, and so they could usually run circles around less experienced parties—if they were so inclined. Secondly, KPIs, targets, goals, and any metrics can be manipulated to suit either party. For example, if a KPI is to make 100 phone calls per day, the BPO could

ensure that this is achieved; however, they might compromise call length, call quality, and could even cause damage to your brand or reputation in striving to achieve this KPI. So, be careful what you wish for.

6. **Win-Win**

Any negotiations have to be sustainable and a win-win for all parties. Typically, a BPO becomes a close operational partner, so you need to start things off well, and both parties will need to be able to profit from the interaction. In fact, for the arrangement to work, the BPO—and the BPO staff who will be working for you—all have to benefit from the terms of the engagement. So don't battle too hard at the start on price or terms so that you destroy any goodwill and end up with a begrudging partner.

Like any long-term partnership—even marriage—the relationship will develop over time. Both of your needs will likely evolve over the many months or years ahead of you. In fact, you probably have zero visibility on exactly what you will need and how it needs to be delivered a few years down the track. And if you aren't sure what you will need, then it will be pretty hard for the BPO to know and cater to those future needs. So flexibility is king, alongside the conscientious development of a mutually beneficial and understanding partnership with your BPO.

Is It Safe?

The Philippines is generally a very safe place to do business. This is especially the case if you're working from within the protected 'air-bubble' confines of a reputable BPO. And this is even more the case, if that BPO is working from within one of the main 'air-bubble' central business districts of Makati, BGC, or Ortigas in Metro Manila—or the IT parks of Cebu, Davao, or Baguio.

The Philippines is indeed a developing economy, and like any country and any business dealings, there are some unscrupulous parties. However, I can honestly say, hand on heart, that I have found the vast majority, if not all, of the business dealings and business people I have been involved with in the Philippines to be upfront, uncomplicated, and honest.

However, I do caution that the Philippines can most definitely be highly bureaucratic and any process can involve a huge amount of red tape. If you expose yourself to the external bureaucracy of the country, then you can get quickly and easily bogged down— and once you're in the bog, it's hard to get out. The Philippines is bureaucratic for everyone but can become especially so if you are identified as a foreigner. Once identified as such, you can find that the endless official red tape is augmented further, and things can become very slow indeed.

From what I understand and have read, there is a reasonably high amount of corruption, bribery, and payoffs in the country. This is a deep-seated custom, and one of such complexity that I can't begin to comprehend nor explain. However, I have never generally seen any overt corruption in my personal dealings. I would suggest that it is generally not something that you should fear. Again, this is most certainly the case if you build an offshore team from within the safe confines of a reputable BPO. However, if you opt to step outside of the cushy BPO environment, things don't necessarily become corrupt by default, but they can quickly get complex.

As a foreigner, a simple sanity and survival tip is to stay well away from the coalface of negotiations. The trick is to, wherever possible, avoid all operational and structural dealings yourself. Labor is cheap in the Philippines, so if you need to get involved in any bureaucracy, it is best to avoid getting directly involved. Try to ensure that someone else is 99.9% managing all the external activities as your proxy. In this respect, it is important to find a good solicitor that can help advise you in any dealings and help you navigate the environment. It is important to remember that the Philippine business and legal environment is very different to the native environment that you are already familiar with. When you are working from within a BPO bubble, it is very easy to become complacent and take for granted how easy everything is. It quickly becomes a very different world once you choose to step out on your own. And once you step out, it's not always so easy to step back in.

There is a lot to learn about doing business in the Philippines and it can take you many painful years to learn how to navigate its many complex official and unofficial bureaucracies. My suggestion then is that you generally do all you can to avoid it completely—for as long as you can. If you feel brave and become emboldened to go out on your own after a while, try and remind yourself that dealing with endless bureaucracy is not your core commercial activity.

You and your business are most effective if you concentrate on your company's high-value and core activities. You and your staff can do your best work, if you are insulated from all external noise and complication so that you have the space to just concentrate on the critical and key value-add tasks. Navigating Philippine bureaucracy is likely not, and never will be, one of these core tasks. So do everything you can to avoid it. The Philippines is a lovely place, it is friendly and inviting. But don't become complacent and think that 'doing business' in the Philippines is as streamlined and transparent as it is in your own home country—it most certainly is not.

Fortunately, BPOs, and the outsourcing industry generally, provide the safe bubble that you need. It is one of the many central—and most easily undervalued—functions of a BPO to shroud you from all of the backend complexities and external goings-on related to running facilities and employing staff. BPOs even de-hassle the HR component of running a large team of people. The enormous value-add of a BPO is that they allow you to just concentrate on training your team, and best optimize your core competencies and tasks.

Judge a Book By Its Cover

In summary, the Philippines is a safe and great place to do business. But don't kid yourself that it isn't a developing nation, and as a result, complex and highly bureaucratic.

Thus, the best way to form an office in the Philippines, is to do so from within the coddled supported environment of a BPO—at least at the beginning. Aside from shrouding you from the country's bureaucratic hubbub, they commonly handle all of your recruitment, HR, employee welfare, and payroll. In every way, they protect you from the many high-touch, high-complexity, but low-contributory activities associated with running a business. And so my best suggestion to you is to let the BPO deal with all the local bureaucracy, employment, compliance, facilities, and infrastructure, while you just get on with 'your job' of running your business.

It's important to do due diligence on your potential BPO partner. As mentioned, a successful BPO relationship will likely last many years, and they can become a close ally of your business. So choose well, as it can be a pain to switch BPO providers later on.

Without wanting to simplify it too much, my rule of thumb is to 'judge a book by its cover.' If a BPO can tick most of the boxes I mentioned earlier, then they're probably pretty reliable. I say this because the sector is by now a pretty mature and reliable sector. The outsourcing industry is well established, highly competitive, and has reasonably low margins, so any con artists and underperformers generally don't survive too long.

There are, of course, good and bad providers within the

spectrum—as is the case with any company or service provider in any market or country. So do your homework, but don't overthink it.

It is easy to get hung up on selecting the best BPO provider in the world. However, it is not necessarily the BPO itself that determines the success or failure of a particular project. For example, consider that you do find the best BPO firm ever, but you might happen to be allocated to a poor-performing and inexperienced account manager. Or maybe the account manager is great, but your initial employees by chance turn out not to be the best hires. Again, these are all common scenarios, which can be found in any aspect of life and business. There are a lot of potential points of failure, and also any new process might take a certain amount of trial, error, improvement, and iteration. This is all normal. So try to have faith in the process, and don't throw in the towel too early if you're met with initial unsatisfactory progress.

A Contract and an SLA

A contract is the primary written agreement between you and the other party—in this case, the BPO. This legally-binding document details the approach, services, duration, resources, and costs of doing business together.

Meanwhile, the service level agreement (SLA) is often an independent document that defines the minimum service levels you will receive as part of the engagement. It outlines what service levels are acceptable and the corresponding consequences if these levels are not met. It should also spend time to clearly define each service and the basis of which each service is measured for performance.

A separate SLA document enables you to review, revise, and iterate the performance objectives of a team without having to alter the core contract. This allows the team's performance objectives to be more easily iterated over time without undermining the core agreement about the basic foundations—such as costs, facilities, and employment. Keeping the two agreements distinct helps reduce the administrative strain of regularly reviewing contracts, while enabling operational agility.

Contracts and SLAs come in all forms and most are designed to be customized for each particular client. Below are some critical items that should be covered in either the contract or the SLA:

1. **What You Get**

   There should be a comprehensive list of what your support agreement covers including what kinds of infrastructure, facilities, software and hardware are included, as well as the nature of the employment of the staffing.

   The agreement should also identify the level of operational support you will receive. First, second, and third-line support tiers can reveal an organization's foresight and capability in handling issues with differing levels of complexity or difficulty.

2. **What You Don't Get**

   A good agreement should also identify any exclusions or limitations of the partnership. This is basically the things that are not included, but might possibly be required. It's natural for companies to leave out certain items from the services they provide. This might include IT issues outside of your service provider's control, specific hardware requirements or upgrades, or operational downtime due to natural calamities.

3. **How Long You Will Wait**

   The 'response time' refers to the time taken for the support provider to recognize and respond to the issue you have raised.

   The 'resolution time' refers to the time taken to fix the issue.

The response time is commonly defined within the SLA, but the resolution time can change depending on the difficulty and severity of the problem. Many agreements will have a list of response and resolution times relative to different levels of priority or issue severity.

4. **What You Have To Do**
Check for conditions or responsibilities that you have to follow to honor your side of the contract. This may include things such as:

- Identifying any system requirements that need to be put in place before the contract starts.
- Getting approval from the IT support before making changes to your system.
- Having a designated person in your team in charge of collaborating with the provider.
- Meeting minimum standards for security and safety.
- Employee welfare and performance management reporting requirements.
- Invoice payment schedule and implications of delayed payment.

5. **What It Costs**
The bottom line is pricing. Knowing what you are paying, for exactly what you are getting, is critical. Is the support price calculated per seat, per employee, per incident, or per day? Do you have a fixed monthly bill or pay-as-you-go credits? Don't forget to check for hidden costs such as excess charges for special conditions or additional personnel. Are these agreed in advance, or on a case-to-case basis?

6. The Price of Exiting

Time will come when a client might decide to finish operating for any reason, transfer to a different provider, or to incorporate the outsourced personnel into their company and move out from the current provider. There is usually a cost involved with doing this, as the provider will be losing both the staff and the client with any of these decisions.

Also, bear in mind that the staff are real people, and have rights to a stable employment and fair treatment if their employment finishes. There are costs and considerations associated with the separation of employees as defined by the labor laws of the land, as well as any administrative costs and fees associated with the terms of the BPO agreement. Be sure that all of this is laid out clearly in the contract. Ensure that all costs and conditions are clearly identified from the beginning.

Payment Considerations

If you set up an offshore operation, you will likely be paying a large amount of money regularly to a foreign business in a foreign currency. Making international payments used to be quite difficult, however, things have gotten much easier over the last few years. Most outsourcing firms should now offer easy payment solutions. It is certainly worth exploring the expected payment methods before you engage with a provider.

It is worth noting that the payment systems in the Philippines are quite antiquated. Many of the standard payment platforms available in most countries are not yet available in the Philippines. This is quickly changing though.

Bigger BPOs will ensure that payment processes are easy, cheap, and convenient, however, this is not the case for all. To avoid over-complicated payment processes, ensure that you clarify the options from the start. The setup for each will vary depending on who you are talking to.

If you are doing business with an established BPO, then you will want to pay just one payment monthly—regardless of the size of your team, or the number of individual activities you have in each month. Payroll is super complex in the Philippines, so a singular monthly payment to a BPO provider—especially if you have a large team—is worth its weight in gold.

Ideally, you want to be able to spend time on your business and not worry about making numerous small payments for a load of small invoices to a troop of employees or contractors. If you are using a standard means of international money transfer, then the fees and unfavorable currency exchange rates can end up costing you many thousands of dollars annually. It is worth exploring better and cheaper ways of paying your provider. Once set up, they can be incredibly quick, easy, and cheap to maintain.

It is also worth considering that if you pay for your services by credit card, then you will have an extra layer of security if there is any fraud or non-delivery of services. Credit cards generally insure all payments, under most conditions. This might not be relevant after the first few months of service, but it could be a valuable asset in the early days of exploring a new offshore partnership.

Currency Exchange

All currencies have a certain amount of volatility and the Philippine peso (PHP) is no exception. The entirely export-based BPO industry is vital to the Philippine economy and is heavily impacted if the exchange rates for the Peso get too expensive. So many stakeholders pay close attention to the Philippine Peso-to-US Dollar exchange rates. The US is the major buyer of Philippine outsourcing services, and so the USD is most commonly tracked, but all other major currencies are considered.

When the prices start to get expensive, it erodes outsourcing's primary competitive advantage—which is cost savings—and so the industry starts getting uncomfortable. However, the Philippines has remained politically and economically stable for many decades and the Peso and its inflation rate has followed suit.

If your company is spending millions of dollars on offshore salaries each year, then a movement of 10% to 20% on the exchange rate can have a big impact. Within a period of the last two to three years, the Peso has moved about 15% against the US Dollar, 17% against the British Pound, and 42% against the Australian Dollar. However, the peaks and troughs generally average out over the medium term. So keep the exchange rates in mind but don't spend too much time worrying about currency fluctuations.

Many BPOs might offer to invoice you in your local currency. This is especially the case if it is a US-owned BPO serving a US client, or an Australian BPO serving an Australian client, for example. However, all costs generally occur in the Philippines—for salaries, facilities, and general overheads—so exposure to the Philippine Peso can not be completely avoided. If BPOs do offer a local-currency invoicing option, the contract might have a clause allowing for adjustments in case of significant currency fluctuations—so keep an eye out for this.

If you plan to have a big team in the Philippines, then it might be worth looking into some currency hedging options. There are plenty out there, usually offered by banks and currency providers, but they are generally pretty advanced and aren't worth the complexity unless you deal in big numbers.

4.2.4

Inquire, Negotiate, Hire!

A Gentle Entry

I have suggested above that with outsourcing, you should 'just get started.' In doing so, you will learn a lot of skills and gain valuable insights—just by setting up and managing your first offshore employee.

However, not everyone is ready to jump straight in and get started. And to be fair, employing someone, offshore or otherwise, is a pretty significant commitment—on both a financial and operational level. So there are some options to get you started with a little less risk, less commitment, and less cost.

An easy and common stepping-stone to get started is using a freelancer or virtual assistant, sourced from a freelancer site or VA agency. This person start part-time and eventually move up to a full-time role. They might even be able to transfer into a BPO facility as your team grows. While I don't think this is the best way to build an offshore team, it certainly minimizes the risks involved. It also offers a cheaper, more gradual way to test the waters, and iterate your approach—and so I do see some value in this option.

This approach is easy and gently introduces you to outsourcing while exposing you to the lowest possible cost and risk. If you are cautious or uncertain, this might be a good approach to getting started.

The downside with this model is that it might not allow for an easy or natural expansion of your team. It would be a shame if the freelancers you have hired won't transition to become full-time staff in your team. Or they might want to stay home-based when your ideal vision is to have your entire team sitting within a centralized office. It would be a shame if the remote team were scattered around the country and wouldn't be a part of the maturing office and business.

Obviously, every approach has its own pros and cons; however, just like building a team anywhere in the world, it takes a great deal of time to train and develop your people. If you have invested considerable time into training your remote team, it would be a shame to lose all of this organizational learning if you have to later let them go just because they don't align with the next step of your expansion plan.

Thus, planning for your future early on, and laying foundations that support your future direction, makes great sense.

Compared to a part-time freelancer, the formal BPO option is certainly more expensive. As I mentioned earlier in this book, you would need to pay both the salary and desk fees (i.e., recruitment, guidance, and expertise) right off the bat. You will generally be expected to hire a full-time person instead of a per-hour freelancer, and in many cases, a BPO will want you to sign a minimum 12-month contract. However, the total costs compared to hiring someone in your own country are generally pretty attractive, and if you have reasonable ambitions to grow your business, starting out with a BPO might be your best option.

BPOs can assist you greatly with your outsourcing journey. It's within a BPO's interests to see you succeed and expand. So you might be even more successful on both your journey and in your business simply as a by-product of choosing a well-suited BPO partner from the start.

If and when you have mastered early-stage outsourcing and do want to scale, then most BPOs should be able to scale your operation from one person to 100 effortlessly, as needed. The considerable upside with this optionality is that you only pay for desk space when you need it—there are few excess or unattributed overheads. This makes scaling your team and business highly cost-effective and incremental, and is just one of the many extra profound perks of outsourcing.

Inquire, Negotiate, Hire!

Finding a suitable long-term partner for your outsourcing future is a critical part of the puzzle. It is probably one of the biggest predictors of long-term success and could even make or break your outsourcing experience. So choose wisely, and make sure that the partnership is a win-win. However, don't overthink it at the start, try to minimize the downsides, start small, and do it now.

Try to enter the partnership with an open and considerate mindset while ensuring reasonable allowances for future flexibility.

Consider that your chosen BPO will be working closely beside you for at least the next five years—and they will accompany you through some of the most vital growth phases that your business might ever go through.

Once you have a team in a BPO, it's generally a sticky relationship, and it's a pain to switch once you're there. Equally, incorporation and moving out 'on your own' is tough, even when you have the full support of your BPO. So finding a good BPO to help you along your journey can be a vital and valuable ingredient in your outsourcing endeavor and business success.

Action is Essential, Experience is Irreplaceable

You cannot learn what you need to learn just by reading books or completing courses. Establishing an outsourced function within your business will prove to be one of the biggest learning curves you'll ever have—maybe second only to your initial entrepreneurial journey.

A BPO partner can be an invaluable aid throughout your journey. They generally have a huge amount of expertise in the areas of offshore staffing, employee management, and operational design and delivery, and you can benefit greatly from their support and guidance. So heed their advice, and show appreciation for their involvement.

Time to Hire!

Now that you have a better understanding of how outsourcing can help change the way you do business, it's now time to start working with your offshore team!

Learning is great, but applying what you're learning is so much better. Congratulations on taking action and making the first crucial step to start your own outsourcing journey.

In summary: choose wisely, negotiate fairly, get started, and iterate as you go.

Part 4.3

Training and Skill Development

Key Performance Indicators

Train the Trainer

Once you have found the outsourcing firm and team that you'll be working with, you will need to integrate those people into your own headquartered team and company. You will want to train them well and align them with your culture and mission to ensure they have the resources, buy-in, and potential to do the job as smoothly and effectively as possible.

For many new people to outsourcing, the beginning of the offshore journey can appear a little daunting. The good news here is that this journey you're starting is just another day at the office for the BPO firm. Equally, your new employees will also likely have a lot of experience in working with an offshore boss.

Outsourcing firms specialize in facilitating operational activities for every kind of company you can imagine. They service businesses from every country, timezone, and industry sector, and provide staffing for almost any role, profession, or skillset. Their familiarity with business operations across the spectrum is part of the value proposition that outsourcing offers its clients. As a client, you get to piggyback on the vast expertise and sophistication that these outsourcing firms have developed since they have provided staffing and overseeing processes across a wide range of global businesses.

The big scary outsourcing journey you're about to embark on is also pretty normal to the average BPO worker. The majority of outsourcing staff have already been working in the industry for many years, so they are used to working for different accounts, across different functions, and serving different timezones.

So the main difference is you—the business owner, manager, or company who has decided to outsource for the first time. Everything is new to you, and there are a lot of little things that you'll be learning and getting used to over the coming weeks and months.

Therefore, when starting your new team, it is you, the business owner, boss, or department manager, who often needs a little bit of training. There are many small but collectively significant differences when it comes to the nuances of running a team and doing business in the Philippines. These differences aren't necessarily any better or worse, they're just different. If you are aiming for early and sustained success with your team, then the aspects discussed in this next section are valuable to understand and embrace.

Starting this journey with an open mind and a positive, optimistic frame will help you succeed. When you greet your team for the first time, give them a warm welcome, and introduce yourself, the company and the mission that you're on. Be prepared to trust your team and give them the benefit of your enthusiasm, confidence, and support. The way that you start the relationship is critical. If you start with mistrust, a rushed greeting, and swift marching orders, you may inadvertently undermine the entire foundation of your future success.

Your staff—if selected well—will be highly capable but they won't yet be competent at the role you are setting for them.

The burden of training the team, providing the process and an environment that allows them to succeed is up to you—and also possibly your outsourcing firm—but a lot of it will come down to you. However, the time and energy you invest into this initial stage upfront will pay off manyfold in the future.

There are many systems and processes for onboarding and training, and you might have your own already in place. Also, there are no better experts to help you through this initial process than an experienced BPO, so lean on your outsourcing partner and allow them to guide you through the initial stages. This is especially the case for the softer side of things—the first day welcome call, the cultural alignment, setting communication expectations, and so on.

Why You Should Care About KPIs

A Key Performance Indicator—or KPI—is a common business tool used to measure a company's performance. It is a quantifiable value that denotes a company's efficacy in achieving its critical business objectives. Organizations utilize KPIs at various levels to identify their core targets and their performance in moving toward them.

In its simplest concept, a KPI is the measurable manifestation of a company's goals. For goals to be effective, they should ideally be structured as SMART goals. The SMART acronym refers to goals that are specific, measurable, assignable, realistic, and time-bound:

- **Specific** – ensure that you target and clarify a specific area for improvement.

- **Measurable** – identify a clear factor that can be easily quantified and serves as a good measure of an outcome or progress toward it.
- **Assignable** – specify who is responsible for this outcome.
- **Realistic** – ensure that the KPIs can realistically be achieved, given the available resources.
- **Time-bound** – provide a time frame in which the results are to be achieved.

The SMART way of setting goals will assist your company in setting targets that are clear and simple. For any business to succeed, especially when dealing with a remote team, it is essential that everyone is aware of and understands the company's goals. If your company has big lofty but ambiguous goals—like, building the best global healthcare company—then a new team will not know what they can specifically do to get closer to that goal. So break those big goals down into smaller clearer stepping-stones, and then provide the means to get there.

Your KPIs are a derivative of your broader higher-level goals. They clearly quantify the desired goal-based outputs of your business. Every company should have a separate set of north-star goals that explain the broader mission, and then have the more functional KPIs in place to provide the pathway to get them there. Some common goals might be aligned to sales, revenue, or profit targets, Net Promotor Score (NPS) or customer satisfaction ratings, and number of users, visitors, or signups.

High-level KPIs are used to focus on an organization's overall performance, while lower-level KPIs are used to focus on department processes and individual contributions such as sales, marketing, or production.

The Philippine workforce is very familiar with the concepts of measurement, metrics, and KPIs in and around their workday. It is an almost ubiquitous operational language within the BPO setting.

Some might see performance tracking as burdensome; however, many staff can feel a little unguided and directionless if they aren't given sufficient KPIs and structure to do their job properly.

How to define KPIs specific to your needs

Properly creating and defining a set of KPIs can prove to be tricky. The operative word here is: 'key.' How do you identify your 'key' indicators? And how do you ensure that those indicators are easy to measure correctly and that those indicators are actually indicative of the greater outcome that you want to achieve?

Every KPI must have significant relevance to a particular business outcome. However, there can't be too many key foci of a business. If there are too many KPIs, they can create more confusion than clarity or simply dilute their relevance. It is also easy for some KPIs to conflict with others. For example, a quality KPI could easily conflict with a cost-saving KPI. So the KPIs need to be carefully selected.

KPIs must be defined in line with the critical business objectives. Here are key considerations when identifying these:

- What is your desired outcome?
- Why does this outcome matter?
- How are you going to measure progress towards this outcome?
- Are the measurements quantitative and easy to do, or are they qualitative, subjective, or difficult to obtain?
- What is the process for measuring, recording, and reporting the activities and outcomes?
- How can the people in the team influence the outcome?
- Do the people in the team have the means to achieve the desired outcome?

- Could the team have conflicting interests when achieving the outcomes?
- Are any of the outcomes in conflict with another desired outcome?
- Who is responsible for the business outcome?
- What is the way to know you've achieved your outcome?
- How often must you review progress toward the outcome?

As an example, if your objective is to boost sales revenue for this year, your KPI might be called 'Sales Growth KPI.' Here's how you might define this KPI:

- **Objective:** To boost sales revenue by 20% this year.
- **Justification:** Meeting this target will make the business become profitable.
- **Measurement:** Progress will be assessed as an increase in revenue, measured in dollars spent.
- **How:** Hire additional sales personnel and promote to existing customers to purchase more products.
- **Responsible party:** The CSO (Chief Sales Officer) is responsible for this Sales Growth metric.
- **Outcome:** Revenue will have soared by 20% this year.
- **Review:** This KPI will be evaluated monthly.

Simple or Complex

KPIs can be as simple or as complex as you allow them to be. They can be powerful tools providing valuable direction and momentum, but if you aren't careful, a KPI could steer a team down the wrong path.

Isaac Newton's third law of motion says that "every action has an equal and opposite reaction." This means that an action can have several unintended consequences or side effects resulting from taking that action—aside from the intended consequences of that action. This is most certainly the case when setting up company KPIs.

For example, if you set a KPI to 'answer 100 phone calls per day per agent,' then your KPI is indeed simple and clear. However, this KPI does not consider the quality of the call, length of the conversation, quality of the outcome, or customer satisfaction. You could, of course, add extra KPIs to measure and track these sub-considerations, but then if you're not careful, your small set of focused KPIs can balloon into dozens or hundreds of analysis factors, at which point you have lost the point of having a small set of key indicators.

You need to set KPIs that can easily be assessed and monitored. If you create a key metric that's too difficult to measure or monitor —despite maybe being the best metric in the world—it could be as good as useless.

There's also the natural tendency for the people who are subject to the KPIs to learn how to manipulate and "game" the system. Of course, you can't blame people for this; it's human nature when faced with a specific problem to find the most efficient way of solving it. It is not uncommon for KPIs to impact people's salaries through bonuses, for example. So they might be driven to achieve the set KPIs—possibly to the detriment of the company's welfare— because they need to feed their family.

Finding the perfect balance of KPI—simplicity, clarity, and complexity—is not an easy task. But this is not to say that KPIs don't work. They are probably the 'best worst' option out there.

It would be wise to set some basic KPIs initially and then continually assess and reassess their relevance, accuracy, and whether they positively impact the way the team carries out their job. Ultimately, the KPIs need to align well with a company's expected outcomes and make it easier for the team to do their job well. KPIs should be seen as organic and evolving, not set in stone.

So when initiating KPIs, make the team aware that they will

be iterated as you generate more data and experience with them. They should not be changed all the time as this creates confusion. However, they will, without doubt, have to evolve, just as other aspects of the business do.

In creating your company's KPIs, it is valuable to identify the main processes that drive your company forward and the people responsible for those processes. Some people might feel that a business can become very rigid if everything is written down and mapped. They might prefer a more free-flowing company culture where people figure things out as they go along. There is definitely validity to that argument, and I'm not here to suggest how one should best run their business. However, at the beginning of launching a new team that are doing new processes, it is safer and prudent to have more documentation rather than less.

If you don't currently have a lot of documentation in place, don't stress. Don't let the lack of documentation stop you from building your team or getting started. But just be mindful that it could be slightly harder to build a remote team and process without it. Sometimes businesses can get caught in a Catch-22 with growth and resources. For example, you might need more people to get the work done and formalize processes so that you can grow, but in order to bring more people on, you need to formalize the processes. While it isn't ideal to bring a team on without structures, it is still very possible. And the good news is that once you bring on your first key people and get up to speed, they can start documenting the processes and start to map the journey themselves.

Staff Onboarding

The Art of Onboarding

For all the advantages that an offshore team can bring to your company, the part of onboarding and orientating them remotely can prove to be a little more challenging. Because of these reasons, more care and attention should be given at the starting stages, compared to your traditional hires. When onboarding a remote team, you need to be more structured, explicit, and comprehensive with your approach.

With communication, they say that speaking in person to someone is much better than a phone call, as you're conveying the full range of verbal and nonverbal communication prompts. In comparison, a telephone call is less effective, as you're only conveying a fraction of the total communication signal with the rest of the nonverbal nuances being lost through what is effectively a filter. An email is worse still, the filter is even stronger—the message is still there, but you lose more components of the total communication, including tonality and pace. Texting is at the furthest end of the comprehension spectrum. We all know how easy it is to misinterpret some texts; sometimes you can't even tell if a close friend of yours is happy, sad, or joking when they send a text. If it is easy to misinterpret a close friend in a simple chat conversation, then just imagine the opportunity for error when trying to communicate complicated concepts incompletely or over the wrong medium.

Not only is explicit communication slightly harder when done remotely, but all aspects of building a team are slightly hindered. If this is your first remote team, then it might take a while for you, your company, and your new staff to adjust to a new way of approaching your communications.

People, in general, are tougher to motivate when working remotely. Just the fact that they aren't in the same room immediately adds a filter. Combine this with a range of other factors: (a) differences in culture, (b) time zone differences, (c) different communication styles, (d) different skillsets and functions within the company, and (e) different shift patterns; and you can see that the filters, which stack on top of each other, can create some significant obstructions.

In short, the more points of friction and filtering a team has, the more effort you need to invest to ensure a cohesive, successful unit.

Let's take differing time zones as an example. The fact that people are working synchronously across the globe, and thus contending with different time zones can in itself prove a difficult operational hurdle to cross. It is interesting to observe that while various technologies have miraculously enabled us to almost completely eradicate the relevance of geographical distance, it has not and will never be able to tame the impact of time zones.

Today's technology is incredible. Someone in New York can now have an almost 'as-real' in-person meeting with their Manila team over Zoom. However, despite this magnificent technological feat, it will always annoyingly and inconveniently be someone's nighttime and someone's daytime. The different time zones is one thing that technology will never be able to solve. It's not an unassailable challenge, however, but it's always going to be a bit of a pain. Rest assured though, the Philippines is completely primed for 24/7 shift patterns, so having them work night shift to suit your local schedule is not a problem and should not become an impediment to you building your business. However, the subtle impacts of this factor should certainly be considered when building your remote team and onboarding and motivating the staff.

So as you are setting up the team and their routines, just spend a little extra attention to make sure that you are mindful of all the little filters, friction points, and hurdles that are different to working with a traditional localized team. For example, you can establish communication tools, standards and protocols early, and be considerate when setting meetings.

This process of you getting to know your team and your team getting to know you is all part of the onboarding. A successful onboarding won't necessarily make or break the outcome, but it can certainly determine your team's ability to quickly get up to speed with your company's culture and operations—and it will have a big impact on their first impressions and sentiments toward you. It's an old throwaway trope that 'first impressions, last,' but they really do. For best results, it's important to capture someone's understanding, attention, and loyalty quickly and comprehensively from the start—and with a little planning, it is relatively easy and cheap to do.

Aspects of the onboarding can start as early as the hiring process. It's better to move as 'upstream' as you can. So, if you're using a BPO to do your recruitment, make sure that you are up-to-date with their hiring processes and at least semi-involved in them. At a minimum, it's good to get involved in the latter stages of the interviews, personally have at least one final-round interview with the candidates, and use this time to introduce your company and explore whether the candidate's work ethic and cultural alignment are in sync with your business.

As you onboard your new team, try and provide a strong support network for them that reaches across the other parts of your company. This is, even more, the case if you start with just one person, a small team, or building a group of home-based virtual workers. Try and avoid situations where your new staff members are working alone and cannot reach another teammate for help, or even just a chat. In the beginning, a new employee might come across innumerable little uncertainties that could easily be resolved with a quick chat or question. If they don't have access to an easy resource or a friendly colleague to check in with, it can dramatically hinder their progress and quickly stifle their confidence and early enthusiasm for the job.

So it's worth spending some extra time, in the beginning, to build the initial onboarding process and consider the necessary ongoing training and support systems required for your remote team. At a minimum, some simple outlines of these programs will mean that your new employees are better equipped with the tools, resources, and confidence they will need to get on board with your company's mission, get up to speed quicker, and get their work done well.

Setting Expectations

Part of the onboarding process will include the setting of expectations. It's important that you set and communicate your expectations with your team clearly, and early to facilitate a good working relationship. Below are some considerations that can help establish a solid foundation for your outsourced personnel.

1. **Provide structure**

Providing structure begins with defining a set of objective goals and setting unambiguous boundaries around them. Your goals can stem from you and your vision for the future, your consumers, or the collective inputs of your team. Regardless of how they are sourced, they need to be articulated clearly and spoken about often. This ensures that everyone is on the same page regarding what needs to be accomplished.

Likewise, setting unambiguous boundaries involves defining the details within the scope of work and how they should be carried out. This could include how you expect the staff to conduct themselves at work and what appropriate behavior and productive work is or is not. This may come across as slightly overreaching—since you're telling people what they should or should not do—however, when people can operate within clear given guidelines, they are more empowered to act, take the initiative, and innovate.

Often, companies provide less guidance, less structure, and less clarity. It's argued that they want their staff to be treated like adults, so they are left to their own devices. This is a fair argument and might suit some companies better. But generally, the reality is that spending the time to set proper expectations clearly takes more time and energy, than an employer is willing to spend. Or, possibly, they don't realize the value in spending some time to set proper boundaries. And so by default, most companies revert to a complete blank canvas and endorse a 'freestyle' culture. It is generally only as companies mature that they realize they need clearer structures and more defined environments for their staff.

Contrary to the common belief, a clear structure and defined parameters can provide an enhanced level of freedom and autonomy to a workplace—when people know the framework they are working within, they are able to move about more and flourish.

2. Share Culture and Build Rapport

It is valuable to introduce your new remote team to your company's values, mission, and culture as early as possible. This is important for every employee you have, but it is even more important when the person is sitting in a different office in another country. If you get an early heartfelt buy-in to your culture, then you will have an eager and very loyal employee for a long time to come. If you don't invest in the person upfront, then you will just have a 'worker'... and there isn't a lot of longevity in that.

When a traditional business has all of its staff in one central office, the company culture is more naturally formed, communicated, and assimilated. When new staff are added to that office, they can passively observe and absorb that culture with relative ease. However, if someone works remotely, it is much harder for them to absorb or even notice the company's culture. Therefore, it is important to be more proactive and intentional in acknowledging your culture and propagating it to the new people in your team.

There are many books on how you do this, so I won't go into it here—the principles of culture are all the same, regardless of whether your staff are working remotely or not. However, I will say that culture needs to be proactively nurtured—it will not just passively appear. Culture does not just 'happen.' And also, culture needs to be seen and felt. It is the company's actions that determine its culture, not its words or cliche maxims.

There is a common—and crazy—misconception that outsourced employees don't need to be managed or cared for quite as much as the 'real staff.' People often work with a remote worker and just recognize them for the work that they produce. It is critical to realize a remote offshore worker is indeed a person—just like your other staff. They have the full spectrum of hopes and dreams, adversity and successes that every normal employee has.

It's important to engage with your remote workers on a level that reflects this—and on both a business and a personal level. So spend some time building rapport with your team. Let them know that you care for them as a sentient human being. When put in the context of a Filipino team, it can be even more important to develop a strong rapport with them. They are generally a very community-based culture and highly value interpersonal communication.

3. **Clarify Roles**

Recheck your job descriptions and responsibilities. Do they match the work that is currently being done? Are they an ideal fit for the structure that you have set? And are your expectations clear to your new workforce?

Generally, a job description is the minimum baseline expectation of a Filipino team. If you have people on your team doing well and looking for advancement, then a career development conversation can link back to their original job description and how they are performing in relation to that initial agreed expectation. If they want to progress, then they should go above and beyond the expectations within their job description. Having this document in place provides them with a clear pathway for performing and outperforming their objectives.

As mentioned previously, the Filipino workforce is used to very structured environments and roles. In this respect, they commonly place a lot of emphasis on their job description to form the basis of their expected daily tasks. This is much more the case than for most Western employees.

If you want a more freestyle employee that will proactively develop themselves and the role that they are doing, then you need to set these expectations early, and also write this down in the job description. For example, you can simply say something broad like: "roles will vary from day to day, and shall be set by the line manager, in line with the company's broader objectives." But make sure that the nature of the role and these expectations are clearly understood from the outset.

4. Set Motivating Goals

Spend time on setting good clear goals. Getting your goals right sounds easy, but it can be a lot harder than it sounds. When the goals are aligned with the company's strategy, and support important processes, then they have the power to direct work in an almost effortless way. They can not only set you on the right path, but they can keep you on track whenever stressors pile up and you start to lose sight of what to prioritize.

Goals should directly motivate and be relevant to each employee. Try to have goals in place with short-term horizons and clearly visible endpoints, as long-term and ambiguous goals are far less impactful psychologically. The time period for any accomplishment should be much shorter than a year, and ideally just six to 12 weeks. If you have some big long-term goals to reach for, break them down and create a smaller set of stepping-stone goals. Tie a measurable accomplishment to them once achieved, and have them sound inspiring. There should be an unmistakable and ideally quantifiable difference between a goal's success and failure. The completion should create a sense of pride.

5. Give and Receive Feedback

As cliché as this may seem, nobody is perfect. Allow people to make mistakes and feel okay about that and grow as a result of the experience.

Enabling open communication and a conversation that encourages a two-way feedback is one of the best means to guarantee continuous improvement, constant progress, and high-level performance. Likewise, engaging in a genuine conversation where you can both seek and accept feedback, without resorting to excuses or defensiveness, builds significant trust between you and your team's relationship.

Close feedback and guidance is infinitely more important at the early stages of a new engagement. This is where the foundations are set for mutual understanding of expectations, culture, and output.

4.3.3

Developing Talent

The Importance of Training

As the platitude goes in a discussion between a CFO and his CEO:

CFO: "What if we train our employees and then they leave?"
CEO: "What if we don't train them and they stay?"

On the surface, training and investing in your people might seem expensive and time-consuming. But if you really want to build a great high-quality team, there is really no alternative. The importance of training both your new and experienced employees cannot be overemphasized. Effective training of your people results in a team who:

- Know what they're doing
- Get up to speed more quickly
- Do better work
- Save time and work more efficiently
- Feel good about their job and development

- Appreciate the investment and repay it with loyalty and effort

Before beginning the actual training, review your training content, materials, and procedures first. As a company owner or boss, it is not necessarily your job to do the training. But as a senior executive of the company who is responsible for the success of your new offshore team, you will want to make sure that the training is accurate, valuable, and highly representative of your company and its mission. So try to spend a little time to review your materials before you share it all with your new recruits.

If you are the owner of a younger company, then you might not have any materials prepared. It might be the case that as the owner, you yourself know everything about everything, and know what each employee should be doing. You know exactly what needs to be taught—however, the training materials either don't exist, or they don't reflect the vast wealth of knowledge that you have trapped in your own head.

When it comes to training, they say there is a 'curse of knowledge.' This is a commonly referred cognitive bias that occurs when someone trying to teach others assumes that they have the requisite background knowledge to understand what they are trying to teach. Often, the informed expert assumes that people can see or understand concepts from the same perspective that they themselves can see. And it is rarely the case. This is why domain experts rarely make good teachers. The skills required to be a domain expert compared to the skills needed to teach the principles of a certain domain are quite different. A teacher's skill is to break down complex concepts into simple messages and communicate those messages clearly.

When building your company's training materials, the trick is to break everything down into simple concepts and never assume the things you might take for granted.

Try to go through your training materials from a beginner's mind. Or try to experience the process from a new hire's perspective for the first time. Experiencing your company and its processes from an outsider's point of view can help you clarify the critical messages and materials that need to be communicated. To help you with this process, you can also ask for inputs and feedback from your existing employees and recent recruits. While they are already company insiders by now, at least they will see things from a fresher perspective. They will generally have a wealth of different perspectives and opinions.

Early Weeks of Training

As you begin to train your team, start things gradually. Don't overwhelm or intimidate your new trainees or they might get despondent and shut down a little bit. If their head isn't in the right place, then they'll find it hard to retain information that may be crucial to their work.

Observe your employees and see how they are reacting to the process. Different people have different thresholds when it comes to digesting information, and some might have a different starting point to others. If they find it tough, then slow down a little and engage them more in two-way conversations. If they find it easy— or aren't bringing relevant experience to the table—you can speed up the process and raise the bar to their level.

Once they get the hang of things and build some confidence, you can start to challenge them a little. Provide achievable goals and responsibilities and watch their performance. Throughout their training and onboarding period, try to ensure that you're available if they need support but don't micromanage them. Availability is the key here. Try to ensure that the employee feels supported, and that they have help on hand if it is needed. If they feel that they are on their own, or it is a hindrance for them to ask a question, then mistakes will happen, and bad practices will become instilled. These things are harder to correct or improve later on.

Try to render praise and constructive criticism in equal measure. If they're just starting, praise is more important, but it's good to give a balanced approach at all times. People want to do well, and they will try hard to get praise from their mentors. People also want to feel good about their work and their workplace—so make it a warm and safe environment for them to learn.

On the other hand, criticism, when used constructively, can also be very valuable. It can intercept and correct wrong behavior before it becomes a habit. This shows that you are paying attention and are keeping everyone on track. Judicious use of both the carrot and stick is often the best approach to get best results.

Cultural Awareness

Spend some extra time on being culturally aware and exploring your team's cultural differences. Be aware that Filipinos come from a different country with a different language, have a different culture, and have different insights to yours. It's okay to acknowledge this. It is naive to treat everyone the same. Explore this with innocent curiosity and a beginner's mind.

The relevance and impact of this cultural difference will vary greatly depending on what your business does and the roles of your staff. You might be surprised by what you expected to be different —but wasn't—and what you thought would be the same—but isn't.

People who have not traveled much or have not worked internationally before can get tripped up by this more than others who have done more travel. Unless you step outside of a certain culture, there are nuances in everyone's cultures that are not really noticed.

For example, if you are an interior designer in Norway, then there are a few aspects of your business that Filipinos would have very little firsthand understanding of. They might be highly qualified and understand all the business aspects of your business, but they would probably have gaping knowledge gaps when it comes to the specific domain knowledge of interior design and the Norwegian context. Most likely, they won't be familiar with Norwegian fashion trends and common furniture found in a Norwegian home, for example. This unfamiliarity might even extend to auxiliary—but important—localized references such as towns, styles, genres, locations, books, magazines, and many other aspects. All of these things come naturally to the client and would probably come naturally to any Norwegian for that matter, but none of that knowledge would be inherent for Filipinos.

In this case, if you are hiring a Filipino to be an accountant for the business, then much of the knowledge is generic and transcends the culture—so it would not be a big issue. However, if you are hiring a Filipino to contribute to the creative output of the product or to interact directly with the clients, then it could be difficult to get them up to proficiency.

Try to take an outsider's view of 'what you know' to really appreciate all of the tacit pieces of knowledge that you might take for granted. The curse of knowledge affects almost everyone. Your business, clients, culture, community, and country are unique to you. You have probably spent years working on every part of your business in your own particular way, so don't expect that people will know what you know in a matter of days or weeks.

Cultural differences are not always relevant, though. There are many aspects in a business that are generic and internationalized. For example, if you are a web designer, product manager, or accountant, there is significantly less cultural divergence. But there is still more than you might give credit for.

Cultural Subservience

It's also important to note that Filipinos have a very traditional approach to respect and hierarchy. Filipinos are commonly taught not to question authority, to follow orders and do what they are told. While this obedient nature is very much the antithesis to Western millennials in the workplace, and is possibly dismissed as subservience, this approach can have certain advantages as well as some disadvantages. As a result of this nature, Filipinos can be very diligent with their work and can be very happy and perfectly content just to get on and get through their work. This is in many ways a virtue, although it can be a double-edged sword.

Additionally, Filipinos have default respect for, and a slight sense of inferiority, around foreigners. They are enormously respectful of hierarchy and they by default assume that foreigners are superior to them within the hierarchy. This means that they might take a subservient or passive approach when dealing with foreigners—especially if new or nervous.

So if your team are going to be working or communicating with overseas customers directly, then it is important to brief them on how you would like them to communicate. In the West, it is more common to talk with customers on an equal level. Not only is it more effective, but customers generally appreciate this more than having someone sounding gratuitously polite. Filipinos can generally lather customers with a nervous over-respect, which has good intentions, but can produce less-than-optimal results. It can take a while for your new team to get used to talking to foreigners as it can be a little intimidating at first. So the key is to be aware of this cultural difference, set your expectations, and support your remote team in this journey. Empower them to feel confident by training them well, providing a supportive structure, and gently reminding them to talk as equals.

Ongoing Feedback

Designate a weekly contact session for review and feedback, especially at the beginning of their working relationship with you. This contact session is the place where concerns are aired, feedback is given, and healthy communication is fostered. This doesn't need to be maintained forever, but it is essential in the early stages of a relationship. By setting a good routine early on, you're making a point that you're available to listen to their needs, and are there to support their performance development and concerns at any given time. The key is to maintain alignment, continue to clarify goals and objectives, provide feedback regarding the objectives, and encourage their own problem-solving and creativity.

You might also want to cultivate an atmosphere of creativity, ingenuity, and innovation for your employees by encouraging them to think outside the rules and use their own problem-solving initiative. Blindly following the rules is possibly the preferred default for a traditional Filipino workforce, and it can leave you with placid and ineffective employees and processes. So it can take a little extra encouragement and support to bring a Filipino workforce to a stage where they are comfortable to exercise their own autonomy and initiative. By encouraging and developing them to think outside the box, they will improve your company's process and output. It's a win-win for all.

Training Content and Tools

When trying to convey the core cultural principles relevant to your business, there are three macro concepts you should consider:

1. **Broad Business Concepts**
   There are broad concepts in business such as sales, marketing, administration, and bookkeeping. You will want to train your

team regarding these things, but many of them are already fairly standardized. And the staff should already have considerable experience and transferrable skills in these roles that's why you hired them.

Since these concepts are fairly generic, there will already be countless training resources online that you can tap into. If you do need any training content, learning resources can often be found for free or at a minimal cost. Find good educational resources online and make sure that they're used. Don't spend time unnecessarily reinventing the wheel with these aspects.

2. Cultural Training

Cultural training, or 'culture 101,' refers to the items more specific to your own company's macro-culture, environment, and country. But again, you should be able to find all the content and resources you need online, and mostly for free.

Taking off from our earlier example, if you want your new remote team to know more about Norway, Norwegian customs, and Norwegian interior design, then find existing resources that can help them with that.

For my UK business, the team needed to have firsthand familiarity with key aspects of London. So we provided a framework and set a challenge for the team to find the best and most relevant YouTube clips that best captured the knowledge we wanted covered. We offered a small prize, worth around $5, for the best submission, which got everyone eager, onboard, and contributing. Afterward, we aggregated all the submissions to have a huge training resource for all future trainings.

This interactive approach to education was a winner in many respects:

- It showed the team that they could do their own research.
- It gets the team used to searching and finding answers to

their own questions.

- It opens their eyes up to the amount of easily accessible information available out there.
- It generates a list of great content that could be accessed for free and used over and over again.
- It sources free content, which was exactly what was needed to fulfill their educational requirement.
- It gets the team to invest in their own education and educational resources.
- It gamifies the entire process for the team and makes learning fun and engaging.

In summary, there's generally no need to spend time making your own content to cover these sorts of things. Instead, spend some time—or get your team to spend time—searching for existing content that will fulfill their learning requirements. YouTube, Wikipedia, online magazines, and Google are generally full of videos, articles, infographics, and content that can easily impart the key insights you're trying to convey to them. Again, don't spend time reinventing the wheel regarding culture.

3. **Business Specifics**

No doubt, your business has many specific and unique processes and contexts. Most likely, you will need to make training resources specifically for these things. These aspects of knowledge could be as varied as: (a) where to file expense receipts; to (b) what is your company's vision and mission, and why they are so; and (c) how to learn the deep knowledge and understanding required to contribute to the company's service or product line.

This knowledge is taken for granted in smaller companies, and new employees typically just learn from peers or 'organically absorb' it by simply being part of the organization. As your business grows and matures, and especially when you build a remote team, you will need to crystallize this knowledge— otherwise, it won't naturally spread. You can crystallize this knowledge in the form of articles, mind maps, and videos, or a mix of all. What's important is that this knowledge is captured and distributed.

Unfortunately, most of this knowledge will be specific to you and need to be created by you or your team. It is important that you spend the time going through the process. On the upside, once the document is done, you have managed to crystallize the essence of your company, which is actually more valuable than you think. Congratulations! It is worth the effort and time you'll have put into it.

Once you have completed your training content and process, and have trained your pioneer team, you can already assign a task for that team to keep the document up-to-date. Having the team update the training documents can even form a part of their ongoing training. It is then a living document, which will grow and evolve as your business does—with relatively minimal further involvement required from you.

Systems and Tools for Training

Launching an offshore team can often inadvertently force a standard Western company to mature its own documentation, processes, and infrastructure. Previously, a company might have operated and scaled by way of word-of-mouth teaching and training. But as the company grows, or sets up a remote office, they soon realize that an informal word-of-mouth approach to onboarding and training is no longer sufficient.

Also, the fact that your team is remote and might be working in a different timezone means that resources need to be available asynchronously so that they can be referred to as needed. In addition, the Philippines is used to a more structured environment and training process, and responds better to a more formalized approach.

Below is an outline of some common resources to help you build a program to train your new team and align them with your existing staff and company mission.

1. **"Buddy" System**

   To help with initial integration and bonding, it can be a good idea to buddy up one of your new offshore staff with an employee at the main office. The incumbent employee can act as a guide and mentor. Just try and ensure that they are both working on the same time zone shift. The new employee can then be trained using traditional old-fashioned methods where basically they just observe, slowly pick up basic tasks, and then progress to more complex ones.

   The buddy system can either be used to onboard and train people formally, or it can be used equally for socializing and bonding. It can be a good idea to have one buddy for training and support, and another buddy for cultural and social alignment.

2. **Cultural Exchange**

   Most of your remote employees will likely never get to step foot in your home office, which makes it easy to overlook the importance of sharing your company culture. When onboarding the new team, getting them aligned to your culture is arguably as important as the daily tasks and responsibilities. As your company expands and starts hiring more remote employees, you might soon realize that your culture has not evolved with the process—and cracks might start appearing. You can prevent that from happening by sharing your company's culture through coaching, mentoring, and technology, and consciously making it a core part of your onboarding process.

3. **Video Handbook**

   Video tutorials are valuable. Staff across the company can record short videos that offer advice to new members. They could be about a specific process or problem or offer broad introductions to the company, product, and culture. Videos are a great way of demonstrating things quickly and easily, and they are better at conveying more subtle nuances, feelings, and emotions.

   Videos are very effective; however, it's worth noting that it's generally hard to edit or revise a video. Unlike written text where you can dive into a passage and change some parts of it, a video has to be re-recorded from the start when it needs updating. This doesn't sound such a pain initially, but if you have hundreds of videos, it can become a burden to maintain and update.

4. **Social Media Groups**

   Consider using an internal social media platform like Discord, Slack, Campfire, or now even Facebook for Business. Set up an online group that allows remote workers to connect with their coworkers and other necessary resources. You can use a standard Facebook group as well if you are okay to allow the site to be accessible to your team.

5. **Resource Wiki**

   A resource wiki allows remote workers to share resources, advice, and tips in a 'live' document that can be collectively managed and updated. These could be accessed and stored via

Google Docs or a self-service help center. This system might be started by you or someone in your company, but as the team grows, the resource wiki is then managed and maintained by the team for the team.

◇◇◇◇◇◇◇◇◇◇◇◇◇

Below are some common training delivery methods that you can use. Try, test, and explore to find what works best for you and your team.

1. Documents

This is the most traditional form of training materials. The leadership writes down the entire business process, composes them as a document, and sends them over to future employees to read over and master. This may seem boring but it is a good solid reference point for employees.

Before you start producing a massive training tome, check out Google for existing resources—you'll be amazed at what's already out there, ready to be used, and mostly free.

2. Class Lectures

Think of yourself as the teacher and your employees as the students. By having a curriculum set, you should be able to train them at a reasonable pace. You can give these lectures in person or over some sort of video conference. You can also pre-record lectures or record live ones so that they can be re-consumed.

3. Video Lessons

The goal here is to make the training as engaging as possible by creating walk-through videos of particular processes and explaining them to your employees.

4. **Online Courses (Self-Paced Training)**

   Online courses can be a great way to consolidate your company's knowledge base and present it in an easy and approachable way for your employees. Creating the actual course may take some time, but it can be infinitely better than just handing over your documents to them.

5. **Job Shadowing**

   This is a classic way of leading by example. It is one of the most common approaches to "show" your employees what they need to do to grasp the entire process comprehensively. Your employee observes you or a team member closely while doing the work in order to learn how it is done.

6. **Reverse Shadowing**

   In this method, the employee does the work while being supervised by the client in every step of the way in order to coach the material or process completely.

Part 4.4

Managing a Filipino Workforce

4.4.1

Becoming a Great Boss

Conscientious Leadership

There are many macro and micro skills and endless subtle nuances associated with effectively managing a team. Bookstore shelves are filled with management textbooks, memoirs, and how-to strategies. Society has been debating management approaches for centuries— and yet—we are still learning how to do it. There are some clearly better ways, and some clearly worse ways, to manage, but there are not necessarily any clearly right or wrong ways. Management is highly personalized to the people involved, the mission they're on, and the environment they're in.

Managing a team of people requires the successful utilization of a vast array of varied skill sets, disciplines, and routines—and all these things need constant evolution and adaption. The broader concept and application of management fundamentals are well beyond this book's remit, but it is absolutely critical for success. Furthermore, effective management becomes even more mission-critical when you're working with a team that is both remote and a team that is made up of a different country's culture.

The fact that the remote team is physically distant from the company headquarters inevitably adds a slight 'friction' to any interaction. It is slightly harder to communicate due to the email or Zoom interface instead of in-person, and there are timezones and shift schedules to consider, among others.

In this section, I'd like to go over some core considerations for managing a remote offshore team and review some popular management fundamentals that can help you get the best out of your Filipino workforce.

A Great Client

I have seen many clients begin their outsourcing journey that typically starts with great excitement—as it should.

Within the entrepreneurial community, those that are often doing the hiring, there's generally no shortage of bravado, enthusiasm, and ego. By definition, successful entrepreneurs are generally effective and... successful.

But that doesn't mean they know everything, and it doesn't mean their successful traits translate by default, across to all other areas and skill sets. I commonly see entrepreneurs start their outsourcing journey with great gusto and confidence—and then they start to encounter the 'fritction.' Shortly after starting their journey, instead of encountering easy success, many are met with either frustration or worse, failure.

It is best to try and avoid this fate.

To prevent this from happening, it's valuable to understand that as someone who is new to outsourcing, you'll need to become a student again. For any entrepreneur entering this world, it's critical not to overlook the nuances of setting up a new remote team and see the value in learning and embracing the new skill sets associated with outsourcing.

Outsourcing in many ways is a quick and effective turnkey human resources solution. It can transform businesses. But it isn't a magic bullet. And it isn't really all that turnkey. It most definitely isn't something you can just throw cash at in exchange for easy results. Instead, it's a delicate operation, which at its heart involves people, personalities, egos, and emotions.

First of all, to master outsourcing, you really need to become a great client. To become a great client, you'll want to acknowledge and work with these two considerations:

1. You will need to invest 'you' into the operation. That's your time and your personal connection.
2. Initially, you will need to be humble, and approach setting up this offshore team as a student, not a master.

Good clients invest their money into a project, whereas great clients invest their money, time, resources, personal energy and spirit.

A great client realizes that the necessary learning, improvement, and progress in developing a team is a continual process. One that is more a way of life rather than a quick end-goal. One that takes continual work.

A great client appreciates the value of his virtual team. He treats them not as a commodity, but as an equal, and a part of the company's core 'family.' A great client realizes that a remote team takes even more attention and consideration than a normal team because they are remote—and thus need extra care to ensure that the company culture and processes are properly transferred to them.

Great clients are prepared to dedicate their time and effort throughout their business relationship. Great clients realize that they have a lot of learning to do and will need to adapt their processes to suit the new requirements of having a remote team.

They are comfortable at becoming a student again—for a short time at least.

Below are the 12 characteristics of a great client and successful student of outsourcing. The reward for being a great client is the success of your project, outsized business outcomes, a happy team, and a relatively stress-free ride.

1. Communicate expectations clearly

The number one characteristic of a great client is that you can clearly express what you want and need. This ability is vital for the virtual team to deliver the right output. The extent of this communication will vary depending on the size and complexity of the team and its functions. Clear communication might require just a few emails or phone calls. Alternatively, it might mean a full program of training manuals and sessions, protocols, SOPs, process maps, and KPIs.

2. Expect evolution

No plan goes completely to plan. If you are building a team and process, then accept that the process itself will involve planning, testing, feedback, some failure, and a lot of learning and iteration. Very rarely is a process completely clear from the beginning. So allow for mistakes, errors, and iteration within any plan, process, or team.

3. Allow a reasonable time for the work to be done

The outsourcing world is filled with clients who want it all done 'yesterday.' Often, what these clients actually get in return is a rushed job full of mistakes and needing a lot of rework. You, however, need to understand that quality work takes time to set up, time to properly execute, and so plan for that accordingly.

4. **Be available for questions and check-ins**

   While most consultants and advisors can and do work independently, there's no greater impediment for a new employee than being faced by an obstacle in being unable to reach the client. Smart clients know that it's cheaper to get it right the first time than to fix it later. Make yourself available to your outsourced team for questions or feedback.

5. **Pay a fair amount for work done**

   A bargain is a bargain, except when it's not. Often, paying less than the market rate for any job results in less than average quality work. Set a reasonable budget properly before you choose to outsource.

6. **Pay in a timely fashion**

   Once you commit to a team and cost structure, ensure that you pay quickly and graciously. With outsourcing, the vast majority of your cost goes into the salaries of those working for you. Any employer realizes the mission-critical importance of having their own staff salaries paid in full and on time. It is no different with the outsourcing staff.

7. **Have high integrity**

   Honesty is at the core of every successful business relationship. Conduct all of your business honestly and transparently. Not only is this a great way to conduct yourself in general, but it will also enhance your business reputation.

8. **Allow the outsourced team to perform**

   If you've hired the right team, then trust that they possess the talent and skill to do their job well. Keep an open mind about what your outsourced team proposes. Don't be constantly second-guessing their abilities.

9. **Delegation, not abdication**

   Giving your team the space and trust to perform is critical. Likewise, effective delegation is essential if you want to scale your company. However, this doesn't mean you can hand off tasks with no framework for training, oversight, measurement, or support. If you are delegating jobs, it is initially up to you to make sure that the team can get those jobs done.

10. **Establish an ongoing relationship**

    The best clients understand the value of an ongoing relationship with your team and outsourcing firm. A successful outsourcing relationship will likely last many years, if not decades. Play the long game.

11. **Give credit where credit is due**

    Simply recognize your outsourced team for the quality work that they have done. Usually, when you start outsourcing, you will realize that it is not quite as easy as you thought. So frustration can arise, and then any gratitude is lost and compliments are gone. Play the long game though—recognize the wins and encourage the good outcomes you want to see more of.

12. **Committed to quality**

    Filipinos mostly take pride in their work and want to produce high-quality work. They dislike it when a client asks them to take shortcuts. Encourage quality, and give enough space to allow it to happen.

4.4.2

Key Cultural Differences

Culture and Communication

One of the key considerations to effectively manage a Filipino workforce is understanding the differences in culture between you and your remote team. As discussed in a previous chapter, there is a myriad of small cultural differentiators between your existing workforce and a Filipino team. Over time, you will become familiar with the differences and adapt. But in the short term try to be conscious of these differences, and don't just assume that your way of doing things is universal.

There is a risk that this following short section could appear to be casually typecasting an entire population of 110 million diverse people. This is, of course, not my intention.

I am personally a super-proponent of the Filipino people and the Philippines itself. I am somewhat paternalistic for my adopted home country and have the highest hopes and expectations for the country's development. On balance, the Filipino people are one of the warmest, kindest, and most gentle people I have ever met. They are supremely loyal, hardworking, and generally of superb moral code. I have utmost respect and admiration for the Philippines.

However, there are certain obvious cultural differences when working with a Filipino workforce, and I feel that it is better for everyone to discuss and adjust for these openly.

The skill of a sensitive manager when working with a group of people is not to treat everyone as the 'same.' People are not pressed from cookie cutters; everyone is complex and unique. Great managers acknowledge and work with these individual nuances. Great managers know how to identify and double down on the team's strengths and mitigate the team's weaknesses. If managers can have more insight into the workings of their team, and have a better set of skills to make the team and their environment a happier and more productive place, then this is a great thing for everyone involved.

So, let's take time now to explore some traits and considerations specific to a Filipino workforce.

Communication

Filipinos are naturally quite quiet, unassuming people. This is, of course, unless you meet them during a karaoke session, when they will no doubt surprise you with their charismatic extroversion. They are very courteous people and have a somewhat traditionalist observance and high regard for hierarchy and authority.

It is very common for them to greet superiors with a 'Sir' or 'Ma'am,' and it's hard to get them to stop this even once they know you well, or even if you explicitly request them to use your first name. Traditionally, they have been taught not to question or talk back to their superiors nor question 'established' processes or procedures.

While foreign bosses tend to dismiss the concept of hierarchy, it is still very relevant and present within the Filipino culture. So, even if you ask people to just call you by your first name and ignore job titles, they might awkwardly do this to comply with your wishes, but they will revert back to a more standardized hierarchy within their own team.

You should try to be sensitive to this, and make sure that you don't recklessly undermine the hierarchical structure and traditions they have. This means that you have to respect the team leaders in front of the staff, and respect the management in front of the team leaders, for example. It is easy to casually usurp the established hierarchy when you're the boss, but this will unsettle and undermine your team, so it is much better to observe and respect it.

If you need to correct people, it would be best to do this in private, and certainly don't do it in front of any subordinates, or they would lose their respect for their leader, and the person could easily feel irrevocably 'shamed.'

People don't like being embarrassed or spoken harshly to in front of their coworkers. Taking discipline conversations into a private space is critical. Keep in mind that it will need to be subtle and sensitively communicated for your message to be effective. Filipinos generally avoid confrontation, and so if they are confronted or offended by a brash conversation, they can completely shut down or walk out. Any issues related to performance must be dealt with in utmost confidentiality. If you are managing the team remotely, it is better to do so with a video conference call to visually assess your team's non-verbal reaction. At the same time, you give your feedback and adjust the tone or strength of your message accordingly.

It is good to spend extra time with the team, especially at the start, to ensure that they have understood your instructions and expectations. If they don't clearly understand the requirements, they might feel slightly awkward, but they're certainly not going to tell you that they are confused and not following.

Filipinos generally have excellent English, and generally you would hire people based on their strong—English—communication skills. While English comes very naturally to many Filipinos, most would still speak their local language, Tagalog, outside of the professional setting. The Philippines also has a hybrid English-Tagalog dialect, colloquially referred to as 'Taglish,' which many would use in most circumstances. Despite generally having great English, their formal English pronunciation, accent, and phrases might still be a little different to yours. This all means that when they are in a fast-moving meeting, discussing technical issues, their comprehension might drop a little, and their ability to contribute at speed might wane.

So it's considerate to speak a little slower and clearer than you might usually do, and also try to give them a bit of space if you see them start to get flustered. As a meeting concludes, to ensure that they understand, you can get them to summarize the discussion back to you in their own words. But make sure that this is not done in a confrontational or demeaning way.

Complex communication is generally less successful if done over the phone or chat as they might just send a quick appeasing response saying that they understand and will do the task. Instead, taking time, doing a video call, observing their body language, and digging a little deeper will generally reveal if they can do the job or need further guidance.

Standard 'rank and file' workers are not commonly used to directly speaking to you, the big boss. Because of the hierarchical nature of traditional workplaces in the Philippines, having a direct conversation with a senior boss would be highly unusual and a little scary. In addition, they would be even more daunted by the fact that they're talking to a 'senior' foreigner directly. So the combination of these two things can mean that they can become enormously shy, and sometimes to a point where they are almost unresponsive.

You can get them to become more comfortable, over time, with regular direct warm-hearted interaction—but don't expect this to change overnight. Also, if any of your interactions become terse or agitated, because they may have made a mistake with some work, it could easily undo any of the prior bonding and push them right back into a defensive hermit mode. So if you feel that you are starting to get frustrated in a conversation, suggest taking a time out and then revisiting it later. Try to keep your emotions in check. An emotional flare-up from a senior foreign boss can be enormously intimidating for the average Filipino worker.

Behaviors can certainly change. And it is a wonderful thing to see junior staff build their skill sets, as well as their own confidence and capacity to work directly with senior foreign staff. But it can demand a lot of time and energy, which is in short supply in most businesses. So instead of shooting for the stars, just work on building a basic rapport and a comfort level with your staff, and eventually, their interaction with you will become more normalized.

As mentioned, Filipinos generally have a fantastic grasp of the English language. Many of the younger generations are now mostly bilingual to a native-speaking level. Their accent is neutral—though definitely leaning toward an American accent—and many of the nuances of their communication are very similar to our own.

However, not everyone is great at English, and not everyone is necessarily 100% comfortable at speaking it. So be aware of this when you establish who you want to hire and for what role. In your home country, where English is the native language, it is just assumed that you know it. But in the Philippines, you have to treat 'native spoken English' as an extra specific skill on a CV, and you cannot just assume 100% English competence for everyone.

If you are hiring someone for a telesales job, English competence should be very high on your requirement list. Their accent, and spoken and written communication skills will also need to be assessed. Beyond this, take note of the person's confidence in communication. Are they happy to speak to foreigners? Do they have a natural confidence and bubbly nature to speak to people on the phone for hours? Many Filipinos might be unsuited to this communication style, so if you do require good communicators, make sure that you specifically filter for these attributes.

If your team is doing cold-calling outbound sales, you will need to carefully choose your staff. As I mentioned earlier, Filipinos are naturally quite quiet. They are a little daunted by talking to foreigners, so boiler-room type hardcore cold-calling does not come naturally to many of them. Though, with good recruitment, careful selection, and adequate training and support, you can build a world-class Filipino team for anything.

When you build your team, be cognizant of the roles you're selecting and the typical profiles and capabilities of the people that are attracted to those roles. Certain roles typically attract more introverted people. Again, this is a generalization, but roles such as accounting, data science, research, and web development generally attract the quieter kind of person. There's also generally a pretty direct correlation between someone's introversion and their comfort with the English language. So to cut a long explanation short: Basically, don't expect an introverted web developer to make the best outbound salesperson. If you force someone like this to do a tough communication-based task, then you will probably get enormous resistance, poor performance, and they will leave soon after.

These basic principles can apply to everyone across the world, but I think it might be even more acute when working in the Philippines. The lesson to be learned here is twofold: (a) be aware of the typical attributes of specific roles; but also (b) in the beginning, don't expect someone to be successful at two or more tasks, especially if those tasks are significantly divergent to each other. Early on, for best results, be specific about the role, narrowly focus the function and expectations, and hire people who have the best attributes for the said functions.

It's also worth noting that when dealing with quieter,

more introverted people or teams, you might find it harder to communicate effectively with them. This might result in poor performance and output, unless you establish a degree of trust and a good communication protocol from early on. It can be worth spending time upfront to learn the communication styles of your team and adapt to them to ensure that you're working to their strengths.

As a manager, it is important to acknowledge your people or team's different learning, communication, and interaction styles. Some people are quiet, some loud, some introverted, and some extroverted. People do communicate in different ways. Outbound communication styles may differ, and also people prefer to receive information in different formats. Just as people might learn better through books, videos, lectures, mentors, indirect, direct, or on-the-job, everyone is built a little bit different. In the office, some might prefer emails and written proposals, while others might work better with meetings and brainstorming sessions.

This means that as a team leader, manager, or boss, you not only need to be aware of your communication style and preferences, but equally the individual communication styles of everyone else. This applies to all teams across the world, but it's probably a little more important for your remote team, as they will most certainly respond a little differently to the traditional team that is sitting next to you in your own hometown.

Filipinos certainly have some common communication traits which are easy to spot and valuable to accommodate. Despite being quiet in nature, Filipinos are generally quite warm, social, and highly chatty people—and they can often be quite wordy with their communications. This means that emails or presentations might take a little longer than necessary and their communications might wonder off a bit or be a little discursive. This can quickly become highlighted within higher pressure professional environments, where clear, concise, and direct communication is important. If this is an issue for you, work with them on this, gradually get them to better summarize, condense, and communicate their thoughts.

In stark contrast—and worth mentioning here—I have come across many people in the West where their written email and text communications are nothing more than an inattentive shorthand and completely stripped of any personality, niceties, or warmth. They mostly aren't trying to be cold nor offensive—they're just being efficient and functional. Short emails might not be a problem if you are going to see that same colleague a bit later at the water cooler or canteen, but when you are working with a remote team, that email that you send might be the only contact that your team has with you. If you are one of these 'minimalist' communicators, it might be worth spending a little more time on allowing your warmth and personality to show through your written communications.

Punctuality and Attendance

Manila has some of the worst traffic in the world. Rush-hour traffic in the metro travels at about three to four miles per hour, and 'normal' traffic flow is perhaps just double that. Generally, it can take you one to three hours to travel a reasonable distance in Manila. Even between the peak rush hours, arterial roads are usually clogged and major junctions become gridlocked with a melee of entangled vehicles all sounding their horns. There are a range of jeepneys (local minibuses), tricycles, buses, and limited train lines for commuters, but these are also overcrowded and frequently suffer interruptions. It's not uncommon for office workers to commute for two to three hours each way, and travel conditions are commonly overcrowded, hot, and dirty.

It all gets even worse every year when the rainy season starts. The Philippines is a tropical country with a wet season that spans about five months each year. The torrential rains, which can appear with little warning, can instantly double road congestion, cut the traffic speed in half, and drench the throngs of commuters.

As a result, people can commonly come in late to the office, and a bit of a lax permissive culture has been developed where it's understandable to be late 15 to 30 minutes for any given appointment. However, this can often be used to justify tardiness and can degenerate into a general acceptance of turning up late for meetings and work.

This issue needs to be acknowledged early on with your team, and a clear policy should be put in place so that people know where they stand. Generally, you have to take a fairly firm stance on punctuality as it can quickly get out of hand. A common telltale sign of it being a behavioral thing is that the same people are always late—and it is generally never the star performers. While zero tolerance to punctuality is a hardline approach to take, it can sometimes be the fairest approach over the long term and easiest to implement. Some companies offer their employees a bonus based on their on-time attendance, although others would argue that punctuality is a basic condition of the job, and employees should not be unduly rewarded just for turning up.

If you are hiring staff to work from an office, you need to consider their commute. Make sure you know where they live, how they plan to commute, and what their typical commute time will be. If people desperately want the job, then they will understate the commute time—and the pain—that it takes to get into the office. So don't just take their word for it, make sure you understand the reality of each person's commute, as otherwise, in three months' time, even with the best intentions, it could come back to bite you.

The severe traffic issues generally only impact the people who travel within the peak hours of the day—although, the hours of peak gridlock do seem to be getting longer by the month. However, since the outsourcing industry caters to global businesses across all time zones, depending on where your company is based, it is likely that your staff won't be commuting during the standard domestic peak hours. If this is the case, the roads will generally be significantly faster and more reliable. However, bear in mind that not all commuter transport services are available through the night, so it could limit the mobility of your staff.

There are many roles within an organization nowadays that are not time-sensitive, in fact, most roles can be done completely asynchronously. However, there is definitely still an advantage to having everyone work alongside each other following a set coordinated schedule. Alignment of work hours can increase collaboration, peer-to-peer training, and an improved a sense of community and culture.

There are good arguments for having people work the same hours and from the same office space. If you are offshoring for the first time, I would certainly advise you to start with aligned hours for all staff and have them come in to and work from an office. While it is no longer essential to work from an office during the same hours, it is generally the safer, more conservative approach, and is easier to onboard and get the results you're after. If you are determined to have a free-flowing culture, then remote asynchronous work is definitely an option. But I would suggest that you start with the easier centralized approach first, and you can later ease off the restrictions at a later point and move over to a decentralized operation, if you prefer. It is easy to start centralized and then decentralize, but it is very hard, if not impossible, to move the other way. If you start a remote decentralized team, it will generally be impossible to get them back into an office—not least because the team might be spread throughout the country—or world.

So just make sure that you set clear expectations for the operations from the beginning, and ensure that you get the understanding and buy-in from the team. However, try and avoid setting strict rules, just for the sake of them. If a set start time is not critical, then maybe a strict enforcement of the start time may not be required.

There are no right or wrong approaches to these sorts of issues, it's really up to the preference of the business owner or manager. I would generally recommend that a new team be started with a more conservative framework initially, with the option of lightening the framework later. Working from home and flexi-time should be seen as a benefit, not a right. Flexible work arrangements can be offered once a certain level of discipline and track record has been established with individuals on the team. The benefits can be withdrawn again if performance levels drop or the company needs change. It is very easy to hand out additional benefits and to increase flexibility as you go, whereas it can be very difficult to go the other way.

◇◇◇◇◇◇◇◇◇◇◇◇◇

Filipinos are very close to their families. Almost everything revolves around the family unit in some way. If you offer a job to someone, it is common that they would have to consult with their family before taking the job. When considering a role, the Filipino employee is often not just thinking about their own welfare, but the welfare of their children, spouse, parents, and even the extended family and possibly their village.

Paradoxically, Filipinos aren't necessarily desperate for work though. This is a common misconception of many foreign employers. For one, there are a lot of job opportunities out there for the Filipino workforce at the moment. The economy is healthy, and offshore staffing is booming. But beyond that, if a Filipino feels that a job isn't working out for them, they will just simply leave. For example, if they become unhappy with their boss, despondent with their work, or they have been shamed in front of their colleagues or forced into an awkward corner, it will not end well. Many will just resign on the spot—and you might not even get a notice of their resignation.

In the same way that the employee will consider their extended family and community before taking a job—they also have the support of that same community to fall back on if they don't have a job. So in some ways, despite generally having less money, resources, and savings, they have more security than their comparable contemporaries in the West. If a worker lives with their extended family, it would not be unusual for them to have very few overheads, which means no car costs or loans, no insurance costs, very low housing and food costs, and certainly no mortgage payments. When you combine this, with the support of their extended family, which can act like a micro-social security network, the typical worker can appear to be fairly secure—at least in the short term.

If a family member gets sick, it's not uncommon for an employee to file for leave to assist their family. Generally, if anyone is hospitalized, then the family will organize among themselves to have one or multiple family members sit with that person 24/7 during their time at the hospital. This is a wonderful trait in many ways—people from the West could maybe learn a lot about the Filipino devotion to family and community. But Filipinos generally have huge extended families, and it can certainly affect productivity in the workplace if policies are not established from the outset.

It's also important to realize that genuine sick leaves for things such as colds and flu can be frustratingly high. Again, it's hard to generalize, but the average Filipino BPO worker can lead a pretty unhealthy existence. Their diets generally aren't great, they eat a lot of fast food, and there's virtually no exercise culture. BPO workers commonly work a lot of shift work, disrupting sleep and compromising health. They are usually at the mercy of overly intense office air conditioning, tough crowded commutes to work, and frequent tropical rainstorms. So sickness is not uncommon in the outsourcing industry. But again, it's almost certainly a fact that sick leaves are far more common among non-performers and rare among star-performers.

Generally, as soon as a worker becomes demotivated or distracted for any reason, you will start to see it in their punctuality and absenteeism rates. It's important to set expectations early here, as with everything. The key though is to find great employees from the start and ensure that you offer a great employment opportunity and a compelling mission to be a part of. It is very rare to have punctuality and attendance issues for star players. So the key is to build a recruitment process and team environment that attracts and nurtures the star players and filters out the non-performers.

Work Motivation

Outsourcing workers are extremely well-paid, compared to traditional domestic employment opportunities. For example, a qualified nurse working in a medical-related outsourcing role might earn two-to-three times more than a professional role working within the nursing profession within a domestic hospital.

The high pay rates of outsourcing consequently attract a lot of applicants, and a lot of young graduates, all eager to break into the industry. Previously, the early call center industry—from which the outsourcing sector emerged—was not a highly regarded career choice. However, since then, the outsourcing sector has matured, jobs have become more specialized, and the sector now attracts star candidates for all fields.

The candidates are generally savvy, know the salary and benefits they can expect, and also all the training and career progression that the job should provide. Candidates are less likely to negotiate over the salary than their Western contemporaries, but it doesn't mean that they aren't choosey. Despite being a well-paid job with many ancillary benefits, good employees are generally in short supply and high demand. It is very much an employees-market.

The outsourcing industry has been growing at a breakneck speed over the last three decades, resulting in a lot of job vacancies and a shortage of great staff. This presents a huge opportunity for the upwardly motivated star employees, but also for the mediocre—and bad—ones too. Many mediocre employees are happy to just put in minimum effort into their job and then move along if challenged. If these people feel a little pressured, under-loved, or demotivated, they can easily 'hop' from one BPO to another. This 'job-hopping' can be a big issue among BPOs and it should be a warning sign to prospective employers if there are signs of this on their CV.

If you are like many new clients to outsourcing and think that Filipinos are desperate for the money and will take anything that comes along, you might be surprised by the reality. It is very much a workers-market at the moment, where good people are hard to come by, and great people are worth their weight in gold. So make sure that your hiring processes and retention strategies reflect the state of the market.

Ironically, the younger people aren't as motivated by the salary compared to their contemporaries in the West. Again, the default assumption is that these 'poor people' are all desperate for a job and money. The reality is very different. The reasons for this are manifold.

Most Filipinos live at home with their family until they get married, which means that many of them would have no rent to pay, enjoy cheap board and lodging, and some might even have a maid or two to take care of the household cooking, cleaning, and laundry. Even once Filipinos are married, they still often live within a multi-generational household.

While Filipinos mostly aren't rich, they generally don't have the stifling student debt, credit card and mortgage obligations, car repayments, and insurance costs of their Western counterparts. For these reasons, most staff can be quite happy with the money they make, and it is seldom a primary cause of discontentment.

The money earned by an employee is rarely kept to themselves or counted solely as their own. Their salary is usually taken home and shared between the wider family, or sometimes even with the whole community. This salary distribution can make people less sensitive to the amount they're being paid. What's the point in working hard to get a bonus, if that money is going to be distributed among the entire family. For these reasons, they might value auxiliary non-monetary incentives more than pay rise or bonus—such as staff getaways, Christmas parties, pizza or movie offers, and travel or training opportunities.

◇◇◇◇◇◇◇◇◇◇◇◇◇◇

There is also quite a stark difference between Filipino workers and those of the West regarding job title, job promotion, aspirations, and application. It is a common trope that junior staff in the West only want to work for six months before they feel they deserve a promotion, and then expect to be the boss within a year of working at the company. This is commonly referred to as the Gen Z's feeling of entitlement.

In the Philippines, I generally find that it's the complete opposite. I find that the typical Filipino worker is reticent to progress, or apply for promotions, until they feel they are completely capable of that next role. You will commonly get Filipinos saying that "they feel they need one or two more years in their role so that they can master it before they feel ready to progress to the next level."

I find this quite endearing, as it is typically the antithesis of workers in the West. But I have found that even excellent workers with high aspirations can stunt their own progress and opportunities, because they are too limited in their belief in themselves and their ability to learn, grow, and adapt. So if you spot good people in your team, then take the time to nurture that growth and support them in developing their skills and encouraging them to extend their responsibilities and progress through the ranks. It can pay off in spades.

Retention and Community

Ensure that you spend time to build rapport with your remote team, and make sure that you stay in touch with them regularly in both formal and informal capacities. Considerate communication will mean a huge amount for your Filipino workforce. Any time you invest into this will certainly pay off many times over.

It is sometimes easy to forget that your remote workers are people too. Since you're likely never to meet them in person and the interactions all happen through a computer screen, it is almost natural to dehumanize the person behind the productivity. It can be easy to focus on the production of the emails, documents, and reports that pop up on your screen and forget that there is a human somewhere back there that's producing all of this.

It's common for companies in the Philippines to offer regular activities and events for their staff. In fact, visitors to the country are often shocked at the extent to which employee engagement activities are embraced. Everything from employee awards, birthday celebrations, competitions, fancy dresses, karaoke nights, to summer, anniversary, Halloween, Christmas parties, and even company-wide retreats are all standard fare for many outsourcing companies.

Most companies create a summer sports league offering basketball (the top sport in the country), badminton and soccer leagues, and it's not unusual to have the Christmas parties hosting extravagant company-wide singing, dancing, and talent competitions.

The facilitation of a strong office community is vital in the Philippines. Known for being community-minded, Filipinos usually develop a close friendly bond with their colleagues due to sharing the same office for much of their waking hours. This can most certainly work to your advantage, as it's easier to build a strong culture and rally the troops behind your mission. However, the darker side to this same coin is that the strong bonded culture can create unwanted friction and dramas if the team becomes demotivated by the work or disenchanted by the company's decisions.

Office gossip, politics, and group dynamics can get pretty complex within a Filipino office. Filipinos form strong community bonds, so almost inevitably, a part of that includes gossip and a range of possible negative aspects that can occur within tight-knit groups. Office gossip and rumourmongering can get particularly intense and pernicious if it isn't managed properly. Instances of office bullying can also appear. These considerations are all part of running a team, but it needs to be handled sensitively and urgently quelled if issues are identified before they get out of hand.

Considering my emphatic support for proactive management fundamentals, my next suggestion might take you a little by surprise. It's generally best, as a foreigner, to not directly manage the individuals on your team. This is, of course, a little difficult if you only have a small team. However, do what you can, and try to build the team with that ultimate aim in mind. It's a good idea to develop at least one layer of separation between yourself and the rank-and-file staff as early as possible. There are a lot of nuances of office culture in the Philippines that are hard to understand or even notice as a foreigner sitting many thousands of miles away, and it is even harder to manage these properly. So it's best to either lean on your BPO account manager, or place an operations- or office-manager of your own to oversee the team as early as possible. Ideally, the majority of day-to-day staff management can be handled by this person and escalated to you if necessary. But avoid direct escalation of non-operational activities. You want to be available to your staff for their work needs, but you want to avoid getting dragged into the adjudication of day-to-day office dramas at all costs. This will save you a lot of time and stress in the short term, and prepare the foundations for a stronger and more scalable team structure over the long term.

If you are managing a remote team, try to ensure that they do not feel segregated from your headquartered office-based team or their other coworkers. As mentioned earlier, onsite office-based teams maintain a healthy relationship by engaging in regular team-building events. Although these activities might be tougher to coordinate when the team is remote, they are still important and arguably even more important since they are physically apart. You can build a strong virtual community by providing them with perks, rewards, and opportunities to have fun and socialize, and remember to stay in touch with them through regular check-ins.

Training and Processes

Employee performance will markedly improve if you offer a clear set of goals and performance metrics, such as KPIs, for each worker. Provide them also with development support structures such as formal training processes, quality control (QA), career ladder opportunities, and on-hand senior support via supervisors and team leads.

All these things are almost standard in even the smallest Philippine BPO settings. So, if you cannot provide all of this support to your team yourself, make sure you set expectations early on, and provide at least a basic outline for their support, opportunities, and resources.

It is important to have at least some established processes and structures in place. Roles should be clearly defined, and ideally, processes should be mapped. Filipinos are very process and KPI-driven. This can be a good thing or a bad thing depending on the tasks at hand and the structure you provide for them.

If you're looking for more autonomous, free-thinking, and self-directed work from your team, then it's vital to build them up to this. Work toward this goal and remind them that they need to be proactive, to take the initiative, and not just follow orders blindly. This applies particularly to younger staff who are used to following a set of orders and almost blindly following them, without considering a more global perspective.

Generally, people work in far more specialized roles in the Philippines. Employees often prefer to stick within clearly defined lanes, focus on limited tasks, and work to diligently complete them. There are far fewer generalists to be found than in the West, and people usually prefer to have a narrow, rather than a broad, work remit. They appreciate having very set and clear functions, as they don't like role ambiguity. If you want a more freewheeling team, you can change this approach, but it takes time, and their transition to the new paradigm will need to be patiently supported and encouraged.

Holidays and Labor Laws

Know that there are a lot of public holidays in the Philippines. There are about 20 standard public holidays each year, and then it's not unusual for the government to add up to five more, sometimes with little notice, during the year. Plus, the staff typically get 10 to 20 days of a combined sick leave (SL) and vacation leave (VL) quota each year. That's potentially a lot of time off in a 12-month period, which can make it difficult for some companies and especially smaller teams to manage operations and cover those days. And if nothing else, it can make the home team a little jealous of all of the Philippine holidays.

You can, of course, make your team work some, or all, of these holidays. Philippine BPOs are known for their 24/7/365 day operational coverage—and the teams are used to this requirement —so it wouldn't be seen as unusual. The Philippine workforce is used to working for foreign clients, and so abiding with the foreign holidays structures is commonly understood and accepted. However, you will, of course, have to pay the government-mandated holiday rates for asking them to work on these special days—but the total cost for this is generally relatively insignificant. There are so many holidays that most Filipinos don't worry if they skip a few, they enjoy the extra money. However, Filipinos are very family-oriented, so it requires a certain sensitivity if you expect someone to work through any of the important major holidays— like Christmas, Holy Week, Easter, All Souls Day, and so on.

Most employees, particularly seasoned ones, would be filing their leaves in advance toward these big holidays. Although this practice is fine, problems may arise when more than half of the workforce file for a certain holiday leave. You would need to decide how to schedule them accordingly during these days. Fortunately, not everyone takes advantage of these holidays. Certain employees prefer working on holidays due to the increased pay rate mandated by the law.

The Philippines is especially strong on labor laws and the employees are extremely aware of this. Therefore, if you ever need to reprimand or terminate an employee, the due process must be strictly followed. You can avoid a lot of these headaches if you have strong policies in place and have already built a good working relationship with your staff. If you are managing your team from within a BPO, then the BPO will generally take care of all the technical aspects of employee management for you, or at least, with you. Terminating an employee can be a hornet's nest if done improperly, so do lean on your BPO for advice—and try and offload a lot of the burden onto them.

As previously mentioned, Philippine law mandates companies to pay out a 13th-month pay to Filipino workers. This is standard and compulsory, and is paid out to the employee just before Christmas. You generally don't have to worry about this annual lump cost if you're working with a BPO, because they would usually bundle this extra cost consideration into the service fee or monthly salary computation. But it is important to know about this possible liability, so make sure that you discuss it with your BPO.

As mentioned at the beginning of this chapter, management is more of an art than a science, and regardless of who you are managing, it will take continual iteration and refinement to get right. Be as versatile as you can be when dealing with your team, especially if they work for you full time, and particularly if you plan to retain them and groom them as part of management. The key is to gain their loyalty, trust, and commitment, and get them to a state where they're working efficiently for you, and then you will have an invaluable asset and a most rewarding relationship going forward.

'English-only Policy'

Some BPOs enforce an 'English-only' policy in their offices. This policy can sometimes be limited to just the work floor, but sometimes also the entire company—including lunch areas and meeting rooms.

This rule could be seen as draconian and insensitive, but it is not uncommon, especially in many of the bigger call centers. Most staff are comfortable with this. The rule was not created to belittle the country's national language, and it's generally rare that Filipinos would take offense to it. Though, many might quietly resent it.

Filipinos are most comfortable speaking their own native language. Speaking English all day, every day, can be quite mentally draining and does not allow them to fully 'relax' into a conversation. Restricting them to just English can drain the work environment of fun conversation and banter, and negatively impact morale.

From a commercial point of view, it can be more advantageous for the employees over the long run to follow the English-only rule, as they will get fully immersed into the English language and will develop an almost native-speaker competence. For the BPO and its clients, the 'English-only' policy can be beneficial in the following ways:

1. It can ensure that the end-customer will feel at ease by not hearing any foreign language in the background of a call.
2. It can further enhance the employee's English learning and proficiency.
3. It can maintain an atmosphere of Western professionalism.
4. It can demonstrate a professional courtesy to foreign clients.
5. It can minimize unnecessary office chats among workers.

This policy is most applicable to voice-based call centers where the staff regularly communicate verbally with foreign customers. For those that focus on back-office support (i.e., web development or accounting), there isn't a need to be as strict as others. Needless to say, it is up to the client to make a call on their preferences for their team and workplace in this regard.

4.4.3

Reward and Recognition

Staff Performance and Appraisal

The Philippine workforce is used to structured appraisal and performance management. If you don't provide a good structured approach, the team might think that you're not investing into their career, that the company isn't a proper company, or that they aren't doing a good job.

As with management generally, personnel management and performance appraisals have a million different methodologies. I've outlined the fundamentals of a basic approach below, but you might also have your own systems already in place. You can also buy endless books on the subject or quickly download tools from the Internet. The key though is to select and stick to some sort of process. Without one in place, the staff will start to feel quite unloved.

Performance management doesn't really differ when applied to the Filipino workforce, except that they prefer it to be done, rather than not. However, there are subtleties in terms of how you run the performance processes and how they respond to certain incentives and disincentives. Also, as previously mentioned, make sure that any appraisal is done privately as Filipinos are vehemently opposed to being critiqued in public.

Performance Management vs. Performance Appraisal

Depending on your resources and goals, you can either do performance management or performance appraisal.

Performance management aims to ensure that employees contribute positively to business objectives. It is generally applicable for entire teams or departments and is best applied to outsourcing companies with a dedicated HR department.

On the other hand, performance appraisal is a more limited method where managers make top-down evaluations and performance ratings of their subordinates at a yearly performance appraisal meeting. Its individualistic approach is equally applicable to individual employees, freelancers, and contractors, since they report to the client directly.

In summary, you will find the difference between performance management and performance appraisal as follows:

Performance Management	Performance Appraisal
Joint process through iteration	Formal top-down evaluation
Continuous review including one or more formal reviews	Annual or semi-annual appraisal meeting
Ratings are less common	Use of ratings
Flexible process	Rigid system
Focuses on values, behaviours, and objectives	Focuses on quantified objectives
Less likely to be directly linked to pay	Often linked to pay
Documentation kept to a minimum	Bureaucratic - complex paperwork
Owned by line managers	Owned by the HR department

You may also have your own performance management systems which will more or less contain the following features:

1. It typically defines the goal and responsibilities of an employee for the next performance period. This includes period-specific objectives backed up by a job description that contains the expectations for the position.
2. It is performed formally on a quarterly, biannual, or annual basis with inputs all year round.
3. It is a review of remuneration and bonuses once goals are met.
4. It is a review of objectives related to personal development.
5. It is generally fully automated where the information is readily available to all participants at any given time.

A regular performance appraisal where you provide positive and constructive feedback, coupled with frequent rewards and incentivization, is a great way to build and maintain a strong and healthy Filipino workforce. So It's worth investing some time into this process.

Rewards and Recognition

Job-hopping can be a big problem in the Philippines. This is when people repeatedly switch jobs every three to 12 months, creating a lot of churn and disruption in their wake. This has become almost commonplace in parts of the outsourcing sector. As mentioned above, it's really a result of an oversupply of jobs and an undersupply of good staff.

There are hundreds of BPO companies, all looking for staff, and so people might only stay three to six months if they are not treated well. The BPO industry traditionally has one of the highest attrition rates with most employees citing 'better pay opportunity' as the main reason for leaving. Ironically though, most employees are not motivated just by salary, and many have the propensity to become lifelong dedicated employees if they are paired with the right environment that allows them to flourish.

Again, the principles of employee retention are pretty much the same across the globe. However, localized cultural nuances need to be understood and embraced when designing the implementation of such programs in the Philippines.

Below are some winning ways that can help you retain your star performers, as well as engage, align, and motivate your team to stay with you for the long haul. They are all effective ways to reward good performance and encourage growth and improvement.

Simple Recognition

Aside from making employees feel special through a range of extravagant annual activities, the best thing that a manager can really do for their team is to simply cultivate a channel of high-quality communication with each of them. Managers should frequently and proactively communicate with their team and foster an environment where the team can do the same back to their boss.

Micromanagement isn't necessary, nor advisable, when handling remote employees. It is better to spend more time listening to them, greeting them in the morning at the start of their shift, and being readily available to them. This is more valuable to your team and will be greatly appreciated by them.

The concept of 'visibility' in the workplace is a tough challenge to conquer and one that both managers and workers must overcome. Visibility in a normal office setting is taken for granted. People see each other around the office, and so there are constant reminders that people are there, and by association, committed and working. This is not the case with remote workers. The visibility of a remote employee is determined by their deliverables or the chats, emails, or calls about their deliverables.

Workers and managers alike need to work to avoid the 'out of sight, out of mind' spiral. As is necessary to strengthen any team dynamic, both parties must actively work on cultivating open communication, providing praise and constructive feedback, and building high levels of trust and autonomy. The solution to this can be something as simple as a short greeting at the beginning and end of the day. It need not be complicated or costly, but it can so often be overlooked or de-prioritized.

A Job Well Done
Sometimes, the best way to reward people is by just acknowledging the work they have accomplished. This is a surefire way to motivate people. It risks sounding condescending, but it is usually a big deal for a Filipino employee to be personally commended by their foreign boss.

Aside from the obvious fact that a simple compliment is the cheapest—i.e., free!—and quickest form of recognition, it is often overlooked as being one of the best ways to engender loyalty, increase output, and lower attrition. Plus, handing out compliments actually also feels good to the person giving the compliment. Try it. It provides an instant psychological boost to both the giver and receiver.

As you already know, Filipinos are very socially-oriented, so it is immensely valuable to acknowledge and reward people in front of their peers publicly. A public commendation will 10x the impact of the recognition. Conversely, it is even more important to make sure that you discipline people in absolute privacy.

Doug Conant, the former CEO of the Campbell Soup Company, became celebrated for his habit of writing handwritten notes of gratitude to his staff. Despite the company going through hard times, and employing over 20,000 people, Doug personally handwrote 30,000 notes during his 10-year tenure. That's 10 notes that Doug wrote every day for 10 years! Doug said that he was encouraged to write more and more notes, as he witnessed the incredible impact that a simple handwritten gratitude had on its recipients.

Here are some other ways that you can recognize your team by rewarding them in simple ways that will have the greatest impact:

- Bring the team for an in-office retreat that allows shadowing, team-building, planning sessions and bonding exercises. Finish the day with a team meal, awards ceremony, social event, or happy hour.
- Reward individuals with gift cards simply sent to their email for doing a good job or hitting a specific goal. Random and unexpected rewards at unexpected times or intervals can work even better than anticipated recognition events.
- Encourage and support attendance at conferences and learning events. This will enable your team to feel important and prized, as they travel to different locations, learning something new, and sharing their experiences with each other afterward.
- Acknowledge success. Remote workers especially will appreciate being recognized for the times they've gone above and beyond the call of duty or performed well at their work.
- Give simple pleasurable benefits that your team will appreciate. Do an in-house activity such as a half-hour back massage or an in-home ergonomic consultation. Fruit or cookie baskets and even food deliveries will be dearly appreciated.
- Simple things like being treated to pizza, happy hours, after-work drinks, cinema tickets, and karaoke are all appreciated by Filipino teams.

- Consider upgrading tools that will enhance your team's efficiency at work such as tablets, headphones, or phone upgrades.

- Are you also willing to budget for a yearly team raffle? This would give your team something to look forward to.

- BPO workers also love company-branded items. They love to belong and fly the flag of their mission-driven employer. So get some T-shirts or hoodies printed with your logo on it. Most BPOs require their staff to wear their ID at all times. So make sure that you have your logo branded on their lanyards. You'd be surprised at how keen they are to wear your logo, to show it off to their friends and family, and say that they belong to your tribe.

Many of the above suggestions might seem a little grandiose. You might argue that you are paying them a salary, so they should work hard for you in return. Period. However, many of these activities are now relatively common, if not standard, within most BPO settings. So in some ways, you have to work hard, just to keep up with the pack and be seen as an exciting place to work. It's also important to realize that things are much much cheaper in the Philippines, so it is infinitely more affordable to treat your Filipino team to pizza nights, team-building events, and Christmas parties.

Incentive Types

Any successful performance system needs a blend of incentives and disincentives. Put more simply, for a system to work, it needs both a carrot-and-stick approach. The carrot refers to a reward for good behavior, and the stick refers to a consequence for poor behavior.

We will explore more complex motivational structures later in this chapter. But for now, let's first outline some of the more basic, yet most efficacious of incentives.

This section outlines some of the easy-win incentives that you can offer to your team. Most of the items listed below are not difficult to do, can easily be systematized, and can yield huge positive returns. It's a shame that so few companies do it well or in a regular, sustainable way.

Because motivation systems are so important, and staffing is so cheap in the Philippines, it is best to put someone in charge of social events and incentives early on. You can even form a committee to do this. It's a fun thing to organize, so staff usually jump at the chance to participate. For your incentive scheme to be sustainable, have the committee create a schedule and policy for the incentives, apply a budget, and then automate it as much as possible.

To balance out the incentives, you need to have a range of disincentives. Common disincentives can simply be the loss or removal of anticipated bonus incentives. Standard human psychology responds very strongly to losing things. This is known as 'loss aversion,' and people will work much harder to prevent the loss of something than gaining something. Put simply, it is generally considered to be much worse to lose $1 than it is to gain $1.

Be careful that any disincentives or punishments don't publicly shame anyone in front of their colleagues. It's fine to reprimand people, but make sure it is done privately, following due process. Disincentives should be real, but not punitive or long-lasting.

Below is an outline of some effective incentive and disincentive options:

1. **Compensation Incentives**
    This type of incentive includes items such as salary raises, bonuses, profit-sharing, sign-on bonuses, and stock options.

Bear in mind that monetary rewards are typically one of the more expensive forms of compensation—and often least impactful. And as previously mentioned, basic cash bonuses are less effective within the Filipino community than they might be in the West.

Also, while employee stock options are becoming commonplace in the West, it is not yet common or expected in the Philippines.

2. **Recognition Incentives**

Recognition incentives include simply acknowledging and praising employees, presenting them with a certificate of achievement or announcing an achievement at a company meeting. Employers can likewise offer recognition incentives as part of the company's overall employee recognition program. They can also integrate recognition into the daily interaction of managers with staff.

Recognition is such a cheap way of rewarding someone, but it can be incredibly effective and powerful. It is one of the best, yet least utilized reward systems available.

3. **Rewards Incentives**

Reward incentives include items such as gifts, gift certificates, cash rewards, and service awards, among others. A common example are employee referral bonuses that some companies offer to encourage employees to refer job candidates.

These are often awarded in line with recognition incentives to align them with contributions and behavior that their employer desires to see. Small gestures can cost very little, yet can have a big impact on an employee. A reward has the dual benefit of being both a gift or consideration, plus the recognition of the action. The effect of a reward is especially heightened if the employee is rewarded in public.

4. Appreciation Incentives

Appreciation is usually shown in the form of company parties and celebrations, company-paid outings, family and sporting events, paid group lunches, and sponsored sports teams.

Filipino BPO workers are no stranger to some quite grandiose parties. It is common to have one retreat each year, where they have their accommodation and parties paid for. It's also pretty common to have reasonably big parties for each major calendar event, such as Christmas, Halloween, and the company anniversary. However, don't be too worried by all of this cost. Generally, things are pretty cheap in the Philippines, so they never break the bank—and they are great for team building.

However, you don't need to have massive events. It's all about the conscious and regular effort, not necessarily the size and scale of the event. An obvious example is simply buying your team a pizza or a few drinks after work if they finish a project, reach a goal, or take on a new team member.

Incentives Fit for Your Team

Incentive structures can be a highly cost-effective way of reaching company targets. Incentive schemes can backfire though, if not properly thought out or incorrectly implemented. For example, it can be hard to calculate appropriate incentives for appropriate targets. If targets are too hard to reach, then people can quickly become despondent and give up. If targets are miscalculated and become too easy to achieve, the company might have to readjust goals, which can cause the team to feel like they have been ripped off.

It may be a little counterintuitive to think that you can actually make money by paying out incentives, but that is exactly the case.

There is nothing more powerful than having a committed and engaged workforce—so it's at your own cost if you don't optimize these options.

Incentives need not be expensive, and most of the best incentives can cost very little. Rather, the true cost of running an incentive program is the time invested, the process consideration, and the discipline to maintain it. These are often the biggest inputs into a successful incentive program.

Cash (or its equivalent)

Cash is usually king! But it is less the case in the Philippine workforce. As previously mentioned, the Philippines is a highly community-based society, so typically, a person's salary might be distributed between their larger family and even the broader community.

There are few social welfare programs in the Philippines, very little retirement funding, and high unemployment in the provinces. So communities group together, and distribute incomes among their group—creating a microcosm of a social welfare system. It is not uncommon for family units to consist of grandparents, multiple siblings, and descendants in one dwelling.

The sharing of income applies to their base salary, but also to any extra bonuses. Therefore, many people might not be as motivated to put in the long hours, or work a little bit harder, as the upside of their salary and bonus is significantly diluted. Generally, people aren't going to work hard and chase rewards if it is just distributed to the family when they get home.

But of course, cash is still cash, so people won't turn it down. But bear in mind that cash is one of the most expensive forms of remuneration, and there can be other more effective options.

The process of establishing incentivized targets is valuable to both the employer and employee as it forces the company to clearly identify the desired outcome and provide a clear process to achieve the desired goal. This process in itself can be difficult to do and might take a lot of initial iteration.

There are many roles where a target-based cash incentive is not easily applied. Target-based performance can only be effectively implemented if the target and the means of getting there are easily measured. Sales and customer service performance can easily be measured and metrics of success are readily defined. However, other roles that produce less objective outputs can be harder to directly measure and reward. For example, a developer needs to write good code and ship great products. This is clear. But it can be very hard to measure this. A developer cannot be rewarded simply based on the number of lines of code that they write, because it's about the quality of code and the sophistication of its architecture. If you force someone to perform based on an irrelevant metric, then their output and your results will be negatively impacted.

It is common for high-repetition roles with easily observable performance metrics, like customer service and sales for example, to have incentive schemes attached to them. In fact, it can be difficult to get the best out of a sales team, unless there are clear success metrics and cash incentives associated with them.

However, bonuses are typically only the icing on the cake. They might represent a maximum 20% to 30% boost to the base salary only. It is rare in the Philippines to offer a very low base salary and high-commission structures. Well, it might be happening, but it is generally far less successful. The Filipino workforce—and their extended family—prefer the security of a reasonable base salary. They will respond well to cash target incentives and strive to meet KPIs as a result, but you very rarely get someone good working for a huge commission on a very low base salary.

If you do provide cash incentives, make sure that they're planned meticulously and monitored. You don't want to end up paying significant bonuses for results that, as it turns out, a standard team would be able to achieve without much effort.

Also, you can try mixing up the incentives a bit by providing alternative non-cash incentives like gift certificates for groceries, baby products, and clothes. This can be better since it can be used to purchase goods that will help both your employee and their family.

Social Events

Filipinos love celebrating, whether it be in the form of a party or a company-sponsored family event. Social events are a highly effective way of improving staff morale and engagement.

The family and community are very central to the lives of your team. Also, the staff are generally proud of where they work, what they do, and who they work for. So it's a savvy move to plan at least one social event each year that involves the team's family and community. More commonly, this happens during a company's summer outing, Halloween, or Christmas party.

Paid Holidays

By law, a worker gets only five paid service incentive leaves for the whole year. In practice though, the outsourcing community generally gets a combined 10 to 20 days of sick leave and vacation leave in the same period.

Offering extra days off is a perfect opportunity to incentivize people by giving them more time to spend with their family. By giving them more paid leaves, the argument goes that they will be more productive at work to maintain this incentive.

Health Insurance

Public healthcare coverage, to a vastly varied extent, is standard in most countries. However, the Philippines and most outsourcing destinations generally have a very low standard of public healthcare coverage. There is a mandated employment contribution to public healthcare, but the standard of the public services are, unfortunately, well below acceptable.

For the Philippines, it is not required, but is now almost standard for BPO workers to get a reasonable HMO private healthcare insurance coverage of some sort. There is a huge spectrum of policies out there though, with the expensive ones costing a king's ransom, and the cheaper ones being close to useless.

Filipinos are aware of the need for good health cover, and they really do value it. So by investing some time and a little more money into finding and selecting a better health cover, it can really be a huge benefit for, and highly appreciated by, your team. Having better health cover also has a mutual benefit for the employer. It can, in theory, reduce the amount of sick time your company and staff are exposed to.

Good health insurance will mean more to some people than others in your team. Obviously, the young single employees think about it less and won't value it so much. However, for most of the mid- and senior-level employees that might have a young family of multiple kids, and maybe some ailing parents nearby, a good HMO cover is like a golden ticket.

Because of the extended codependent nature of Filipino families, it is very common to have an allowance of a certain number of 'dependents' within an HMO policy. You need to decide what approach you will take in regards to this. A dependent can be defined as a child, spouse, and also a parent, or even an uncle or distant cousin. Some companies offer a policy of allowing one to two dependents for free, and then people can opt to add additional dependents for a set amount. Consult with your own team, and gauge their interests and needs. But be mindful that adding dependents, especially children, onto a health policy can become a very expensive exercise —especially if you have a large team with many kids.

There are different approaches to optimizing HMO benefits.

Some companies might offer increasingly better HMO coverage based on the length of service or the seniority of rank. Some companies offer staff access to better options, and extra dependents, if they contribute a little money themselves. There is no right or wrong way to do this, but usually being generous with health insurance will generate a lot of goodwill among your staff.

Be warned that it is easy to increase the HMO provision, but it can be very difficult to reduce coverage, or in some cases, even change the HMO provider. Your staff will take unkindly to any downgrades, so make sure that whatever you implement is sustainable over the long term.

It's not easy to please everyone: if you offer a premium health insurance for an unlimited number of dependents, this will impress those that need it no end. However, the young people with no health concerns or dependents might complain that they're receiving significantly less benefit—as a monetary equivalent—than their colleague with eight children. Sometimes, there is just no winning. So just be careful what decisions you make, and always consult with someone local before you lock things in.

If you are hiring freelancers, contractors, or people from Upwork and other freelancing platforms, these people generally won't have access to health insurance. So offering health cover can become a big point of difference for your company and can really impact performance and loyalty. While it's not common, a few service providers offer HMO health cover for contract workers. Do note though, that many freelance and contract workers do not declare their income, pay any tax, nor make any SSS or social security contributions. So in some ways, they create their own vulnerability. Philippine contractors are faced with the difficult decision to go legit and pay taxes or stay off the grid but have no social safety net. Unfortunately, many typically opt for the latter. And so it can be difficult if you, the client, want to try and formalize a freelancer's employment and benefits. The freelancers would also like to do this, but they often aren't willing to sort out the paperwork or pay the requisite taxes.

Gamification

The Gamification of Incentivization

Employers generally use rewards to cultivate a particular performance that they believe is vital to the company's success. A successful incentive campaign aligns individual employee goals and ambitions with that of the company.

This seems simple in theory, however, humans are a pretty complicated bunch. And no two of us are quite alike. So creating a system that equally encourages everyone on a team in the same way is no simple task. However, there is hope. Despite humanity being incredibly diverse, we all share many of the common psychological triggers.

A successful incentivization program should be careful to reward people based on directly controllable behaviors and output, not on indirect goals or results. It is critical to focus on your team's actions and not the outcomes. If the system is properly designed and the team executes the desired actions according to the established process, it should hopefully translate into the desired results.

If this sounds a little esoteric—allow me to simplify. Try to build an incentivization system that only rewards people for things they are in direct control of.

You can typically control most inputs but not most outputs. For example, you cannot completely control whether a prospect buys your product. However, you are in control of whether you make 10, 50, or 500 sales calls in a day. You are not in direct control of how the prospect responds on the call, but you do control the process that you follow when on that call—which might mean following a certain script and offering certain discounts. Once you build a reliable process, you can identify and emphasize the specific inputs which have the most impact on positive outputs.

If you link incentives to things that are outside of a person's direct control, then it dilutes their ability to impact their performance and can disenfranchise them from their incentives and objectives. It is a lazy and ineffective incentive system that overlooks a process's critical inputs and instead blindly rewards just the outcome.

For an incentive program to work well, you need to clearly identify the behaviors you wish to encourage and know how those behaviors impact the desired outcome. It's sometimes easy to be misled by focusing on the more obvious overt behaviors— often unwittingly—but they might be the wrong behaviors. For example, is making 500 outbound sales calls necessarily better than making 100 calls? Or is the desired result of making more sales better determined by what is said on the call, how it is said, and the quality of the conversation?

An Intentional Process

Gamification is the art of turning a one-dimensional top-down incentive program into a sustainable, self-motivating ecosystem. Card games, board games and video games all have an almost mysterious intrinsic motivational momentum to them. Good games are characterized as activities that are relatively easy to learn but hard to master. For example, the rules of chess or poker can be learned in a few hours, but it can take years to get good and a lifetime to master. Games are not necessarily easy or enjoyable—many of them can be challenging or downright hard. Yet, people love games. Some can get addicted to games and spend hours trying to improve and win. Most people do not earn money for playing games, and other than bragging rights, they get nothing for winning. There is an intrinsic motivation to a good game. The action of playing the game is in itself the reward for playing the game.

Video game and mobile app developers are conscious of the power of gamification and work to incorporate its principles into the program's design. Some video games are now so immersive and compelling that people can spend endless hours playing the game, sometimes forgetting to eat or sleep. In some extreme cases, people become addicted to the game itself and need medical treatment to break the cycle.

Now, game and app developers are under pressure to moderate the addictive qualities of their creations as society realizes the powerful tenets of gamification. People now see that gamification can leave such a strong manipulative, and even destructive, impact on people if left unchecked.

So, gamification is a powerful tool. It can be used for both good and bad. But, just imagine for a moment if you could gamify your company's work process so that your employees turned up to work every day, excited to get started, dedicated to improving their skills, and determined to win at your defined 'game.' It's possibly the holy grail of process design. This is gamification.

Bringing gameplay into the workplace is no easy task. Why is it that people associate work with work? Yet after their workday, they might take a grueling Crossfit class or a play a demanding game of chess—and they call that fun, play, or a hobby?

Many products and industries have learned to harness the power of gamification, however, unfortunately, employers, HR departments, and general businesses don't feature much on that list. Conversely, the gambling sector, mobile app developers, video gaming, and even Facebook have done well in mastering the art of gamification.

Like any tool, gamification can be good or bad, depending on its application and intention for its target audience. But it is not fair to simply dismiss gamification as divisive and resolve that people are better off without it. One could argue that expecting people to come to work every day to do a lousy job for 40-plus hours a week for 45 years of their life is also an undesirable proposition. If businesses can find ways to engage intrinsically, motivate and encourage their team, and reward them for doing well, this is inarguably a fantastic outcome for all.

Successful implementers of gamification—whether it's an incentivization program, gambling, or Facebook—basically work to get the participants 'hooked' on the particular activity. Getting someone hooked has a fairly negative connotation, but in this application, it means that someone is engaged in an activity and has the motivation to do it more, leading to more compounding motivation and engagement in the same activity. If you want to read more about this fascinating human science, there is no better book than *Hooked: How to Build Habit-Forming Products* by Nir Eyal.

There is a lot to be said about this super complex field, which at some points blur the lines between incentivization, motivation, manipulation, and addiction. There is a slight ethical consideration with the more extreme application of gamification, so it is worth declaring that my aim is by no means to get people addicted or to take advantage of anyone at any point.

However, consider for a moment this hypothetical scenario—where your team is addicted to coming to work and they're obsessed about achieving every goal given to them, to the best of their ability. They come in the office every morning, focused and eager to get started, so that they can get back to work on moving closer to their goals. As the team achieves their goals, they get increasingly rewarded, encouraged, and engaged. Next thing you know, they are leaving work later, shortening their breaks, and turning up earlier.

The scenario I have just suggested sounds ridiculous for a work environment and might even sound a bit like a zombie-movie dystopia, but these intensive behaviors are commonly seen in video gaming fans, young kids taking up a new sport, or even people who fervently pursue their hobbies. So what is it about some of these things—like a kid getting addicted to soccer, or chess—that applies only to activities of 'choice,' and not to someone's job or their workplace? How can we get that kind of passion back into the workplace?

A New Era for the Workplace

The workplace is getting pretty old now. The traditional office environment hasn't really changed much in the last 50 years and has barely even changed in the last 100. So it's no surprise that 'going to work' has all got a bit monotonous by now. Guidance, feedback, reward, engagement, and encouragement are generally in short supply in most workplaces. It's no wonder then that most people don't feel the same engagement when sitting in their office, as they do playing a newly released first-person immersive video game.

If you take a quick look at a casino poker machine, they don't look like the most engaging of apparatus at face value. Most would find it a confounding proposition if you were told that you would have to sit on a stool facing a flashing box, just to press a few random buttons for endless hours per session. If poker-machine playing was turned into a job, prospective employees would probably complain that the work is unfair, and the conditions are inhumane. Yet, the casinos have perfected this 'engagement' to such a degree that people spend all day on them, barely taking time to go to the bathroom, and draining their bank accounts to keep going.

Equally, Facebook, mobile games, children's TV shows, and popular Netflix series all take advantage of the principles that tap into the psychological triggers that turn something normal into something compelling.

The leaders of gamification know exactly how human psychology works and how best to trigger the reactions they want. Casinos, for example, offer the full range of 'inducements' to make sure that their customers stay glued to their seats. They dangle the carrot of the huge potential jackpot—inviting you to play that next round because you could just be one game away. In the meantime, to prevent possible distraction, they offer a full raft of flashing lights, hypnotic noises, and small motivational rewards along the way. In addition, they make sure that the environment is perfectly comfortable, bringing free refreshments, controlling the lighting, and hiding all clocks and any reference to time. There is a method to this madness.

Gamifying Your Workplace

While I don't suggest that you try and fully 'hook' your team, there are many things that can be learned from gamification principles and applied to business processes to make them more palatable and engaging for the workforce.

Slowly but surely, we see that process gamification is finally entering the workplace. I do not doubt that its influence will eventually become commonplace. An example of early-stage gamification can be seen in Slack. This hugely popular workplace chat app provides a useful communication system. It works on all of the habit-forming trigger and reward systems, which ultimately aims to get people hooked on internal work communications.

Getting people hooked is not necessarily the main intent when using gamification techniques, but getting people engaged and aligned to the company's goals is certainly a good objective. As previously mentioned, the Philippines is very conversant with process mapping, KPIs, and target-based systems. They are relatively sophisticated in this sense, and I do not doubt that the BPOs and workplaces in the Philippines will be leading the charge in terms of process optimization through gamification.

As an example, Alorica, one of the 10 largest BPOs in the Philippines, implemented a gamified approach to its recruitment. With 40,000 staff, they needed their recruitment process to be as self-sustaining and streamlined as possible. Partnering with STORM Technologies, a subsidiary of Xurpas, they implemented an incentives-based motivational platform to acquire new talent and increase employee engagement.[38]

As they studied their recruitment process, they discovered that their top source for successful hires was through employee referrals. They also found that referred recruits also had a higher retention rate of 70% compared to other recruitment channels such as job fairs and online portals. As a result, Alorica set about finding innovative ways to encourage their employees to refer their friends. Xurpas created an Employee Referral System (ERS) to help them automate the processing of referrals and to track them more efficiently, which ultimately enabled the company to streamline internal processes and generate significant company savings.

The ERS was integrated with Kudos, an online rewards and

---

38 Inquirer.net. (2017). Alorica doubles down on employee recruitment with Xurpas Group. Retrieved from https://business.inquirer.net/238412/alorica-doubles-down-on-employee-recruitment-with-xurpas-group%E2%80%AC#ixzz7KTpAFE7I

recognition platform developed by STORM to motivate and reward their employees for giving successful referrals. Through this digital platform, Alorica could now reward its employees with digital points, which could then be used to redeem items via STORM's exclusive marketplace. The platform also featured a virtual leaderboard that enables real-time social recognition, providing further psychological rewards to its employees. Alorica took a recruitment pain point, identified a solution, and then gamified the process, producing a win-win result for everyone participating in the system.

With the ambition of increasing employee engagement, I completely support and encourage incentive-based gamification in your workplace. But to start with, it is best to keep it simple. Gamification can get complicated, quickly.

If a rewards system gets too complicated, then people will be discouraged from participating. Participation is the lifeblood of any good system. It creates a critical positive feedback mechanism that leads to self-perpetuating outcomes. However, if your system becomes too unwieldy and starts discouraging people, it could be the beginning of the end for your system. Big complex systems can also take a lot of work and resources to maintain. So, try to keep it simple. Remember that the most successful games are often the easiest to understand and play, yet complex to master.

To help get started, I have outlined some key factors that I have found effective in my personal practice when formulating a gamified incentive program.

1. **Carrot and the Stick**

    To properly engage, people need both a carrot and a stick—incentives and disincentives. Suggesting the use of a 'stick' might sound a little controversial and tough, but I believe that we all need both the incentive of a carrot and the threat of a stick in life to really get motivated. When you think of any video game, there is the enticing opportunity to 'win,' but equally, there is the ever-present risk of failing—or 'dying.' What bigger motivation is there in a video game than to avoid dying?

It is just not realistic that a workplace can effectively incentivize people if they can only use warm fluffy positive incentives. There is always the potential threat of an employee losing their job if they don't perform, but generally, this threat is not imminent or of immediate concern, and so it is not really on the radar—and thus not relevant. It sounds tough, but people need a small but present threat of a psychological stick to balance the risk-versus-reward incentive to get real motivation. When offering rewards, if you don't counter this with a threat of discipline or disincentive, then people will become overly comfortable and complacent—this is a basic construct of human nature.

However, workplaces cannot thrive if the staff feel coerced and uncomfortable. People have to feel comfortable to perform well. Some stress is good and stimulatory, but intense or chronic stress can shut down creativity and productivity abruptly. The key is to find the perfect balance of risk versus reward.

Going back to the example of the casino, people would simply never stay there if they weren't having fun. So, for a system to work, it needs to offer primarily positive incentives and feedback. People need to feel good and be rewarded for their efforts, otherwise, they'll quickly become discouraged and will want to move on.

2. **Variability**

Incentives should be dependable but also, variable in nature. Animal studies have shown that if the subject receives an unreliable and variable reward, then they will work harder to get that reward—in this case, by repeatedly pressing a lever. In contrast, if their reward is a reliable known outcome—for example, one reward for each press of the lever—the studies show that the animals will have more certainty about what they're getting and reduce their efforts. The same applies to people.

When applied to a real-life context, there is more of a thrill in getting something that you didn't expect compared to getting something that you did expect. For example, someone's salary quickly becomes unexciting, even though it is really important to them and they could not survive without it. The reason is that it is an expected benefit, it generally doesn't vary, and they have been getting it every month since they started. Also, people feel that they deserve their salary, which significantly reduces the paycheck's impact on them at the end of the month. They probably aren't conscious of it, but once employees get used to their salary, they can start taking it for granted, and they can easily become complacent. This is when you sometimes find that you need to remind people that they are being paid to do their job, and thus they must take it seriously and not take it for granted.

It's bad enough when people start to take their salary for granted, but the same can happen with annual and semi-annual bonuses. You might think that everyone would be thrilled to get a yearly bonus—but as soon as people become used to, and count on, their bonus payout, then they can start to expect it—regardless of their performance for that period, or the performance of the company. People generally adapt quickly, so they can become quickly entitled and blasé about anything that happens with any regularity. Even though a company might remind their staff that their annual bonuses are (a) discretionary, (b) conditional, (c) variable, and (d) uncertain, people will very quickly start to expect a certain payout and can kick up a huge fuss if it comes in lower than expected.

Be careful not to dig yourself these holes.

Try to introduce as much variability to the bonuses as possible. Make it variable in both amount and frequency, and keep the reason for distribution a little more opaque. This will keep people more engaged.

3. **Loss Aversion**

Endless studies have shown that people are far more psychologically affected by a loss than gain. As I've mentioned before, people are more perturbed by losing $1 than impressed by gaining $1. It equally means that they'll go to greater efforts to avoid a loss than to ensure a win.

When applied to the workplace, this suggests that people will be better motivated to mitigate losses rather than gain something extra. For example, you could offer people a $100 bonus pool at the start of the month and then remove money if they fail to achieve mutually agreed goals. This is the same as giving money when they do achieve goals, but the theory suggests that it has more psychological 'punch' if reversed.

4. **High Frequency**

Humans have a short attention span. If a goal is too far away, then its value is depreciated. That's why it's hard to get people to save for retirement or even take the whole topic of retirement seriously—even though retirement is inevitable for everyone.

You may already be aware of the well-known Stanford marshmallow test, which has been running for over 50 years now. The test offers children the option of one marshmallow now, or three marshmallows if they just wait for five minutes. The child is then left in a room by themselves for five minutes, facing the singular marshmallow. They only need to wait five minutes to get all three marshmallows. It seems simple enough.

There was a small minority that opted for the one marshmallow at the start of the exercise. The majority opted to wait for the time to collect the bigger bounty. But it was only one-third of that latter group that was able to wait the whole time for the extra marshmallows. The majority of children eventually capitulated and took the singular marshmallow halfway through the waiting period.

The lesson here is that people are relatively short-term thinkers. If you promise someone $1,000 in a year, it's a nice thought, but it's relatively irrelevant to them. It relies on someone deprioritizing endless instant gratification opportunities for one possible delayed gratification opportunity. We all know that instant gratification is a much more compelling proposition. After all, there is a chance, maybe even a big chance, that the $1,000 reward doesn't even happen—so who would reasonably invest attention into something that is so distant and uncertain?

Humans generally struggle with putting off immediate gratification for a deferred gratification that may or may not happen later. Think of people trying to lose weight. It is hard to battle day-in and day-out for a possible weight loss reward, six to 12 months from now. It is far more gratifying to eat the pizza and have the extra beer—now. People are constantly battling compelling monkey-brain short-termism against the mature sophisticated human-brain concept of long-term discipline.

Most people can rationalize that working hard today will yield better results for tomorrow, but human emotion and short-termism can frequently dominate and give way to the least optimal outcome. As an employer, we can't hope to change human evolution, but we can be aware of it and work with it.

In short, if you offer people a great bonus at the end of the year, it might be completely useless and have zero impact on performance. Similarly, if you need someone to create a huge report and give them three months to do it, you can almost guarantee that the first 10 weeks will be completely under-utilized, and the report will be rushed through in the last two weeks.

So, it makes sense that incentives are frequent and very relevant. I don't know of any relevant studies in this area, but I bet people would opt for smaller, more frequent bonuses, rather than a bigger potential bonus in 12 months' time.

There is a mutual benefit to this approach. Frequent rewards keep people more engaged, feel more relevant, and are usually more representative of the mutually desired outcomes. Imagine a scenario where someone gets rewarded every two to three days. This will give them a thrill each and every time. You might opt to give someone a cinema ticket, book voucher, or greeting card each week. The cumulative cost would still be less than a $1,000 bonus at the end of the year, but it would have a far bigger and more cumulative impact. Remember, though, as mentioned above, if the cinema reward becomes normal, reliable, or expected, then its value will be minimized in the mind of the beneficiary. So make sure that the bonuses are irregular, are varied, and require the successful completion of an activity to be won.

5. **Company, teamwork, and individual contributions**

It's important to recognize the different contributing factors of success. Getting anything done takes a complex interaction of varying contributions from the individual, the team, and the overall company. No one is independent within a company, and someone's success is rarely completely contingent on just their efforts alone. It is important to encourage personal achievement but it is also critical to foster a sense of betterment of the overall team.

Incentive programs can go wrong if there is an overemphasis on personal contribution. It can create unproductive individualism, discourage teamwork, and even cause harmful internal competition and friction. Conversely, if a team's performance is rewarded to the exclusion of the individual, it can quickly discourage individual effort and contribution.

Another common conundrum is whether a sales team should get paid hefty bonuses if the overall company is ultimately unprofitable and underperforming. If bonuses aren't paid, the sales team might perform even worse, further impeding the company's results. However, should the sales team be taking home costly rewards when the rest of the company might be having to slash costs and cut jobs?

As with anything, there is no perfect solution to these incentive systems, but knowing the basic principles and exploring different designs could produce some exciting results for your team and company.

Epilogue

A New World

I'm writing these last pages from my home in Manila, on a characteristically beautiful Sunday, with a bright morning light beaming through the windows. I'm using my Californian-designed, Chinese-built laptop, South Korean monitors, Swedish standing desk, Norwegian chair, and have an Italian coffee and an excellent French croissant in front of me that I'm about to devour. I'm on the 41st floor overlooking the winding Pasig river in a building that would not look out of place in downtown Manhattan. Manila is a vast concrete jungle, imposing a harsh existence for so many, but is filled with tens of millions of wonderful souls, all working together to build a better life for themselves, their families, and countrymen. They are some of the happiest, gracious, gentle, and warm-hearted people I have ever met, and I am honored to call their city, my home.

Despite sitting in Manila, my surroundings and my morning feel no different from others that I have spent in Sydney, London, or New York. That Sunday morning feel, my laptop, and the coffee is all the same—though the croissant is probably a little bit better.

Manila is full of delightful cultural, historical, and traditional tributes, reflecting its unique heritage and vivid identity. Though in other ways, it is a generic international metropolis, sharing all the common traits of other major cities. From shopping malls, movies, cars, universities, and hospitals, to pizza, ramen, basketball, Netflix, and cafe culture. We are all converging into a single humanity and are all much more similar than we are different.

I have lived in the UK, New Zealand, Australia, and the Philippines for many years each, spent many months in Spain, Brazil, Dubai, and the US, and traveled through dozens more. I have always felt like a global citizen, so the concept of a single global marketplace has always felt like a natural point of convergence.

We see the world getting smaller, technology fast improving, people becoming more homogenized, and global trade going through the roof. There are obvious benefits to collaboration and specialization, and we are seeing those benefits increase as the network expands.

For many people, hiring globally is still a novel concept. Yet, they drive a German car, use a South Korean phone, wear Turkish clothes, watch UK movies from a Chinese laptop, and fly an Emirati airline. The concept of global employment is really no different from the free trade and basic consumerism that we are already all a part of and engage in daily. It's simply the process of buying or trading what you want, from who you want, and seeking the best quality, price, and output available.

The ability to hire staff globally is an incredible accomplishment. It is the by-product of humanity's breathtaking technological advancement over many thousands of years. We are all truly standing on the shoulders of giants.

As the world transitions from separate geographical silos into a homogenized single market, there are opportunities right now to access deep pools of talent and significantly lower salaries.

The lower salaries will not last forever; eventually, there will be a rebalancing, but it might take many generations to happen. For now, the salary imbalance is as much a disgrace as it is an opportunity. Outsourcing has not created this imbalance, though, and is instead shining a light on this issue. And with the bright lights of attention and energy, we will eventually neutralize the problem. Offshore staffing, and an increasingly globalized economy, offers a win-win for all participants.

Right now, businesses in the West have a historical opportunity to benefit from this enormous disparity. There has always been an imbalance, but it was locked in place until recently. Now, with technology, globalization, and turnkey outsourcing solutions in situ, along with a normalization of the remote-work paradigm, global employment will quickly transition from obscure to ubiquitous.

Having access to a pool of 8 billion workers dramatically increases the size of the intellectual, innovation, and production pool from which a business can find its resources. They are now no longer limited to their very finite geographical catchment and the benefits of this enhanced network will reverberate through the economy.

Offshore staffing is the single most powerful tool in business. It should not be missed.

However, it is no magic bullet.

It is enormously difficult to build and run a thriving business, and managing a team of people is equally complex. These are universal realities, irrespective of where your staff are sitting.

Offshore staffing does not alleviate these issues. In fact, employing internationally might even add more complexity—due to remote-work adjustments and cultural differences. But if done properly, it works, and there are significant net benefits.

From my years working with offshore teams, I realize that most outsourcing guidance is equally applicable to standard business scenarios and management principles. In some ways, there is no difference, yet in other ways, it is a completely different paradigm.

As with anything of complexity, the devil is in the details. Something as simple as the game of chess for example, can take minutes to understand but decades to master, and this is similar with business, people management, and outsourcing. Outsourcing is very simple in concept, and the principles are mostly the same, but it can take many years of a healthy beginner's mindset to really understand and master its nuances.

There is no economy, business, employment, or consumers without people. People are business. And people are complicated. The efficient win-win utilization of people within a business is a vital element of a company's success, and is so often underrated. If a company can draw on the best talent that the world has to offer, and can get them onboard and motivated by its mission, then there is no limit to what can be achieved.

Below are some final closing thoughts on how to get the best out of an offshore team for your business.

- Change is inevitable. The globalization of the workforce is an inescapable reality.
- There is a big world out there of 8 billion employees. With increased networking and cooperation, there will be increased upside and prosperity for the entire world.
- Treat traditional staff and offshore staff the same—but different. Recognize and adapt to the cultural nuances of each.
- Lean on the expertise and services of the outsourcing firms, and add in the auxiliary support services—at least in the beginning.
- Don't go too cheap. Aim for the top echelons of an emerging economy.

- Try to save 50% to 70% but not more than that. Understand the cost-versus-friction matrix when offshoring.

- Separate out the core aspects of offshore employment from the more flashy additional productivity and process management services.

- Have a clear plan for your business, departments, and processes. Start to build and map processes, but don't focus on them too much at the beginning. Done is better than perfect.

- Start with more senior people first; once they are stable and up to speed, you can fold more junior people within the hierarchy.

- Don't count on hiring unicorn staff. Instead, focus on building strong systems that can enable average staff to thrive.

- Don't count on broadly capable generalists. Instead, focus on a high degree of competency of a very narrow set of clearly defined functions, and then eventually broaden out.

- Understand that designing and building a new process differs from working and managing an existing process. Treat a process' design, build, management, and work as different functions.

- Contrary to assumptions, the risk, exposure, and tie-ins of outsourcing are typically minimal.

- Start now. Start small. You will learn so much by getting your first team member. Learn and iterate as you go. You will never look back.

Welcome to the global economy!

About the Author

DEREK GALLIMORE is a lifelong entrepreneur and global citizen. He built a multimillion-dollar property portfolio and bootstrapped his first business to $20 million revenues in his 20s, and went on to create the world's leading outsourcing marketplace, Outsource Accelerator.

Derek has lived and worked in five countries, traveled through dozens more, and embodied remote, online and global work since 2005. He has been outsourcing to the Philippine since 2011 and moved to Manila in 2014. He believes that outsourcing is one of the most potent and transformative business tools available today, and is a leading proponent for the future of work and the eventual migration to a single global economy.

Made in the USA
Las Vegas, NV
02 November 2022

58631923R00275